ACTING

ACTING
Preparation, Practice, Performance

BELLA ITKIN
The Theatre School,
DePaul University

with

RICHARD AVEN

HarperCollinsCollegePublishers

Acquisitions Editor: Daniel Pipp
Project Editor: Steven Pisano
Design Supervisor: John Callahan
Front Cover Photo: John Bridges
Back Cover Photo: Jennifer Girard, The Theatre School, De Paul University
Production Manager: Laura Chavoen
Manufacturing Manager: Joseph Campanella
Compositor, Printer, Binder, and Cover Printer: R.R. Donnelly & Sons Company

For permission to use copyrighted material, grateful acknowledgement is made to the copyright holders on p. 221, which are hereby made part of this copyright page.

Photographs by John Bridges.

ACTING: Preparation, Practice, Performance

Library of Congress Cataloging-in-Publication Data

Itkin, Bella
   Acting: preparation, practice, performance / Bella Itkin, Richard Aven
      p.   cm.
   ISBN 0-673-46350-8
1. Acting 2. Title

94   95   96   97   9   8   7   6   5   4   3   2   1

*To my father and teacher,
David Itkin,
and to my students*

Contents

Preface

Have you noticed that the best actors exude an energy or are alive in a way that is unique? Their emotional and imaginative capacities overflow. They are dangerous and spontaneous—daring to expose themselves both physically and emotionally.

These are actors who possess talent. Talent is something special which cannot be taught. However, raw, creative, uninhibited talent needs to be challenged. Developing a spontaneous technique is the way to focus and challenge talent.

What is technique? Many times we talk about how amazing an actor's abilities are. However, whenever the audience stops being involved in the play to be dazzled by a particular performance, any technique employed by that performer is wasted. In such cases, we become aware of the technique and not the talent. Technique, therefore, has to include a way of practicing and putting forth the talent of an actor. Technique must serve the talent.

Many young and well-trained actors assume that technique means good vocal training and daily practice of speech exercises; that it requires the physical training of the body for movement, whether it be for dance or musical experience or simply to stay fit and flexible for any physical demands that might arise to challenge the actor in a given role; and, finally, that it means being able to analyze a script, to break scenes down into beats, to determine motivations, and to find a throughline in the character's journey from his or her first scene through the last.

Technique is all of this, but it must include something more. It is my belief that a *complete* technique includes developed sensory skills—that talent is an actor's spontaneous sensory awareness. Developing the ability to respond naturally with the body, trusting impulses and not rehearsed responses, is a neglected and misunderstood part of the actor's training. Actors who possess the skill to trust their spontaneous sensory responses have confidence in their ability. Their acting is refreshingly unique; it does not bear the stamp of cliché. Moreover, good sensory work hides itself as a technique, even as it results in believable behavior on stage.

Above all, I want to see behavior on stage that is believable. I see a lot of acting that is "phoney baloney." The actors tend to be superficial. They are acting up a storm. Their work screams with something that might be called technique, but in reality substitutes energy and noise for believability. I often want to say "Please, stop acting. Just talk. Just listen."

But how to teach acting? It's impossible. No one can teach acting. What I believe is that *the actors must teach themselves*! In this book, I seek to help actors uncover their own sensory responses to the world that affects us everyday. If an actor can discover those responses, then surely there is talent for a career in the theatre.

Sensorially ignited actors possess something I was not able to teach them, but which they were able to learn about themselves. If actors understand their sensory responses, then they have a technique that is self-reliant, and therefore possess a technique adaptable to any situation. In a way, they are director proof. Yes, they listen to what the director tells them, they are respectful of that vision of the play, but they also know how to take care of themselves. They know how to analyze a script and how to break down their beats, and they know how to listen to their bodies telling them if something is working or not—if something is believable or not. They recognize that acting is a lifelong process of discovery and not a set of rules for stage pictures and blocking.

I believe that every actor in my class is talented. Being talented, actors have a responsibility to work on their instrument every day of their lives. There is no tomorrow for this, only NOW! Daily progress is an important element in developing sensory technique. It is necessary for the student actor to be at every session, both physically and psychologically prepared to work. In order for this to happen, the actor should be more than prompt—he/she should be early. And, in order to be alert and observant in class, the actor also must be prepared.

So that the actors, as well as I, can be more physically aware of their responses during the experience/exercises presented in this text, I insist that the actors attending my class dress in neutral apparel, that is, leotards, shorts, t-shirts, and bare feet. Anything baggy which hides the body is not acceptable.

The technique class I teach at The Theatre School Conservatory of DePaul University, in Chicago, meets twice a week for an hour-and-a-half each session. (The ideal time would be three hours, twice a week.) DePaul University's academic year is based on the quarter system; each quarter is ten weeks long. The students attending my class have had previous training in improvisation, scene study, voice and speech, and movement. Typically, they have not had any intensive training in sensory technique.

While teaching, I watch and listen to the experience/exercises, frequently not saying much. I want the actor to sense and listen to his/her own body. (A lot more discussion goes on in the imaginary classroom of this book than in my actual class.) I do not believe in negative comments, and try as much as possible to provide positive suggestions when dealing with the work.

The text itself is set up as a series of lectures, experience/exercises, and class discussions. The discussions are with a fictionalized class of seven acting students. Although the text is intended for the classroom, I hope that its use will not be limited to there. This format was simply the most efficient in offering examples of how the work can be accomplished. It is my intention for the professional actor also to be able to read this text and creatively apply the experience/exercises and their concepts to his/her personal development.

I would like to add that each of the seven individuals that make up my imaginary class bear no direct correlation to the many students of the same names I have had the privilege of knowing over the last four-plus decades. The students in this text are composites of all the many actors I have known.

Would that all the classes I have taught were as articulate as the one that appears in this text. However, the student responses to the experience/exercises are by no means the definitive answers. (Interestingly, some of the best actors I know or have taught were never able to talk about what they were doing in class—but when they got on stage, that was a different story. Their bodies spoke volumes!)

My purpose in including a student discussion was to clarify by example any questions that might arise in the lectures or in the set-up of the experience/exercises, as well as to offer through their questions the typical problems encountered in sensory work. I was not as concerned with writing "great drama" as I was in offering simple examples of diverse responses to the work. The point is for each actor to discover the response that is spontaneous, unique, and true unto him or herself.

From time to time in the various experience/exercises, I ask the actors to record their observations or responses in a journal. The purpose of a journal for actors is to stimulate the power of observation and imagination, as well as to use it as a reference to return to when stuck in the work. Recalling responses recorded in a journal can re-ignite the imagination. Journals are a private matter for the actor, by the actor. I do not ask to read journals.

Actors are encouraged to use the experience/exercises where they may be appropriate for roles they are currently rehearsing. While writing the text, I made the decision to keep specific plays out of the first section. My intention was to focus solely on technique, and not on interpretation. I want the actors to be able to develop a technique separate from playing, as much as a musician develops technique through scales. However, actors at The Theatre School are usually working on roles while also studying this technique.

After having studied sensory technique, I hope that actors will refer back to this text for exercise and improvisation ideas in developing a role. Sensory work, like the development of all technique, is a continuous process. The exercises, responses, or suggestions in this text are not carved in stone.

To the actors reading this text, I want to say: "Use the text as it suits you! No one can teach you how to be an actor better than yourself."

Acknowledgments

I would like to thank a few of the many individuals without whose kind assurance and assistance this book would not have been possible. First and foremost, I am beholden to Richard Aven for his inspiration, knowledge, input, creativity, patience, hard work, and endurance to make the writing of this book come to fruition.

I would also like to thank the following: John Ransford Watts, Dean of The Theatre School Conservatory of Depaul University; Jack and Jane Rollins, for their generous hospitality shown in each visit to New York; my colleagues at The Theatre School—Lisa Quinn (director of publicity), Ric Murphy, Joseph Slowik, David Avcollie, John Culbert, John Bridges, Stacy Gonzalez, and Caryl Givilancz; the preliminary typists, George Mathews, Fran Martone, Morgan Rowe, and Jay Paul Skelton; my students of the last forty-plus years, and especially those who keep returning. Finally, to my beloved husband, Frank Konrath, without whose patience and love this book would not have been possible.

DR. BELLA ITKIN

Foreword

The thing that always struck me about Bella was that she was more prepared than her students. Bella always approached class seriously. There was no laughing or clapping allowed when watching one another work. I liked that. There was no time for back-slapping, or self-gratifying behavior. Class was always quiet, focused, working on the inner self and authentically revealing it. To describe Bella's acting class is like trying to describe a religion, philosophy, or a way of life.

What I remember most about her teaching was the idea of not focusing so much on being, as on doing. At the time I studied with Bella, I was very young, so I immediately translated the idea of doing as a physical process. I later discovered there are ways of doing without being physical. But early on, I just jumped into it literally, *physically doing*—and my simple naïveté served me well.

The best example of this is when I worked on *The Corn Is Green* with Bella as the director. There was one day when this idea of doing—not acting, or being, or emoting, or feeling, but literally, physically doing—really popped into place for me. In the flash of a creative moment, all my past class work and my own intuition came together through performance.

There is a scene in the play where Morgan Evans is taunting Miss Moffat, trying to scare her and speak his mind in a little classroom with wooden desks. Without planning to, I began to stalk her, kind of slowly at first, sliding or pushing the desks out of the way. As I continued to approach her, my actions became more violent and scattered. This physical action prompted a response, naturally, and the whole scene turned into a chase around the classroom, ending with a triumphant leap down the staircase, as Morgan is puffed up with his drunken rebellious nature, trying to deny the gifts within him. The first time it happened, it was totally unplanned, totally spontaneous.

Later, when I looked at it analytically, the scattering of desks was a perfect physicalization of what was going on inside Morgan at the time, wanting to reject the profound gifts or talents burning within him and to go back to his rum-soaked days in the coal mines.

I don't think I could have made that discovery without the specific work with Bella in class, which is presented so clearly and exhaustively in this book. I will forever be grateful to her, and I hope this work inspires and ignites the creative fire within you too.

Kevin Anderson

PART
One

TRAINING THE
SENSORY RESPONSE

Chapter
1

Developing Sensory Power

Recognizing a Kinesthetic Response

The web of our life is of a mingled yarn, good and ill together.

All's Well, That Ends Well

LECTURE: THE BODY REMEMBERS

I was born and lived in Moscow during the Stalin era. During my childhood in Russia, milk was not pasteurized. It had to be boiled to make it safe to drink. There is nothing worse than boiled milk that has been standing for a few minutes to cool off. As the milk cools, a yellow, disgusting-looking skin forms on the top. I was once ordered to drink that cup of milk. As I think of this, I can see a very dark room with a long table. The cup of milk is on the table, the yellow skin on top of the milk. These images are very vivid. I see that yellow skin very, very clearly. I can feel the texture of that skin in my mouth. I want to vomit. My body remembers involuntarily the taste, the texture, the disgust, the hate I have for the milk. Even today, years and years later, I cannot drink plain milk; it has to be mixed with something.

I was very young when I had that experience, so I don't remember the specific date or year, but I do remember the evening I arrived in Chicago in 1932. My sister and I were left sitting in our father's car. My father forgot to put the brake on and the car started to roll down the street. My sister and I screamed and someone jumped into the car and put the brake on. Subsequently, I never learned to drive. Now, whenever my husband gets out of the car to fill it up with gas, I ask, "Is the brake on?" He reassures me it is. Nevertheless, as I sit there in the car, my *kinesthetic* memory takes over. I have the sensation of rolling down the street and I feel panic. My body remembers!

The clearest meaning of the word kinesthetic is "the involuntary sensation of movement." The word comes from the Greek *kinesthesia*. *Kinein* means "to move" and *aisthesis* means "perception of movement." This implies the *awareness* of the *sensation* of movement. In order to create a sensation of movement, various parts of the body are activated or stimulated through a sensorial/psychological response.

One year as I was discussing how the body remembers, an unexpected event interrupted the initial meeting of class. Workmen in the alley below the window began to use pneumatic drills. The unnerving sound penetrated the room through the open windows. The entire class responded immediately. Eric jumped up, swearing. He quickly went over and slammed one of the windows shut. He was followed by Martha and Larry, who were relieved to shut the other two windows. Their behavior was an example of a kinesthetic response. I asked each student to recall their behavior in response to the pneumatic drill.

DR. BELLA: Let's discuss your kinesthetic response to the sound created by the pneumatic drills. How did each of you respond physically?

ERIC: I got up and shut the window.

DR. BELLA: Is that all, Eric?

ERIC: I was swearing. The sound was frustrating. I guess I was angry.

DODI: When I jumped up, I needed to cover my ears with my hands. The sound hurt. I wanted to run away. I was frightened, scared.

DR. BELLA: Good! Those are both examples of kinesthetic behavior. You reacted immediately, involuntarily, with a physical action. Now, suppose I said this was the same thing as a "sensory" response?

LARRY: You mean my ears *heard* the sound of the drill?

DR. BELLA: Right! And your sensory life was stimulated by what you heard.

LARRY: Our kinesthetic response led to a behavior or to an action.

MARTHA: My spine still hears the sound.

DR. BELLA: That's marvelous. Can everyone still hear that sound?

DODI: What do you mean, Dr. Bella? They've stopped working.

DR. BELLA: Can you repeat the experience by using your imagination?

LARRY: How?

DR. BELLA: Start with the environment.

DODI: It's our classroom. We're already here.

DR. BELLA: Be more specific in your observations. Class, close your eyes. Keep them closed. What are the vivid images you see of this classroom?

MARTHA: It's a quiet room. The colors are dark. There are blackboards all around.

JOHN: High ceilings and fluorescent lights.

LARRY: There are some exercise mats on the floor. I see the windows open. It's hot!

DR. BELLA: Fine, that's specific. Larry mentioned the heat. In recalling the images of the room, Larry also became aware of the sensory condition of heat. That's good. What were each of you doing before that dreadful sound penetrated the room?

MARTHA: I was listening to you tell us a story about yourself. I felt good, comfortable. I was flashing on some images from my own childhood.

DR. BELLA: Do you remember what they were?

MARTHA: No, not exactly. The drill scared them out of me. And now we're on to other things.

DR. BELLA: Try to recall them specifically and begin the exercise by writing them down.

DODI: If I go through the steps of creating the details, the imagery of my environment, and of what I was doing, will I be able to convince myself of the kinesthetic response?

DR. BELLA: Not quite. A kinesthetic response happens involuntarily. You won't need to "convince" yourself; you'll *be* convinced. It doesn't always happen on the first try, but we are going to investigate many "experience/exercises" to discover and practice kinesthetic responses.

MARTHA: I'm having a problem imagining a response to those pneumatic drills. My spine still wants to arch just at the suggestion.

DR. BELLA: That's marvelous! Martha, your spine is your kinesthetic memory! However, try to repeat the experience several days from now to check it out. If you still have a strong sensation, recall the experience again in several months. See how long you can recall the experience vividly.

DR. BELLA: Class, you all responded involuntarily to the pneumatic drill, but will your body and psyche remember the experience creatively? Will you be able to transform this experience into a sensorial memory you can relive kinesthetically on cue?

Having had the opportunity to demonstrate through real experience how the body responds kinesthetically, the class is now ready for their first experience/exercise. In order to recreate this experience, I side-coach the actors' activities and imaginations in order to help their bodies remember.

EXPERIENCE/EXERCISE 1: RECREATING A KINESTHETIC RESPONSE TO AN ACTUAL EXPERIENCE

Objective   To make the unreal real—using imagination.

Format   Side coaching.

SECTION A: PREPARATION—HELPING THE BODY TO REMEMBER

Place   The classroom.

1. Repeat the activity you were performing while I was lecturing. Your physical activities included:
   a. sitting, laying on floor, finding your physical posture;
   b. hearing/listening to the lecture;
   c. taking notes.
2. Hear the noises now present both inside and outside the classroom.

SECTION B: THE KINESTHETIC RESPONSE

1. Now hear the unexpected sound of the pneumatic drill.
   a. Re-hear the sound. Hear it in the mind's ear.
   b. What do you want to do? Perform that activity. Allow yourself to experience the physical response by changing your posture and activity.
   c. Allow yourself to experience the feelings and sensations connected with your physical response/activity.

SECTION C: FOLLOWING THE EXPERIENCE/EXERCISE, EVALUATE THE KINESTHETIC RESPONSE

1. What sensory conditions did you believe in?
2. Could you sustain your belief through a behavior?
3. Was your response to hearing the pneumatic drill involuntary?

ASSIGNMENT: PRACTICE

Repeat your experience of hearing the pneumatic drill at home. In the next class session we will again explore this experience/exercise.

The following is a discussion in the next class session after repetition of Experience/Exercise 1:

ERIC: I didn't have any response. I couldn't believe in the sound.
DR. BELLA: How did you prepare?
ERIC: I tried to remember the sound.
DR. BELLA: That is too general. Remember by what you were doing when the actual sound occurred. Where were you? What was the temperature? What were you thinking about? Were you performing any physical tasks when you heard the sound? Recreate the situation.
DODI: I did the same activity as when we were last in class. The only difference was that I didn't want to run away. My belief in the imaginary sound was not very strong.
DR. BELLA: You are not ready to hear kinesthetically. Practice and time will develop your kinesthetic ability and stimulate your imagination.
MARTHA: My spine still hears the sound!
LIZ: I tried to believe, but I couldn't remember everything specifically. I kept changing my activity and behaviour, but I couldn't get it exactly like before.
DR. BELLA: You are trying too hard to remember. Don't work so hard on the

remembering, just the doing. Trust your imagination.

JOHN: I began by walking around the room. I can hear the drill real good, but my response is not always the same. I can remember my response and I keep trying to duplicate that, but it doesn't seem to work. I get frustrated.

DR. BELLA: You are trying to plan your response.

JOHN: Of course. I need to know what my response is going to be.

DR. BELLA: Part of the fun of acting is knowing, but not knowing. In doing this experience/exercise, what will you discover about yourself?

JOHN: But aren't we trying to recreate an experience? How can you do that without knowing how it all turns out?

DR. BELLA: Wasn't part of the experience unexpected? When you first responded to the real sound of the pneumatic drill, did you know the drill was going to interrupt the class? An involuntary response is spontaneous. You can't plan it.

SUMMARY OF EXPERIENCE/EXERCISE 1

1. The body remembers by doing.
2. Practice and time will strengthen an ability to relive a kinesthetic response.
3. Recreate the sensory life and activity, not the response.

EXPERIENCE/EXERCISE 2: DISCOVERING A KINESTHETIC RESPONSE TO AN IMAGINARY EVENT

Objective   Stimulating the imagination.

Format   This is an in-class exercise. I again side-coach the actors through the experience, often making spontaneous suggestions for them to discover changes in behavior.

SECTION A: PREPARATION—CREATING AN IMAGINARY PLACE

Part I: Physical Relaxation

Objective   Getting rid of physical tension.

1. Stand up.
2. Stretch. Keep stretching.
3. Shake out. Really shake out every part of your body.
4. Stretch again. Ask yourself if you feel relaxed. If not, keep stretching.
5. Shake out. Shake out. Shake out.
6. Repeat stretching and shaking out until you feel physically relaxed.

Part II: Creating an Imaginary Environment

1. Turn the classroom into any street of your choosing.
2. You are walking.
   a. You have a destination.
   b. You have a purpose (going home, to work, etc.).
3. See a dirty alley.
   a. Does the alley smell?
4. Decide to take a short-cut through the alley.
5. You see a dead rat.

SECTION B: THE INSTINCTIVE RESPONSE

1. What was your instinctive physical response to the suggestion of the dead rat?
2. What sensory conditions did you believe in?
3. How was your belief sustained through a physical behavior?
4. Did your response to the dead rat physically take over? Was your response involuntary?
5. Was your response tied to a specific memory?
6. Can this response be used again?

The following discussion took place after Experience/Exercise 2:

LARRY: At first, I just walked around the room without a purpose. I couldn't decide where I was going or what street to imagine. Then, as I was walking around the room, I got the image of being on Fullerton Avenue on a supper break. I decided to cross in the middle of the street and walk through an alley next to the dime store. I saw the dead rat—the image of a dead rat—near the garbage dumpster. My stomach hurt. I started to walk faster.

DR. BELLA: I'm happy you didn't stand still trying to consider what to do. A simple physical action such as walking fired your imagination, and when I introduced the image of the dead rat, your body reacted kinesthetically. Good.

ERIC: The exercise didn't work for me. I had a hard time believing in the circumstances. I started, but then stopped participating. I couldn't believe anything.

DR. BELLA: Next time, as you begin the physical action—for instance, walking—also *talk* about the images of your given circumstances. "I am on Lincoln Avenue. . . . There is a lot of traffic. . . . It is noisy. . . . I am going to cross the street. . . . It is hot." Before you know it, your body will respond to these visual, aural, tactile images.

MARTHA: I had a hard time believing in the exercise too. I stood in the corner of the classroom trying to decide where I was, where I was going, and why. I was trying to pick something I thought would be really interesting. When you told us to cross the street, I just decided to do it, but I didn't believe anything. Then when you said, "You see a giant, dead rat," I felt numb. I didn't respond in any way. But as we've been discussing the exercise and while I've been talking, I can see the image of the dead rat. I have this sensation of a smell and my eyes burn a little.

DR. BELLA: Martha, during the exercise, you were trying too hard. But when you started to speak about the image of the rat without worrying whether you were supposed to react or not, you kinesthetically began to have a reaction. Don't play head games with this, just experience it.

JUNE: I believed in the rat, but it was so awful. I didn't want to get involved!

DR. BELLA: But you are involved as you speak. What are you sensing?

JUNE: I am trying not to see a large rat, half dead in our basement, but the image is so vivid. I'm scared and I feel shaky. I was afraid, disgusted. I was very young.

DR. BELLA: This experience is certainly part of your psyche. Why were you in the basement? But perhaps it is too frightening to use creatively.

DODI: Dr. Bella, I had a strong image too. I don't remember why I was in the alley, but when you suggested the rat, I saw it. It was real. This happened to me when I was in the eighth grade. I screamed and ran home.

DR. BELLA: Dodi, you were possessed by a *vivid visual image*. This vivid image is in your psyche and consequently, the body remembered its response. June also has a vivid memory image.

JUNE: But the rat was not really in this room.

DR. BELLA: Everyone has a camera inside that records everything he or she has seen. Dodi involuntarily recalled a very vivid image of a dead rat. I am sure others of you were also stimulated involuntarily by this gross image. But an image must have a base in some past reality for the actor to believe it, to use it as an imagined reality in order to stimulate the senses in the present. Actors with technique can recall the images of their experience using their imagination to accept them as real.

LARRY: What do you mean by "technique"?

DR. BELLA: Technique means a way of work, having a specific procedure that stimulates a response on cue. Technique enables the actor to function freely, sensorially, and psychologically. Technique is a method for applying the imagination. But repetition is an important element.

JOHN: Doesn't that make it mechanical?

DR. BELLA: Certainly, that can happen. But hold on! You will discover that repeating won't be mechanical if what you are practicing is recognizing a *kinesthetic* response, not a practiced response.

MARTHA: I am afraid of repeating how I did it last time because it won't be honest.

DR. BELLA: What does that mean? Honest? You're acting.

DODI: Won't repetition kill my instinct?

DR. BELLA: Repetition does not mean responding by rote, by memory alone. You are practicing an involuntary response, a fresh response. At first you might feel uncomfortable as you "try to remember." However, as you explore specific memories lodged in your psyche, or in what I like to call your "Pandora's Box," you will discover that your behavior/response will become instinctive, not planned.

THE PANDORA'S BOX

Each of us carries around a storehouse of all we have learned, observed, fantasized, imagined, dreamed, felt, hoped, and experienced. I call this storehouse the actor's "Pandora's Box". It is the source for self-knowledge and for power to believe in the

THE HISTORY OF PANDORA'S BOX

In its more chauvinistic form, the story of Pandora is similar to Eve's in the Old Testament of the *Bible.* Zeus orders Pandora's creation as part of a revenge against Prometheus, who had cleverly stolen fire from the gods. From the various Greek versions of the myth, it appears Zeus wanted to give humanity something else to be fascinated by, instead of the secrets of the gods. So he has a woman created.

Pandora is molded out of clay by Vulcan or Hephaestus, depending on the particular whim of the storyteller. Life is breathed into her by the four Winds. Minerva endows her with artistic knowledge; Venus adorns her with grace and beauty. She is then attired by the Seasons and Graces. All the gods and goddesses in Olympus contribute to her creation. This is one of the meanings of Pandora's name—"all gifted."

The story continues with several more variations. Either Zeus gives her a beautiful box which contains all the evils known to mankind, or, after being refused by Prometheus, she is married by his brother Epimetheus (which literally means "afterthought"), who has in his house a jar or box which Zeus has ordered never to be opened. Pandora, in her curiosity, opens the box, allowing all the evils to escape and infect the world of mankind. Perceiving the travesty, Pandora shuts the lid just in time to keep hope, the last good or evil contained in the jar, depending on how you look at it, to help humankind endure the pains of old age, labor, sickness, insanity, vice, passion, and all the other ills just released. Hence, woman becomes the bane of man, responsible for all the ills that have plagued humankind ever since. Another story, however, has Epimetheus opening Pandora's box and releasing these same evils. In this version, Pandora is still responsible, as the evils were being released from her box.

During the 1970s and 1980s, scholars recognized that Pandora's story is older than this slightly chauvinistic patriarchal treatment. Before the Greeks, Pandora, Gaia, Themis, Aphrodite, and all of the other goddesses had a more noble and powerful relationship with their followers. In its earlier form, Pandora's name means "all-giving" and she is a form of the earth mother, dispensing all of the nurturing necessary for life. Pagan statues of Pandora and her basket are celebrations of woman's ability to feed all of the hungers and needs of man.

I have enjoyed referring to the actor's Pandora's Box for many years. I suppose I have unconsciously tapped the danger of the Greek myths, but having discovered Pandora's earlier tradition, I am pleased by the balance of both positive and negative forces she releases for all actors.

imaginary. An actor's gift exploits the ability to tap resources in his/her Pandora's Box as part of the technique to recreate a full sensory life on stage.

Figuratively speaking, the actor opens various compartments of memory to allow sensations to fly out. After the actor has been stimulated, the experience automatically restores itself within the actor's memory. The actor must learn how to continue filling the Pandora's Box through an active observation of all that happens in life, as well as to learn how to release the contents of individual compartments lodged deep within his/her psyche.

Frightening, frustrating, or painful experiences; anything that has been somewhat or somehow traumatic; feelings we might consider "unacceptable;" all these emotions can prompt intense responses from the Pandora's Box. Many times, actors want to negate these feelings or experiences, but they exist, waiting to be used. As the self-exploration demanded by this process continues, I always hope the actor will somehow embrace those responses that are considered "unacceptable." Often, they are the most valuable. It can be a painful process, but a necessary one in freeing and stimulating creativity.

The unfamiliar is frightening. Any growth however, depends on a positive approach to change, otherwise, we will not be successful in our training. The objective of identifying the various and specific compartments of the Pandora's Box will enable actors to use these memories in imaginative ways as actors. Actors begin to develop technique when they learn how to consciously select and open the needed compartment of their experience to suit the scene. With practice, each actor will learn how to open and close compartments of memory involuntarily.

The Pandora's Box not only allows actors to investigate and use the valuable past they have accumulated, but also to become more sensorially aware of the present. Often, the memories that have lodged themselves deep in the psyche and that provide the most valuable information, have strong emotional significance. A period of gestation is often required to allow the individual to accept and understand the sensations and feelings associated with these events.

> JOHN: I'm beginning to see a connection here. When you asked us about our reactions to the image of the dead rat, some of us also remembered related images from our past or childhood. But I am confused about being "in-the-moment," or in other words, having a kinesthetic response, and also trying to relate that to a past experience from what you call my Pandora's Box.
> DR. BELLA: Don't try to relate it to a past experience. If there is a past experience to relate it to, the memory will activate your body involuntarily. John, you seem to be worried about how you will control your responses.
> JOHN: I want to be a good actor.
> DR. BELLA: Good acting does not look like "acting." It has all the qualities of natural behavior, and natural behavior is involuntary, that is, it happens kinesthetically, spontaneously. It is a response stimulated through our five senses that expresses itself as a need. When Eric heard the pneumatic drill the other day in class, he needed to make the noise stop, so he shut the window. But his behavior also included a psychology. He jumped up swearing and slammed the window shut.

SUMMARY

Human behavior has two kinds of need: physical and psychological. They are really one thing. Each physical need has a psychology, and psychology can only be expressed through physical behavior. One is inwardly felt, stimulating outward action; the other, vice versa. Therefore, I refer to *acting as behaving, or acting as doing*.

My teaching focuses on the relationship between the inner and outer technique, that is, the relationship between the psychological and the physical. An instinctive response to a stimulus such as a dead rat is an example of involuntary physical behavior. Inseparable from this behavior is the expression of a particular psychology. The students react with fear, disgust, or with memories of a previous experience. My phrase for this involuntary reaction is a "sensorial/psychological kinesthetic response," or simply a "kinesthetic response."

Before an actor can communicate believable behavior on stage, s/he must discover how to develop the ability to uncover his/her emotional/physical responses in life. When acting, these responses are recalled through the use of imagination and kinesthetic technique.

Chapter
2
The Power of Observation

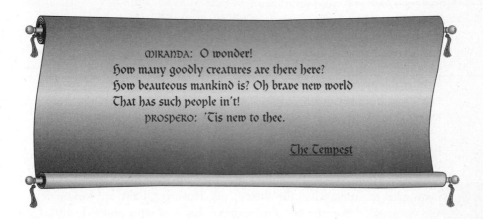

MIRANDA: O wonder!
How many goodly creatures are there here?
How beauteous mankind is? Oh brave new world
That has such people in't!
PROSPERO: 'Tis new to thee.

The Tempest

LECTURE: THE INNOCENT EYE

No matter what age, an actor must have naiveté. He or she must wonder, be aston-ished, and always observe the beautiful and the ugly *as if* for the first time.

We all suffer from the effects of pollution, violence, incessant noise, and the hectic pace necessary to get through each day. In fact, in order to get through each day, we desensitize ourselves to unpleasant and distracting conditions. We undergo sensorial shutdown. An actor, however, must be receptive to stimuli. An actor must make a conscious effort to observe life and to take notice of all sensor-ial responses. Through conscious practice, an actor can revitalize sensorial in-stincts so they will be more readily available kinesthetically when working on a scene. Also, as the power of observation grows, an actor will increase imaginative and interpretative skills, meaning the actor won't need to rely solely on actual past experiences to effectively work on a role.

The important thing is to work without the bias or prejudice of sensorial shut-down, that is, to begin with a clean slate, independent of preconceived thoughts, attitudes, or feelings, and to possess a childlike naiveté that reminds me of Mi-randa in *The Tempest*. An actor who has recognized and conquered sensory shutdown will depend on sensorial instincts for information and not decide or judge beforehand how to react to stimuli.

JOHN: Sensorial shutdown! Why does that happen?

DR. BELLA: There are many causes: not wanting to be sensorially involved because it stimulates physical discomfort or fear of the unexpected. The unknown can cause physical and emotional discomfort. Often, sensory shutdown occurs because an actor is involved with personal problems, such as worrying about success or failure. While self-absorbed, the worried actor figuratively speaking puts on blinders and ear-plugs. If you allow this shutdown to occur in everyday life, how can you hope to be open to a free use of emotions in performance?

LARRY: How do I avoid shutdown?

DR. BELLA: First, become aware of when you are shut down. Ask yourself, "What causes my shutdown?" Second, realize that shutdown hinders emotional growth, and consequently your training process. Third, make a conscious effort to revitalize or activate your senses, to live sensorially in the present, in the moment.

LIZ: How can I start with a clean slate?

ERIC: Yes, I know what I like, how I feel about some things before I see or hear them. Is that a problem?

JOHN: It's impossible not to have preconceived attitudes, feelings.

DR. BELLA: An actor must observe the environment innocently and not *depend* on past influences. I will illustrate. I see the class twice a week. I think I know what to expect when the class meets. However, I also appreciate new and unexpected occurrences. For example, Liz is wearing a new T-shirt. I am aware I have never seen that T-shirt before. On this day, I see the color and the design for the first time. It is a pretty design and it lifts me up. I notice. I am observing. When Dodi entered the classroom, I noticed and saw, today, the look on Dodi's face. I watched the way she walked and dropped her books and coat on the floor. I realize she is disturbed about something. I ask, "What's wrong?" Or I hear laughter in the hall and Larry and Martha enter laughing.

ERIC: Didn't you recognize who was laughing before they came into the room? I mean all that you observed depended on a past experience for you to compare it to.

DR. BELLA: That's true, Eric. However, I must hear the laugh in order to recognize it! Of course there is past experience, but the present must always be acute.

DODI: The present must always be acute.

LIZ: Is that the same thing as being "in the moment?"

DR. BELLA: Yes, responding in the now, . . . concentrating on the present.

DODI: I'm confused. I still don't understand how being aware of my own sensory life will make me a better actor.

DR. BELLA: Babies and very young children use all their senses naturally. But the world is very new to them and so they also use their senses out of ne-

cessity, to make "sense" of their surroundings. However, by the time we be-
come adults, most of us have lost the ability to respond spontaneously and
with curiosity to stimuli. Now you are training to be actors, which means dis-
covering all that is unique. So, we must re-ignite your sensory responses. As
you become more comfortable with a spontaneous, instinctual sensory life,
you will feel free to respond to stimuli in rehearsal and in performance. You
will not preplan your responses. In performance, an actor's response is al-
ways involuntary, even though it is always on cue.

DODI: So, if I train my awareness to sensory responses in life, then I am ob-
serving, and in performance, when I am acting, this ability will help me to be
in the moment and to respond kinesthetically.

DR. BELLA: Yes, Dodi, if you practice!

LARRY: Is observation always sensorial?

DR. BELLA: I won't answer that question with a yes or no. Instead, I will il-
lustrate with a common experience. I will imagine going on a shopping trip
to the grocery market. As I enter the supermarket, my body responds to the
temperature change. For example, if it is a cold winter day, the store is
heated and the hot air warms me up; or if it is a hot summer day, the air con-
ditioning is on and then the cold air hits me.

JUNE: You are saying you respond physically to temperature change.

DR. BELLA: That's right. My body informs me instantaneously. Let's con-
tinue. I hear sounds. At the checkout line, people are talking, children are
crying, or loudly wanting something. I take a shopping cart. As I touch the
handle, I feel its hard surface. I push the cart and hear the wheels squeaking.
The sound is annoying. I pass the flower section. I smell the fragrance and
see the colors of the flowers. They are beautiful. I see the fruit counters. I
notice the orderly arrangement of all kinds of fruits and vegetables. They are
colorful.

DODI: And the prices!

DR. BELLA: That's right. What else might I notice?

MARTHA: If you pick up an apple to examine it, you touch and feel the tex-
ture?

DR. BELLA: Very good. I am interested in purchasing some bananas.

JOHN: When I go shopping, I generally smell the ripe bananas from a dis-
tance.

DR. BELLA: Your sense of smell responds involuntarily. I approach the deli
section. I see the counter full of salads, meats, cheeses. However, a tasty
aroma overwhelms my senses. I see the chickens on a spindle, barbecuing. I
watch the turning of the chickens. I am aware the turning has a repeated,
definite rhythm. I stand watching the chicken sizzle, smelling the seasonings.
With that delicious smell, I get very hungry. I can taste the chicken sensori-
ally. It occurs instinctively, involuntarily—the seeing, the smelling, and the
tasting. The awareness of the smell led to spying the chickens and then to
sensorially tasting them. I am tempted to purchase a barbecued chicken. I
think, "Should I or should I not buy?" I overcome the temptation. I walk
over to the fish counter. I stop being hungry because the fishy smell is not

appetizing. I hurry to the freezer section. My body informs me by respond-
ing instinctively to the change of temperature. Especially when I open one of
the freezer doors, a much colder air hits me. My hands feel the cold pack-
ages.

ERIC: Dr. Bella, the thing for me about going to the market, especially here
in the city, is all the people.

DR. BELLA: How are the people different from what you are used to?

ERIC: Well, first of all, there are so many. I mean the pace gets hectic, push-
ing and shoving. Sometimes, I get edgy.

JOHN: People can be interesting, though. And our neighborhood has such a
mix, both ethnically and economically.

DR. BELLA: You enjoy observing others, don't you, John.

JOHN: Yeah, I do.

MARTHA: The place I notice people is in the checkout line as I am waiting to
pay. That can be fun!

DR. BELLA: What do you mean "fun"?

MARTHA: Sometimes a checkout girl is sharing her love life with the girl bag-
ging the groceries. I always enjoy eavesdropping on what they are saying.

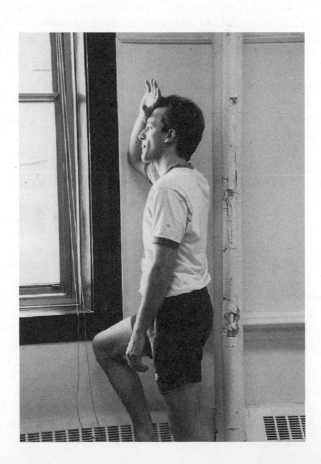

LIZ: I'm very impatient when I hear unnecessary conversation slowing up the line. People around me get angry too.

ERIC: A lot of times the checkout person is slow because he doesn't like his job.

LARRY: Dr. Bella, back when you were describing the chicken, you used a phrase I really liked—"tasty smell." I never thought of smell that way before!

MARTHA: You mentioned temperature changes several times and that your body informed you of the change. Is this what you mean by an instinctive, kinesthetic response?

DR. BELLA: Yes. The instant the sensory response is felt, a behavior is simultaneously and instinctively stimulated.

EXPERIENCE/EXERCISE 3: PRACTICING SENSORIAL OBSERVATION

Objective   Recognizing physical/sensorial responses to visual stimuli.

Place   A window in your apartment or home.

Format   Choose a period of time during the day when you can observe life through the window for five to ten minutes at least three times in one week.

MARTHA: What are we supposed to do, just look out the window?

DR. BELLA: Yes.

DODI: Should I write down what I see?

DR. BELLA: No. Just observe.

DODI: But if I don't write down my observations, I might forget them.

DR. BELLA: I don't think you will forget, but please, do not focus on trying to remember. Just observe the world through the window.

In a session one week later, the actors shared what they could recall about their observations.

DODI: I live in a basement. It was advertised as a "garden apartment," but when I look out the windows, all I see are legs and feet, the wheels of shopping carts and baby buggies. It's very frustrating not to be able to see the sky. Anyway, on Monday, after the rain, around 7:00 P.M., the sky must have still been dark and cloudy because I could see that the streetlights were on and many feet were passing by my window. Lots of people coming home from work. I remember someone ran out of the front door and banged it. I've been thinking about that sound.

DR. BELLA: What do you mean "thinking"?

DODI: The sound keeps repeating in my head.

DR. BELLA: What does your body want to do when you hear it?

DODI: There is a reflex to jump like I did when it happened. I guess I mean I've been thinking about how my body responds to that sound.

DR. BELLA: Continue.

DODI: A woman always passes my window around this time. She wears high heels. I recognize the rhythm of her walk and the click of her high heels. She has attractive legs and she wears beautiful shoes. I also recognized Bill, my neighbor; he wears these boots. This exercise was fun, Dr. Bella, but from my observation last night I have only one overwhelming experience. I was looking out the window as before, and recognizing a few people. Then all of a sudden, there was this crash against my window! This man, I think he was drunk, stumbled and fell against my window. He frightened me, I almost screamed. I got panicky. I was scared he might. . . , well,. . . .

DR. BELLA: What did you do when he smashed into the window?

DODI: I panicked and ducked behind a chair. I don't know why I got so scared, because after a few minutes I felt a little stupid behind the chair, but I was afraid the man was going to be violent and come into my apartment. I haven't been able to think about anything else from last night's observation but my fright.

DR. BELLA: Your reaction was perfectly natural.

LARRY: My window faces a courtyard. I decided to do my observations around 5:30 in the afternoon. On Sunday, the sky was grey. There were clouds and it smelled like rain, but it didn't. The courtyard was quiet; there weren't many people. Monday, it rained all day. The courtyard was wet. People were hurrying home from work. Janet, my next-door neighbor, was wearing a red coat and carrying a matching umbrella as she came home. When Bob and Sue came home—they live upstairs—they seemed tired. They were walking very slowly. A very heavy woman, gross, immense size, probably over 200 pounds, came into the courtyard loaded with shopping bags. I had never seen her before. A few minutes later, she came back out to the courtyard with an oversized bulldog on a leash. I thought how the dog looked like her. I was kind of disgusted by that.

DR. BELLA: Did your body have any physical reaction to this lady?

LARRY: Well, right now, my stomach's getting a little tighter. I remember thinking how people like that just should not exist. That's extreme, but there shouldn't be such ugliness in the world.

DR. BELLA: Continue.

LARRY: On Wednesday, I had the windows open. The traffic on the street sounded very busy. What I mean is, I heard the sound of the cars and buses. It seemed like everyone was going somewhere. Lots of activity: people coming and going with groceries, cleaning, and packages. The air was cool. The feeling of the courtyard was different from Sunday or Monday. More active, not as sedate, or safe.

DR. BELLA: Excellent, Larry. Your observations not only included the visual, but what you heard and smelled as well.

ERIC: I looked out my window beginning on Monday, at 3:00. It was raining. The cars were moving slowly. A few people were on the street with umbrellas. Tuesday, at 3:00, the sun was out. Traffic moved faster. There were more people on the street. Thursday was the same as Tuesday, except it was cold.

DR. BELLA: How long were you observing each time?

ERIC: Oh, about ten minutes.

DR. BELLA: Is that all that transpired?

ERIC: That's all I remember.

LIZ: Monday, 8 A.M.: It was raining. I was sitting at my dining room table, drinking coffee. My window faces LaSalle Street. The window was shut. Traffic was moving very slowly. A driver in a red sedan kept honking his horn. He would always honk two short times and one long. An old woman with boots was walking north. She had a clear plastic rain hat on. Her hair was white. She was carrying a shopping bag from Marshall Field's. At 8:05, two men and a woman ran across LaSalle to catch the bus. One of the men was in a dark long raincoat. The woman had a yellow umbrella. A boy rode by on a bicycle. It was green.

Wednesday, 8 A.M.: My window was open. The air was clean. It was a clear fall morning. Traffic was moving a lot faster than it had on Monday. I tried to watch for specific things to remember, but it was mostly just traffic. Then the same two men and the woman crossed the street to catch their bus. The man who had worn the raincoat on Monday had a green cableknit sweater on. The woman was wearing a shawl. I checked my watch to make sure it was 8:05, and it was.

DR. BELLA: Liz, your observations sound like some sort of list, why so clinical?

LIZ: Didn't I do it right?

DR. BELLA: It's not a question of getting the exercise right, I'm wondering why you felt the need to be so factual in your observations.

LIZ: I was trying to make sure I could remember as much as possible.

DR. BELLA: So your concentration was on the question "What can I remember?"

LIZ: I guess. Was that wrong? I'm not the best student, and sometimes I have a hard time studying. I really wanted to do a good job on this assignment.

DR. BELLA: First of all, Liz, it is an experience/exercise, not an assignment. What do you suppose I mean by the term "experience/exercise"?

LIZ: Well, Dodi and Larry both talked about responses they had while they were observing.

DR. BELLA: Can you recall your responses to the events you witnessed?

LIZ: Wednesday morning I was worried I wouldn't have anything specific to talk about until the two men and the woman crossed the street again to get to their bus.

DR. BELLA: Nothing interesting was going on?

LIZ: No. Everyone was mindlessly going to work and I was thinking about how they were all shut down sensorially and that got me depressed a little. I remember thinking "We live such automated lives." But then I decided that wasn't the assignment and. . . .

DR. BELLA: I don't know about that, you just recalled a very nice response to what you saw. That was the experience/exercise. Very good.

MARTHA: I live on the twelfth floor of a building on Lake Shore Drive, facing the lake. Lake Michigan is wonderful to watch. It's always changing. My first observation was on Monday, at 6:00 P.M., after the rain. The traffic was very heavy going north. The cars and the Outer Drive buses were moving very slowly. All of a sudden, the traffic stopped going north. I saw an ambulance and a police car speed up the Drive.

> *At this point, Martha's body tenses up a bit. She seems to momentarily retreat from the class.*

MARTHA: I was wondering if anyone got hurt. The sky was clearing up, but the lake was grey. Something about that seemed important to me. And even though my windows were closed, I could hear the tires on the wet pavement.

On Tuesday, at 6:00, the traffic was heavy, but moving fast. The sky was clear and the lake was quiet, a blue-green color. I just stood there and looked into the distance, as if I were trying to look across the lake. The lake made me feel very peaceful.

On Thursday, the traffic was heavier than usual, and I was aware of something exciting, but then the phone rang, and I missed the opportunity to do my third observation.

DR. BELLA: Martha, would you like to say anything about your experience during the first observation?

MARTHA: I was aware that the traffic had stopped because of an accident, and, well, . . . it reminded me of an accident I once had, . . . the ambulance, the sirens, my fear. I felt a pressure in my spine and stomach. I didn't want to remember, but the images just kept coming up.

DR. BELLA: That's very interesting, Martha. Thank you.

JOHN: Monday, 8:00 A.M.: I started looking out of my window. My window faces a busy street. It was raining. I looked at the sky, . . . kept looking. It seemed to me it was going to rain all day. I heard the traffic even before I opened the window. Cars on the next street. I stood looking. I closed my window.

DR. BELLA: Both John and Martha have recalled reactions to sound as well as to what they saw. Very good.

JOHN: Wednesday morning, the sky was blue. It made me feel good. I don't remember anything else, except that I was worried about a major paper I had due this morning. At 8:00 A.M. today, I noticed people walking. I think I remember people walking on Monday and Wednesday, but I didn't focus on them. That's about all I remember. I tried to keep focused, but my mind was not on what was happening on the street.

DR. BELLA: What were you focusing on?

JOHN: Well, I had that paper due this morning. I stayed up writing until 3:00 A.M. last night, and as I was looking out of the window my mind was on the paper and on how tired I was. I guess I'm a classic study of how sensorial shutdown works in our lives. I didn't have the energy to allow myself to focus on the exercise, to focus on my responses to what I could have experienced through the window.

DR. BELLA: That's a very interesting analysis, John. You have recognized a problem, but that doesn't mean that your body was not responding to sensory conditions. You mentioned lack of sleep. Your body was aware of this condition. However, it is also true that the pressure of the paper and your lack of sleep interfered with your ability to do the exercise. If this had been an acting scene, you would not have had the energy to focus your imagination to the purpose.

JUNE: Dr. Bella, I had a disturbing response to this exercise.

DR. BELLA: What do you mean, June?

JUNE: Well, my window faces an alley. There are three large garbage containers. I had a cup of coffee in my hands when I first started to observe Tuesday morning at 9:00. Seeing the garbage cans made me feel dirty, but holding the cup of coffee seemed to calm me down in a way. But as I was looking out of the window, this woman stumbled into the alley. She appeared to be in work clothes with a man's cap on. I wondered why she was there, if she was some kind of city worker or if she worked for the electric or gas company. Then, she slipped and fell and I immediately got worried that she was hurt, but she just sat there on the ground. I wasn't quite sure what to feel. She looked young and healthy, but as I looked at her, I began to feel uncomfortable.

On Wednesday, she was back, but this time with three men, and they were all digging through the garbage, looking for soda and beer cans, and then they found some food, which they ate. It made me feel really guilty to watch them. I realized they were probably homeless.

On Friday, they were back again! This time, however, they found an almost empty bottle of booze and they fought over it. I looked specifically at the woman's face, her empty eyes and her puffy, dirty cheeks, and I suddenly realized that on Monday, she had been drunk. I got really angry. It makes me so mad to see people destroying themselves. The minute I realized they were just a bunch of drunks, I stopped feeling sorry for them. Instead, I began to hate them for being so lazy, for wasting their lives.

DR. BELLA: Is this what you found disturbing about the exercise?

JUNE: Well, yes, but also that at first I felt sorry for them, and then when I realized they were alcoholics, I got really angry. That kind of self-abuse totally changed my response. It's like I stopped observing and my prejudice took over.

DR. BELLA: June, that is a very astute observation. Class, almost all of you had as part of your experience a particular response that was not objective. A subjective influence from some past experience or some prejudice interfered with your direct response to the present moment. For Larry, it was obesity; for Martha, it was the memory of a past experience triggered by the possible car accident; for John, it was the belief that an assignment due for another class was more important than this exercise; and June very keenly diagnosed her prejudice. But Eric, what kept you from doing the work?

ERIC: I don't know.

DR. BELLA: Well, think a bit. Are you lazy or are you afraid of the work?

LECTURE: THE SUBJECTIVE SENSORIAL RESPONSE OR PREJUDICE

In Experience/Exercise 3, "Practicing Sensorial Observation," the actors discovered the difficulty of remaining objective. Subjective or prejudiced responses interfered with their ability to stay in the moment. A subjective or prejudiced response is a previous experience that influences our attitude toward the present. In other words, it is how the past influences the present. Experience and human nature naturally lead to the development of opinions, attitudes, prejudices, philosophies, and preconceived feelings. These may be either of a positive or of a negative nature. Frequently, however, the negative reigns, so that a past experience or learned response has a negative or prejudicial influence on our spontaneous, innocent experience of the present.

In order to perform a role, an actor needs to recognize how his/her personal subjectivity differs from that of the character. Or another way of saying it, an actor must understand how a character subjectively prejudices his/her responses in a way that might be different from the actor's. Therefore, it is important for the actor to discover–uncover personal subjectivity. It is not an issue of overcoming. It is an issue of recognizing and understanding the prejudice.

EXPERIENCE/EXERCISE 4: SUBJECTIVE OBSERVATION

Objective   Recognizing subjective responses.

Place   Any public place.

Format

1. Set aside at least two fifteen-minute periods to observe people. Observe people you don't know.
2. Observe during any time of day.
3. Note those responses that are prejudicial or subjective.
4. Type up your responses and hand them in. Do not sign your name.

ERIC: How will you know who did the work? Are we going to share our discoveries with each other, or will these remain anonymous?

DR. BELLA: Certain personal views are private and should remain so. That is the reason your papers should be typed and not signed.

LARRY: Will we ever share our subjective, intimate thoughts and feelings directly with each other?

DR. BELLA: There will come a time when the class will be ready to do so, but at this point, the climate is not conducive for that kind of sharing.

DODI: What do you mean by "climate"?

DR. BELLA: Learning to respect, and understand, and not to negatively criticize or condemn each other's personal subjective views. If you are worried that by exposing a prejudice you will be negatively judged, then probably there would be some censoring of responses. The point is to develop and recognize responses.

SUMMARY OF RESPONSES TO EXPERIENCE/EXERCISE 4

Many ambivalent reactions will result from this exercise. Often the actors berate themselves for being biased or steeped in prejudice. Generally, personal appearance, body odor, unattractive speech (both in the quality of sound and the language), ethnicity or race, sexual behavior and/or orientation, and rude or cruel behavior will reveal negative responses. Occasionally, some positive subjectivity is noted in the respect held for religious people, the elderly, and attractive people. Some students may recognize how appearance can prejudice us to unwarranted positive reactions and in so doing condemn the unhealthy preoccupation of this society for the trim and beautiful.

The actor must not discard these discoveries, but learn how to use them as part of his/her Pandora's Box. It is a complicated process, whereby the actor becomes a Dr. Jekyl and Mr. Hyde, uncovering the negative (generally), but using the discoveries for creative purposes.

LECTURE: THE POWER OF IMAGINATION

Learning to be true to yourself, to be spontaneous in life, is one very important part of the process of becoming a good actor. However, on stage, you are never totally yourself. Plays often explore a time, a place, and a character's journey through a physiology and a psychology that are not necessarily first-hand experience for the actor. A fertile imagination is needed to create a reality out of what is not actually present. To create experience where there has been no experience requires the actor to possess a free and active intellect. An actor knows he is not really Hamlet, but somehow he must discover a way to inhabit Hamlet's world.

Whenever a young actor faces a great role, there is naturally a sense of panic. "How will I measure up to the others? Oh, that great play . . . that great role. What should I do first? How can I do this?" My response is, "Why not start with the sensorial requirements in the text and see how they trigger your imagination." For example, when Hamlet says in Act I, Scene ii:

> Oh that this too too sullied flesh, would melt,
> Thaw, and resolve itself into a dew:

the actor should investigate the sense of feeling dirty and not worry about the psychological aspects of the moment. He should begin with the explicit physical life suggested in the lines.

Another example from Scene iv employs the sensory conditions of the cold and ominous dark night:

HAMLET: The air bites shrewdly; is it very cold?
HORATIO: It is a nipping and an eager air.
HAMLET: What hour now?
HORATIO: I think it lacks of twelve.
MARCELLUS: No, it is struck.
HORATIO: Indeed I heard it not: then it draws near the season,
Wherein the spirit held his want to walk.

The challenge of this scene is met when the actor combines his/her life experiences of the night and the cold with the imaginative experience of anticipating the supernatural. By working on a kinesthetic response to the known sensory conditions of the scene, the actor uses a springboard in reality by which to segue into the unreal, the imaginary.

EXPERIENCE/EXERCISE 5: FREEING THE IMAGINATION THROUGH MAKE-BELIEVE

Format   Observe sensorially something familiar and create something fantastic and unfamiliar out of it; an event or a story.

1. Subjects for observation may include:
   a. people (strangers);
   b. inanimate objects;
   c. nature—trees, plants, sky, etc.;
   d. animals;
   e. painting, sculpture, music.
2. Be prepared to share your imaginative daydreams with the class.

SHARING THE MAKE-BELIEVE

DODI: One night, I looked up at the sky and there was this lonely star. She was twinkling in the sky. I fantasized that she called for someone to keep her company. All of a sudden, my star became a beautiful face sparkling in the sky, sparkling with tears. Then the man in the moon peeked out from behind a cloud. She saw him and her sparkle was a smile. She wasn't lonely anymore!

DR. BELLA: A mixture of fantasy with reality. The star had human elements; tears of loneliness and a face. Dodi called the star "she." Dodi personalized her feelings.

LARRY: My story is the Buddha. I was walking on Michigan Avenue, watching and listening. It was about 4:00 P.M. on Friday. People were in a hurry to get home. The traffic was heavy. I passed an Asian jewelry shop, a souvenir store. I went back and stopped to look into the window. There was a broadly grinning Buddha. He was a carved three-dimensional figure about 3" by 3". His eyes were. . . . They seemed alive. His belly was very large, his arms were outstretched. Around his neck, shoulders, and arms were strings of shiny beads. The beads flowed down his belly. He was in the middle of the window, surrounded by other souvenirs. He was looking at me, smiling, laughing, inviting me to come in and join his party. This Buddha was not a sage or a teacher, but a drunken man, singing, laughing, and inviting me and all the other inhabitants of the window (elephants, clowns, monkeys, jewelry) to join him. He was offering his beads to a clown lady. She smiled and her arms seemed to stretch toward him. All the objects started dancing, laughing, celebrating. I started to laugh, and then I realized I was standing on the street laughing! I felt silly. So I walked home, but all the while I was fantasizing about the Buddha. He was a man who gave up his religion. He loves life, loves the lady clown. I would really like to play a role like the Buddha.

DR. BELLA: Imaginatively bringing inanimate objects to life is a marvelous creative process.

MARTHA: I have a sixteenth-century–looking dagger. I picked the dagger up and kept looking at it and thinking about Queen Elizabeth and Essex. I saw the image of Elizabeth. She was wearing a velvet gown with a farthingale. The gown was bejeweled; her face was very white, heavily rouged. Elizabeth and Essex were lovers. I don't know whether this is fiction or fact, but in my fantasy they were lovers. Once, Elizabeth had given Essex the dagger as a sign of her love. If Essex was ever to betray her, he was to send her that dagger. A messenger brings Elizabeth the dagger to inform her that Essex and his troops are at the palace gates. I am the messenger. I am frightened at her reaction when I hand her the dagger.

DR. BELLA: Martha, I take it you have seen pictures of Queen Elizabeth and Essex and have read some literature from the period.

MARTHA: Yes, a play. I would like to play Elizabeth some day. I think she is a fascinating woman. So powerful.

DR. BELLA: Very good. I hope you do. Objects, historic research, and literature are very productive ways to stimulate the imagination, as well as a means for preparing a role.

JUNE: My story is based on something that might happen. I went to the supermarket to shop. I started to watch the people. As I turned into the aisle of canned goods, there was this grey-haired old gentleman scrutinizing a shelf of canned goods. He was dressed in a dark, pressed business suit with a vest, starched white collar and a dark tie, and highly polished shoes. His black felt hat was propped on top of the cart. It was around 9:00 Saturday morning. He seemed totally out of place. I thought about our assignment. I pretended to read my shopping list so I would not be conspicuous while observing him. I started to imagine that he must be a funeral director. No, I thought, a bank executive, dressed to conduct a board meeting. Probably his chauffeur was outside waiting with the limo. I felt like a spy.

I noticed that he was methodically examining each can, checking the price and size. Finally, he decided on two small cans and put them carefully in his cart. I continued to follow him throughout the store and finally to the check-out counter. He slowly took out and put on the counter the two cans, a small loaf of bread, and a package of lunch meat. He examined his bill, took out his wallet, and gave the checkout person the exact change. He knew her and said, "Good to see you, Ann. How are the kids?" She answered, "Fine. How are you today? Better?" He nodded, "Good." And then she said, "Take care of yourself, Bill." He smiled, put his hat on, and left the store.

I followed him. He walked slowly and with dignity. Of course, there was no chauffeur waiting for him. I stood there for a few minutes imagining what his life might be. I decided that he lives alone, his wife is dead. He survives on his Social Security. Since Ann asked him if he was better, he must have been sick. He can't stand the idea of being retired, so whenever he goes out, he gets dressed up as though he were going to work.

DR. BELLA: Excellent observations. You are a very sympathetic individual.

JOHN: I was sitting in the park trying to decide what I could use for the assignment and a ragged-looking woman arrived with two shopping bags full of clothing and household objects. An umbrella was sticking out of one of the bags. I realized she was a street person. She sat down on the bench next to mine. Her odor was dreadful. I was uncomfortable, but I decided to stay. She was wearing an old, torn, dirty fur coat. The coat must have been expensive at one time. She sat staring into space. Her face was weather-beaten and dirty. Then she pulled out an old yellow newspaper from her pocket, unfolded it, and placed it carefully on her lap. She just sat, staring at the paper, but not really seeing it, or reading it.

My curiosity was aroused. I started to fantasize: She used to be an actress. The paper she had saved was a review with a picture of a role she once played. It reminded her of when she was successful. She was smiling, but the face was dirty and grim. It was tragic. She must be very unhappy, I thought. I could smell alcohol. Perhaps her career was ruined by drink. Or perhaps, even though the review was magnificent, she was afraid she wasn't talented. Her insecurity and pain, and then a tragic love affair, destroyed her. Now, she's all alone.

It started to rain, so I got up to leave but then looked back to see what she was doing. She had opened her umbrella. The newspaper was still on her lap. She was just looking into space. She looked tragic, but funny too, sitting there with a torn umbrella in the rain.

DR. BELLA: John, you made me, and the entire class I think, see specific images and feel pathos for that street woman. Marvelous.

ERIC: Well, I went to the zoo, to the monkey house. I observed several cages of monkeys. They all look so human. They were running and swinging around, making monkey noises. In a corner, I saw three monkeys huddled together. I decided they were a family, and, then, that they were people and not monkeys at all, trapped on an island of monkeys. After that I went home.

DR. BELLA: What!? Excuse me, but that was such a marvelous beginning, why did you stop?

ERIC: I was kind of hoping that would be enough. I knew everyone else would have really inventive stories to share. I only visited the zoo yesterday. The monkey story is stupid.

DR. BELLA: Have you thought about your three monkeys since your visit to the zoo?

ERIC: A little. I decided they were a mother and father protecting their child from the other apes. That's as far as I got.

DR. BELLA: Class, let's help Eric and play a make-believe game. Come, sit in a circle, and, Eric, begin your story again.

Eric stands in the center continuing his story.

ERIC: The male monkey is a human being. I am the man, the male monkey. My name is Mr. Denby. Mrs. Denby, Rose,. . .

Here, Eric takes June by the hand and brings her into the circle.

. . . is my wife, and the mother of our daughter,

Dodi joins the circle.

Her name is Dodi.

DODI: We are on vacation. I am playing with my ball.

Dodi pantomimes playing with a ball.

ERIC: I came to paint.

Eric sets up an imaginary easel, canvas, and paint brushes and starts to paint Larry.

ERIC: Larry is the leader of all the monkeys.

Larry gets up, physicalizing a monkey. John follows.

JUNE: I came to . . .

June pantomimes reading a book.

LARRY: I am the leader of all the monkeys. I don't like these people.

More actors join the improvisation. Larry and John begin running around Mr. Denby.

They look like us, but they are not.

MARTHA: I am the mother monkey. Those people behave strangely. They are dressed in funny clothes.

All the monkeys circle around, touching, pinching the family, and making monkey sounds. They are curious, looking at the easel, the painting, and at each other.

LARRY: Who is that? It looks like your ugly brother, John.

JOHN: It looks like you, Larry.

MARTHA: I don't like this picture. Let's tear it up!

A fight ensues. Dodi crying, runs to her mother June for comfort.

DODI: I want to go home!

MARTHA: I am going to take the child. I like her.

JUNE: Oh, no you're not!

Mr. Denby, Eric throws a bag of clothes at the monkeys. They get interested in the objects.

ERIC: Come, on. While their attention is on those clothes, let's escape.

The improvization comes to an end.

DR. BELLA: Marvelous!

ERIC: It was fun! I felt like a kid again. At one point I thought "This is pretty foolish." But then I looked around and almost everyone was participating, physicalizing monkeys, pantomiming activity, relating.

DR. BELLA: What was important, Eric, was that you were relaxed, not under pressure, and it was a group effort. But Liz, I noticed you did not participate in the improvisation. Why?

LIZ: You didn't say we had to do it. Besides, it was silly.

DR. BELLA: Of course it was! Acting should be fun! The actors were believing in the game of make-believe. Being judgmental is not helpful in creative circumstances. Such prejudice limits your ability to explore all the possibilities. Liz, what observation or fantasy do you have to share with us?

LIZ: I couldn't decide on anything. Everything seemed ridiculous or silly.

SUMMARY

Sometimes an actor is afraid to make a fool out of himself. Consequently, the imagination dries up. In the process of learning to re-ignite the senses, the actors learn that sensorial shutdown is not the only problem they must overcome. Subjective or cultural prejudice often censors responses. The fear of the unknown or of appearing foolish will also interfere with an actor's ability to play creatively. As the professional stakes increase, so do these fears. Unless actors learn to become comfortable or brave with what makes them feel uneasy, real progress is difficult.

Chapter
3

The Visual Sense

The Psychology of Seeing

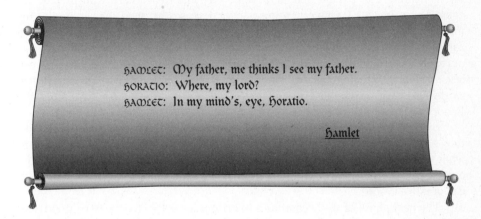

HAMLET: My father, me thinks I see my father.
HORATIO: Where, my lord?
HAMLET: In my mind's, eye, Horatio.

Hamlet

LECTURE: IT'S IN THE EYES

Our eyes continually gather information. We read a book or an article to learn information. We check a traffic light to cross a busy street. We see and recognize (even from a distance) our friends or loved ones.

However, for the actor, seeing *must* be more. It must be special. The eyes must help the actor tell a story. They must be alive with the life and emotions of the character.

Most people look, peek, or glance; they do not really see. The inability of actors to see who or what is in front of them occurs frequently during a scene. When I audition actors, I watch for the following:

1. Are the actor's eyes alive or blank?
2. Does the actor see the images of the speech?
3. Does the actor communicate the meaning of the speech with his/her eyes?
4. Do the actor's eyes tell me he/she involuntarily believes what is being said.

The eyes are an umbilical cord to a complete sensorial life. Seeing and our response to what we see is an instantaneous and reciprocal process. It is vital for actors to develop their instinct to look, see, and respond, as well as to store those visual observations in their Pandora's Box. I often say, "Actors, remove your blinders." Or, "Put in your contact lenses in order to see." If you take time to see, you will remember and be stimulated by what you see.

What we see also stimulates responses in our other four senses. I look into a bakery window. I see the cakes and pastries. My sense of smell and taste are aroused. I can taste the delicacies without actually eating them (I am tasting sensorially). I spy someone I love. The seeing segues into the powerful need to touch. Without actually touching that person, I touch them with my feelings (I touch them sensorially). Seeing a photograph of a person I love may stimulate the memory of hearing that person's laugh or voice. My inner eyes flash with private images. These images frequently arouse several senses at once. For example, my mind's eye sees an image of my childhood, such as the image of a parent and then remembers the *sound* of laughter or of crying. The image also stimulates my sense of touch, as I remember the kiss and then the smell of my mother. Suddenly, I can also smell and taste her cooking. These images are all connected to a psychological world. They are my inner vision. They stimulate emotional responses from the Pandora's Box of my experience.

By now, I hope the actors realize how a physical response to a sensory condition has a direct effect on their psychological life. In seeing and responding to what they see, actors have two sets of eyes; actors have two kinds of vision—the outer eyes (the peripheral, external vision)—and the inner eyes (the psychological, creative vision).

The next phase of study continues to encourage actors to see, to respond, and to remember what they experience, as well as to identify how fully they experience an event with their outer and inner vision.

EXPERIENCE/EXERCISE 6: SEEING AND REMEMBERING

Objective   To recognize outer and inner vision.

SECTION A: INITIAL VIEWING

1. Unfamiliar (and therefore impersonal) objects are placed around the room.
2. Each actor is assigned an object.
3. For five minutes, the actor looks at and sees the object from all perspectives. Touching is forbidden; the actor should touch the object with his/her eyes.
4. The objects are covered.
5. The actor writes down as many details of the observation as he/she can remember.

SECTION B: PERSONAL VIEWING

1. The actor uncovers the object for a second viewing.
2. After this second five- to ten-minute viewing, the objects are again covered.
3. Without referring to the first sheet of paper, the actor records as much as s/he can remember about the object and the thoughts that arose during the second viewing.

SECTION C: THE ACTORS COMPARE AND COMMENT ON THE DETAILS OF THEIR OBSERVATIONS BY READING THEIR PAPERS.

LARRY: This is a statue of a boy in bronze, on a wood base. The boy wears short pants, a short-sleeved shirt with a bag over his left shoulder, and a three-cornered hat with a tiny bird sitting on top of the hat. The boy stands on a log. Two squirrels sit on the edge of the log looking up at him. His left arm and hand are outstretched and a bird sits on his finger. The boy's feet are bare.

On my second observation, I wrote down practically the same details as the first time; however, I missed seeing a detail on the back of the statue. During the second viewing, I walked around the statue and discovered a butterfly propped on the log looking up at the boy! Also, I didn't write this down, but I found myself getting more excited by the carving during the second viewing.

DR. BELLA: Why did the carving excite you?

LARRY: It has a feeling of life, of movement. Also, I was almost ready to begin fantasizing a story or event connected with the boy, much like I did with the Buddha in the shop window.

DR. BELLA: Excellent, Larry. As you began to have a history with the object, you also began to free your imagination, to see the object with inner vision as well as with peripheral vision.

DODI: The stuffed rag doll was lying on the table, so I could only see the front part of the doll. She has red hair with a few streaks of grey, and two long braids. The hair and the braids are made of yarn. It's a soft doll, something nice to hold and cuddle. I can imagine touching the doll, touching the cotton material. The second time: The doll has a white face with eyes that are red buttons, painted brown eyebrows, a painted red mouth, and two small black dots representing nostrils. The dress is red with a brown denim tunic on top of the dress. The tunic has three small brown buttons. The sleeves of the dress are long. The feet are white and bare, and the hands are white fists.

DR. BELLA: Dodi, what were the differences between the first and second viewings?

DODI: It's not so much what I wrote down, but how I remembered the details. The first time I spent a lot of time worrying about remembering and I didn't really remember that much. On the second try, I began to interpret by asking myself where the doll comes from. I think she is from a foreign country of a long, long time ago. Now, as I am talking, I see the image of the doll and her face, and I think she is funny because she is angry about something. I think she is angry about having to wear that dress!

DR. BELLA: Marvelous, when you began to use your creative vision, it made remembering the details easier! Also, I'm really pleased that you allowed your vision to stimulate your sense of touch, as when you imagined touching the doll.

JOHN: The first time I looked at the paperweight, the shapes and colors fascinated me. I was sort of in awe of it. Then I realized the paperweight is shaped like a large egg. I forgot to think about trying to remember the details so when the time came I didn't have much to write down. I decided on the second viewing to pay more attention to the details of my object. I walked around seeing the paperweight from all sides. There were trumpetlike shapes. I think they are supposed to be three white lilies, tinged with green, with a small glass ball in the center of each lily. The glass balls represent the buds of the lily. On the bottom of the lilies there are two green leaves and at the very bottom of the paperweight there are dark blue leaflike flowers floating, or the dark blue shapes are water with specks of red.

DR. BELLA: This is very interesting, John. You began your experience by responding first with your inner vision and then you went back and viewed the object for objective detail.

ERIC: O.K., so, I had the music box to look at. I had trouble concentrating on it, so I didn't have much to write down the first time.

DR. BELLA: Why were you having trouble? What were you thinking about?

ERIC: Well, I started looking at this music box, and then I thought, "Gee, this is stupid. I'm paying all this money in tuition to come here and look at this dumb music box." And then I began to wonder what everyone else had to look at. I saw Larry had that little statue, and I thought that would be much more interesting to look at than this music box. And then the time was up.

DR. BELLA: Continue.

ERIC: The second time I wrote: The music box is round. The lower part of the base is made out of light brown wood. In the center of the box is a merry-go-round. A red hobby horse is in the middle and a monkey is on top of the horse. That's all. I guess I didn't do the assignment. I just peeked at it and didn't really remember all the other stuff there was to see.

DR. BELLA: Eric, I am pleased you understand the phrase "just peeked," and I am glad you have curiosity, as you displayed by being interested in the objects everyone else had to look at, but I wonder why it is you won't allow yourself to do the exercises. What are you afraid of?

ERIC: I don't know what to say.

DR. BELLA: Ask yourself why you want to be an actor and then maybe you'll be able to concentrate.

MARTHA: I began my first observation by recording some facts. This object is a magazine entitled *Horizon,* and it is the Summer 1968 issue. The cover has a reproduction of a painting of a regal-looking Spanish woman wearing two gold rings on her right index and middle fingers. I found myself staring at those two rings with diamonds.

On my second viewing, I forced myself to focus on the black lace mantilla covering her hair and shoulders. She is dressed in an attractive, long, black gown with a vivid red belt. The sleeves of the gown are gold lace and she is wearing gold small-heeled pumps. She has dark eyebrows and eyes. I kept dwelling on the regal look of this unhappy Spanish woman and wondering why she was unhappy. I began searching for clues, but I kept coming back to those two rings.

DR. BELLA: Martha began viewing the magazine with her outer eyes, noting information about her object, but on both observations, she segued into her inner vision. Her curiosity about the woman naturally led to questions about the woman's psychology and history. Martha, the magazine cover reproduces Goya's portrait of the Duchess of Alba. She was his mistress and the two rings that kept attracting your attention were gifts—one from her husband, and one from Goya. It's interesting that you kept focusing on them. You said she was unhappy. How did you come to that conclusion?

MARTHA: I remember some images of bushes or trees and some colored ground. That background seems now to me to have been moody and dark, giving the overall portrait a somber feeling.

DR. BELLA: Very well done, Martha!

JUNE: I was looking at the gold box. I think it is a jewelry box. It looks like a miniature trunk supported by four gold legs. The lid is closed and there is a cameo on top. That was all I wrote down the first time. I was scared I would not remember all the details I had seen. The second time, I tried to take it easy and concentrate on the details of the cameo. I wrote down that the lid is closed: It is encircled with gold patterns. There is a cameo on the very top of the box. The cameo is placed on an oval rose-colored background. The cameo is off-white and is the profile of a beautiful woman's face. She has a white rose on her left shoulder and a string of white beads around her neck. That's all I got. I should have gotten all that the first time, then I would have been able to see the object with more inner vision.

DR. BELLA: June, I have been watching you. When you start working, especially when it is a new experience or something unfamiliar, you tense up; you go into high gear. I frequently feel that you're thinking "I must do it or else, if I don't, I will fail and then I won't be perfect."

JUNE: I find it very difficult not to be successful. I must succeed!

DR. BELLA: Why be so hard on yourself? That kind of challenge impedes your progress. If the actor focuses on having success, the sensory life dies. Try to take each experience on its own. Don't judge it. Just experience it. For an actor to behave convincingly on stage, there is no time to worry about success or failure. If you spend your time focused on that issue, you will definitely fail!

JUNE: I am not a failure!!!

DR. BELLA: I don't mean you are a failure. However, this technique class offers you the opportunity to try—to sometimes succeed, to sometimes fail, but to try and try again. Without failure, success is impossible. An actor can learn from mistakes, from negative as well as from positive experiences. Otherwise, how will you discover what works or doesn't work for you?

JUNE: I worry about what my peers might think about my abilities.

DR. BELLA: I have a slogan you should repeat as often as you need:

I am an actor: I can act, I will act, and no one can stop me!

Remember, you made a decision to be here, to become an actor. "I will act" suggests continuing to learn and practice and experience. Finally, note the sticking point—"no one can stop me!"

DODI: Really, Dr. Bella, none of us will work unless some director casts us.

ERIC: And the teachers are always being so critical.

DR. BELLA: Let me try to convince you that I am on your side. Though at times, I may be critical and I may challenge you to do better, I am guiding your training. As a teacher, I am here to help you, not to hinder you. I hope that's true for all teachers.

LARRY: Dr. Bella, I see now that I am my own worst enemy. I frequently question my ability and not because anyone else questions it.

DR. BELLA: Now you understand.

LIZ: Dr. Bella, I'd like to go next. I looked at the cup. It is a demitasse, a small cup for after-dinner coffee. I wrote down that the object is a demitasse cup on a saucer. That's all I remembered. I can never remember anything. My memory is dreadful!

DR. BELLA: Liz, what did you see on the second try?

LIZ: I tried to pull myself together and convince myself to take time to see. The second time was a little better. I wrote down that the demitasse is white. It has red, painted roses of different sizes, with green leaves scattered through the roses. That's all I remember seeing, so that's all I wrote on my paper.

DR. BELLA: Liz, I would like you to concentrate for a minute. Can you visualize the cup and saucer in your mind right now?

LIZ: Yes, I suppose. I have an image of the cup and there is a gold rim around the edge, and just inside the saucer there is the same flower and leaf design as on the cup. Oh, the handle and the rim of the cup are painted gold.

DR. BELLA: That was specific. You did see and remember details of the entire object very vividly. Why is that? You have a *good* memory!

LIZ: Somehow the pressure of having to remember was off. When we had to write it down, I felt like I was taking an exam. I guess it started in grammar school, about the sixth grade. I was always told I was lazy or stupid. I knew I wasn't lazy, but I would never volunteer in class. When the teacher called on me, I would freeze with fright, even though I did all my homework. I would read and reread my assignments. I knew the stuff, but when the teacher asked me questions, I couldn't remember. I felt stupid.

DR. BELLA: I think Liz is very brave to share with us such a personal problem. This problem is very private. Am I able to help you, Liz? Am I able to give you advice? I'm not sure. One thing I am sure about is that you are not stupid. You *can* remember. The only helpful hint I can offer you is to put remembering on the back burner and try to focus on the task at hand. In this case, looking and seeing, and not jumping ahead to remembering. If you find yourself getting tense or in a panic, just stop, shake out, relax, and then get back to the task at hand. This will allow you to explore the experience, and not worry about the "assignment."

LECTURE: THE BODY NEVER LIES

People-watching is one of the most valuable ways to train the inner eye. Frequently, we tend to take sight for granted. We neglect to see, listen to, or touch those we live with or are close to. However, everyone experiences behavioral and emotional variations caused by daily events or physical conditions such as fatigue, illness, weather, temperature, and so on. These changes in behavior do not have to be traumatic or overt to affect how we relate to one another.

To demonstrate, I would like to share a recent experience. This event occurred in a familiar place, with a familiar activity, and familiar people. On Saturdays, I go to a beauty shop run by three women. They know each other well and have been working together for years. As I came in on this particular Saturday, I recognized that something was wrong. The operator nearest the door always greets me with a friendly "Hello" even before I greet her. This particular afternoon, she looked disturbed and grunted a "Hi."

The other operator did not have a customer and was reading a magazine and never even looked up. The manicurist was hunched over the table finishing a manicure; she looked like she was going to explode. Still, she greeted me politely, finished the manicure, got up, and walked in silence to collect the customer's bill. The place was busy, but quiet; no one was talking. However, their body language screamed loudly. Something dreadful must have happened. I sat down for my manicure; my manicurist was silent. She usually is very talkative. Her face was glum. Whatever happened, no one discussed the problem, but I immediately saw and responded to their body language, the unusual silence, the abbreviated conversation. In all this, I saw the psychology in the room. This is seeing with the inner eye. I allowed myself to see the events occurring on that *particular* visit.

Every time we see someone, whether it is someone we know intimately or a stranger, it should be a fresh, new experience.

EXPERIENCE/EXERCISE 7: VIEWING LIFE WITH OUR INNER EYES

Objective To observe intimately the people we know and people we don't know; to recognize how their body reveals their emotional life.

SECTION A: PEOPLE WATCHING WITH YOUR INNER VISION

1. Make a conscious effort to really watch (with inner vision) the people you:
    a. live with;
    b. work with (outside of class);
    c. encounter socially;
    d. have never seen before.
2. Observe with your outer vision and interpret with your inner vision, in order to discover:
    a. health or physical conditions, and your response to them;
    b. various behavior patterns, and your response to them;
    c. emotional states and your simultaneous interaction with the person.

SECTION B: RECORD YOUR EXPERIENCES IN YOUR JOURNAL AND IN YOUR PANDORA'S BOX.

1. Write down your discoveries and observations.
    a. Allow a few days to pass before making entries in your journal.
    b. After three or four weeks time, re-read your journal and compare your discoveries.
2. Involuntarily, the more significant observations and your responses to them will be stored in your Pandora's Box!

Several weeks after making this assignment, I invite the actors to share the observations they have made using their inner vision.

DODI: I discovered by really taking the time to see a girlfriend of mine that she changes her hairstyle daily, as well as dressing sloppy some days and beautifully the next. It depends on how she feels emotionally. I also realized by watching my boyfriend that he doesn't look at me when he has something on his mind or when he is upset with me. I also learned I often take him for granted because I do not see how he feels or behaves.

MARTHA: I went home for five days. I was determined to focus my attention on observing with my inner vision. I discovered something very upsetting. My parents rarely see each other. They take each other for granted. I decided to watch my mother's eyes. She has blue-green eyes. One day, she was angry at something and I saw her lips get very tight. I couldn't remember seeing that before. The entire five days seemed like I never had seen my parents before.

JOHN: I also went home for a long weekend. During the Sunday dinner, I gave myself a task to see my kid brother. He was watching my father carve the roast. My father always takes his time. I saw my brother was impatient. He kept joking with my father. They have a close relationship. Watching the two of them, I also realized my brother was not a kid anymore. He shaves now and looks grown up. His eyes look older.

JUNE: At work, this guy sits next to me. We both do word processing. As a rule, when he comes to work, he needs a shave and his clothes look like he's been sleeping in them, and during the break, he can hardly keep his eyes open. But the last time I saw him, he came in shaved, hair combed, and had a tie and a good-looking suit on! He looked right at me with his big eyes and said "I got the part I auditioned for!" His body said it too! At the end of work, he ran off without saying a word, and I haven't seen him since! However, his energy gave me a lift.

LARRY: Seeing my girlfriend daily, really seeing her, I realized how beautiful she is with or without make-up. Also, if I allow myself to look and see when she is not aware of me watching her, I noticed she has frequent mood changes. One day, I asked her why she was upset about something. Her reply was astonishing. "I didn't think you noticed or cared how I felt!" The next day, the same thing happened and she felt she could share her feelings with me. I think by really seeing her, it has brought us closer together!

ERIC: I had the opposite experience. My girlfriend wanted to know why I was staring at her. I said I wasn't, but I guess I was. I wasn't very subtle. I tried to explain the experience/exercise and she got angry and told me to practice on someone else.

DR. BELLA: What did you do?

ERIC: Well, at a party last Friday night, I was sitting in a corner watching. Not much was happening. I was going to leave. Then I saw my best friend. I noticed he was dejected, unhappy. I focused on his behavior and I saw him look at his girlfriend. He seemed very agitated and angry. I walked over to Fred—that's his name—and asked, "What's the matter?" He said his girlfriend was through with him. You know, this was a new experience for me. In the past, I would not have seen that look!

DR. BELLA: Eric, do you ever observe as specifically as that while in rehearsal or performance?

ERIC: I don't know. Probably not. It's different when you're acting because you know what you're supposed to see.

DR. BELLA: That is sometimes true, but if you limit yourself to what you're "supposed" to see in rehearsal, you'll probably lose the opportunity to really see and discover the other actors and the true depth of the script. All experience on stage must be unexpected or "as if" for the first time. When an actor practices seeing with inner vision, the unexpected is always there, because each time it is always slightly different.

ERIC: But many times, we're expected to see certain things "on cue." I have a responsibility to the script and the director.

DR. BELLA: Seeing "on cue," as you put it, places a pressure on you to produce a response. Often, that "produced" response has limited believability. However, if you believe in your inner vision and use it to observe each moment and perceive how it is unique, then you will respond kinesthetically, that is, "on cue."

LIZ: I feel I have a difficult time really seeing anyone. My own inner images come up and get in the way. Also, when I was practicing the exercise, I felt self-conscious focusing on people I know. But then something unexpected happened. I went to the same party Eric was at Friday night and I saw this man. I looked right into his eyes and he looked into mine and we both knew we liked each other and I felt we would meet again. We talked, he took my phone number, and sure enough, he called the next day. As I was talking to him on the phone, I kept seeing his eyes, that is, the image of his eyes. His eyes are so alive and caring! We have a date for this weekend!

DR. BELLA: Good for you! Most of us communicate what we are feeling with our eyes. I think you were ready to see.

ERIC: Dr. Bella, I remember watching Liz with this guy at the party, and there was a lot more than just eye contact going on! You could tell by their body language, the electricity between them, this guy was really attracted to Liz.

LIZ: Thanks a lot, Eric. I'm sure the entire class appreciates that you've suddenly developed a keen ability for observation.

MARTHA: Dr. Bella, I already mentioned my mother's eyes and how her lips get tight when she gets angry. I made it my business to look and see her as frequently as I could during my visit. I discovered my mother's eyes are a sure giveaway when she feels angry, or unhappy, or loving, or pleased with someone. They always tell her emotions, but her body sometimes hides what she is feeling. I recognized she was hiding something by how she shifted her vision, avoiding eye contact, even as the eyes betrayed what she was feeling. My father does not see any of this and it makes me very unhappy. It's disturbing, because I have discovered their relationship has some parts in it that are questionable.

DR. BELLA: Remember how I said, "The body never lies." When the eyes speak one thing, and the body and voice say something else, then the person is lying or holding back. This is what you observed in your mother's behavior, Martha.

Now, Martha, I also want to say something important. Trust is a significant step in building your technique as an actor. By sharing this painful, rather personal observation with us, you are also letting us know you trust us, . . . and yourself. I feel honored. And Liz, you also took a risk in letting us know something about your personal life. As we continue to do these experience/exercises, many personal feelings will be aroused and possibly revealed. However, I would also like to make clear to the class that when personal feelings or events come up, you are not necessarily bound to expose them. While it is good to be able to trust the uncomfortable, I want to emphasize, *this is not therapy*. If you wish to reveal something personal in the investigation of your technique, that is fine, even commendable. But many times in rehearsal and performance, personal issues will come up and nine times out of ten, your work will be better served to keep those issues private, to use them without necessarily letting your director or fellow actors know what they are.

LECTURE: INNER VISION: PSYCHOLOGICAL MEMORY AND PHYSICAL RESPONSE

Memory is primarily visual. Think of any childhood memory and an image imme diately pops up in the mind's eye. I decided to test this theory by asking my husband Frank to share with me some of his memories. As Frank began to tell me about a childhood incident, I said, "What do you see?" He got very specific, describing the images of the room, the teacher, his classmates, and how he felt in the uncomfortable situation. An interesting experiment would be to ask your own parents or grandparents to share their early memories. What do they remember? How do they remember it?

When we visualize a memory, we remember facts and events and emotions. If we take the time to carefully investigate the memory for its setting, the sensory conditions, and our physical actions, the process will involuntarily elicit an emotional response. All human experience is emotional (i.e., psychological), and all experience is physical. Emotion and behavior are irrevocably interactive. Emotions are not general categories; they are specific physical responses to specific events within specific environments.

One example I frequently share involves my response whenever I get to a foreign border and produce my naturalization papers. Panic overtakes me. I am overwhelmed with inner-eye images of a very large, empty, bright room. A huge woman is shouting at me to take off my clothes in order to search for objects that I and my mother are supposedly sneaking out of Russia.

I was twelve years old. My mother, my sister, and I were leaving Russia to come to the United States. Being a person of habit, I did something stupid. My mother gave me a small, flat, gold purse to hold. In school, I was taught to put gloves and any personal objects into my hat and put the hat into my coat sleeve before hanging up the coat. Well, of course, that is what I did when we were ordered to take off our coats. The woman searched the coat and found the purse in my coat sleeve. She decided I was hiding the purse. She ordered me and my mother to strip, to undress, to make sure we were not sneaking anything out illegally. The woman was shouting. My mother was trying to explain. I was crying.

For a child of twelve, this was a horrible experience, and it has been deeply rooted in my body and my psyche, ever since. Today, when I travel, I go into a panic whenever I cross any border: emotional reflex and sensorial response. I feel trapped. My body responds. I feel tension and nausea in my stomach. Even when visiting a friendly neighbor like Canada, I know my fear is unfounded, but there it is.

Sometimes I wonder which is first, the panic or the image, . . . the image or the panic. It's like asking, "Which is first, the chicken or the egg?" It's impossible to tell. I suppose I might say I get emotionally and physically prepared when I know I have to produce my naturalization papers or my passport, and off goes my memory camera. Those images of my childhood stimulate my imagination and my feelings. They are an integral part of my psychology.

In the first two exercises of this chapter, the actors focused their awareness on responses to impersonal objects or events as they took place in the present moment. After a period of time had passed, the actors were asked to record memories of what they observed. Through this process the actors not only develop experiences that can be stored in their Pandora's Box, they also become more aware of how the psyche stimulates the vision of their inner eyes. The psyche is that very powerful combination of physical and emotional recall that involuntarily (kinesthetically) stimulates our responses to the present moment.

The purpose in developing an awareness of inner vision is to stimulate the psyche's storehouse of psychological images. Throughout a normal day, events occur that trigger a memory of some past personal experience. Often, we recall the experience without a conscious knowledge or connection as to what triggered its recall. We don't always know why the psyche causes a particular image to come up. Most generally, the memory is founded in some profound experience or a mixture of significant incidents from childhood. The next exercise calls for a more personal investigation of the psyche.

EXPERIENCE/EXERCISE 8: PART I—THE ROOM

1. Select a room you have lived in. You do not need to be aware of the past or attach a special significance to its past.
2. Begin outside the room, on the street. Describe the chain of images out loud as they come to you.
   a. Is it hot, cold, raining, etc.?
   b. What time is it?
   c. What are the sights outside this room?
   d. Why have you come to the room? Why are you here?
   If a number of images fly by, let them. Keep speaking your stream of consciousness out loud until the images lead you or push you into the room.
3. Describe the room.
   a. What color is the room?
   b. Who is in the room?
   c. Why are you in the room?
   d. What has happened in this room?
   e. What other questions do you have about this room?
4. As you talk about the images, walk, sit, stand, keep changing your physical life. Make it active. Occupy yourself with verbal *and* physical action. Walk around the room. Do an activity. Comb your hair; look out the window; say "This is the bedroom door," and touch the imaginary door; or "This is a window," and look out the window; sit down on the bed and say, "This is my bed."
   a. Actively explore your imagination in this way for at least ten to fifteen minutes. Sustain the images as long as you can. Be aware of your

body's kinesthetic responses to the images. (Describing those sensations verbally is not important. Just be aware of how your body informs you of a response.) Which images evoke particularly strong responses?

b. Allow the images of the room to stimulate related images. Sustain these images as long as you can. Physicalize these images in any way possible.

5. After actively exploring the images, silently sustain the strongest image or any related images that have been stimulated. Keep physically still, but maintain the sensorial energy throughout the body.

6. Allow the image of the room or any related images to fade.

I insist that actors talk their stream-of-consciousness out loud during this exercise. When an actor talks about what s/he sees or feels, there is no doubt that s/he is active. *Talking is active.* Talking helps to stimulate sensation, and sensation stimulates the psyche and the body. Talking makes the memory images more specific and keeps the actor from indulging in generic feelings. Unless the actor focuses on specific images (in this case, the specifics of the room), s/he will not have a kinesthetic response. Each question will inspire a particular memory and elicit a specific sensorial response. As each actor develops skill at imagery, s/he will know instinctively when to speak out loud or when to be motivated silently by the stream-of-consciousness.

Generally, I introduce this exercise in class, but I encourage the actors to rehearse and re-rehearse the exercise outside of class and to present their work after a few weeks of private rehearsal.

EXPERIENCE/EXERCISE 8: PART II—THE ROOM

Format The actors continue to rehearse their stream-of-consciousness recall of a specific room. As they rehearse, actors are encouraged to concentrate and actively elaborate on the physical activities suggested in Number 4, of Part I.

1. The actor may use rehearsal furniture to set up the space for "the room."
2. The actor may bring in a key object to stimulate inner-eye images related to the experience.
3. Following the presentation, each actor is asked to share his/her self-observations about:
   a. the preparation process.
   b. the success of their concentration during the presentation.
   c. the ability to allow memory images to stimulate the body.
   d. problems encountered while working and performing this experience/exercise.

The following observations were discussed following presentation in class:

ERIC: When I practiced this exercise at home, I would try to speak out loud a series of images I have of my family's farm in Canada, but I couldn't focus on any specific room and I didn't feel as though anything was happening sensorially to my body. I didn't feel prepared to show anything today. I hadn't made any decisions, so I gave up. I don't really know what it is you want from this exercise.

DR. BELLA: It's not what I want. It's what you want. It's too soon to give up. Stand up. Walk around the room. Stop. What images do you see?

ERIC: It's raining out today. I see the rain outside our classroom window.

DR. BELLA: In your mind's eye, take some time to see the farm in Canada.

ERIC: I can see the rain at home on our farm. The sky is grey. There are leaves in the mud. I feel my father is out in the barn. My mother is sitting at the kitchen table, chopping beans. I can smell the fresh-cut. . . .

DR. BELLA: Eric, why did you stop?

ERIC: I suddenly became conscious of the class.

DR. BELLA: But what you were doing was so clear! You were just standing there; however, I believed you and what your body was communicating.

ERIC: But I wasn't really doing anything; I mean, I wasn't acting.

DR. BELLA: Yes, you were!

ERIC: But that was too simple. Isn't it supposed to be harder than this, more dramatic?

DR. BELLA: Not always. However, with practice, what you allow to happen will become more vivid.

JOHN: When you made this assignment, I knew I wanted to go back to a room from my childhood, when I was around six or seven years old. As I was thinking about this, I kept having an image in my head of a bright green bedroom suspended in midair! The room is not connected to any other part of the house. I figured this was a pretty effective use of my imagination.

Today, in class, I talked my way through a chain of images. I decided it was Christmas. I could see the bright green room, freshly painted, the furniture, the bed, the white desk, a yellow dresser. I surprised myself by discovering some toys, particularly an electric train set. I felt full of anticipation. I wanted to have fun playing.

DR. BELLA: Yes, your body was eager and you seemed to be having a good time. Did you have an electric train set when you were young?

JOHN: No. I wanted one, but my folks didn't have much money then. They couldn't afford it.

DR. BELLA: This is a marvelous mix of the real and imaginary. Build on that.

DODI: My decision happened unexpectedly. I was walking in the park, thinking about what to wear to a party, when all of a sudden, I was focusing on, . . . I had this image of the bedroom my exhusband and I shared. The memory was very vivid, I felt I could almost touch the walls. As I continued to walk and remember, I had an intense desire to touch him again. I went home and tried to repeat this experience, but I failed, so I let it go for a few days.

For the next week, I tried to remember the details of that room. I walked around my apartment talking out all the images I had of the room. Everyday, I just let my stream-of-consciousness go. Once, I absent-mindedly grabbed a pillow and sat down on the bed. Suddenly, I zoomed into the room and very clearly saw my exhusband's eyes. My body had a powerful response to that! I decided to use the pillow as my prop. I tried rehearsing in this way, talking my stream-of-consciousness about the room and the images and then grabbing the pillow. I tried this four more times. Two of the times, it worked very well. However, today in class, it was awful. My concentration felt all off and it seemed I was working at remembering.

DR. BELLA: I think you handled your rehearsal process well. However, you are right, in class, you were trying too hard. You were concerned about repeating the success you had previously experienced, rather than allowing the experience to spontaneously take place. You said that when you rehearsed using the pillow, two of the rehearsals were successful and two were not. Why? Was there a difference in how you talked your stream-of-consciousness or in what you did physically?

DODI: Yes! As a matter of fact, once I forgot to grab the pillow where I usually do because I said something that really surprised me! I don't want to repeat it here, but I saw my exhusband's eyes very clearly that time.

JUNE: When I started to think about this assignment, I kept having a recurring image of my eighth-grade report card. I could see the gold stars and my grades, which were very good. So I went home and pulled out a sheet of paper and made myself a report card: 100 for spelling, 100 for English, 100 for deportment. I folded it up very neatly and put it in a legal white envelope. I started walking around my apartment. I specifically began to recall the road home from school, the other children, my classmates walking with me, my friend Betty, the sky. I just remembered how excited I was to go home and show my mother the report card.

That night, I had a dream about walking home on the road with my report card! Suddenly, I was in my mother's sitting room, which was just to the side of the master bedroom. I woke up with that image strong in my memory. The next day, I decided to recreate my mother's sitting room. She had this large gold chair she sat in, waiting for me when I returned from school. I started to talk my stream-of-consciousness about the room and all my images of it with my mother. I grabbed my report card and kept looking at it. For a moment, I was totally in my mother's sitting room, then I stopped.

The next day, I tried it again. I talked about walking home from the eighth grade, hanging on to the report card. My memory zoomed into the sitting room. I saw the red carpet, the large windows with beautiful curtains, and my mother's empty chair. I started to cry. I kept walking and crying. It seems so clear now. That was the day my mother left me. Today, while I was doing the exercise, I felt many of the same things that had come up in my rehearsals—the anticipation, the rejection, the loneliness, the anger—but I could not cry, even though I easily did at home.

DR. BELLA: June, actual tears are not important. What is important is the need to cry. You chose a powerful, personal experience and I think your success with it had something to do with the passage of time. You were ready to deal with these emotions both personally and as an actor. Each time you return to this memory, you will discover more and more.

MARTHA: I prepared by talking about all the images I have of my grandmother's house, her front porch, the swing on the porch, an open front door leading into the hallway with a telephone on the table. One set of stairs go up to the second-floor bedrooms and another set go down to the basement. My grandmother had the basement decorated and furnished. It was her favorite room. She called it her private room. When I visited, it was the room where I slept. There is a carpet on the floor, pictures, . . . family pictures on a dresser. I can sustain the images of the room and I want to see my dead grandmother again, but, of course, she isn't there. Her smile, sitting on the bed; it keeps coming up. I want to cry, I feel lost. I think I am responding physically, but I don't know how to explain it.

DR. BELLA: Describing the sensations verbally is not important, your body is informing you. You do look "lost." You are physically and verbally involved. Good for you, keep working.

LARRY: I thought I would give myself a challenge! I started seeing my childhood, images of my father, mother, and older brother. I started to see the room my brother and I shared. I talked about the memories I have of my brother when we were kids. I remembered Sam's basketball trophy and a picture of him holding the trophy. I zoomed in on our bedroom and the double bunk-beds we shared. When I see the room, I feel lonely, but it wasn't a lonely room. My brother was killed in an automobile accident. I don't go home too much anymore. Today, in class, I tried to explore the images, but I had difficulty willing my responses and I couldn't sustain the room. I think it is still raw emotionally.

DR. BELLA: How long ago did your brother die?

LARRY: Four years ago.

DR. BELLA: How successful was your work at home compared to what you tried to do today?

LARRY: It was easier to do at home, alone.

DR. BELLA: Maybe this is still too raw to share publicly. Give yourself more time. Keep working.

LIZ: I had real trouble with my concentration today, too. When I rehearsed, I had so many responses I couldn't control them. I'd start the exercise and almost immediately start crying. In class, the images and my responses all dried up.

DR. BELLA: Perhaps you could share with us what you were working on.

LIZ: Well, three weeks ago, a close friend of mine died of AIDS.

DR. BELLA: Oh Liz, I'm sorry. It is necessary to put *distance of time* between you and the memory. The images of your friend are still too disturbing for you to use creatively. Time is a healer and a stimulus. After four or five years have passed, your psyche will have healed this wound. Larry and June both chose particularly painful memories, but I think because a significant amount of time has passed, they are ready to explore and use these experiences. Also remember, you do not have to pick memories that are serious. Happy and frivolous events work too!

RESULTS OF EXPERIENCE/EXERCISE 8: THE ROOM

1. The actors are developing the ability to recognize how the psyche, inner eye images, and physical responses are all simultaneously interactive.
2. The actors learn the value of talking out their stream-of-consciousness in order to discover physical responses associated with specific memories.
3. The actors recognize the value of time and its ability to distance us from the threatening trauma of significant memories, therefore enabling an actor to more easily recall an experience.
4. The actors discover the ability to associate in-the-moment responses to their environment as a source to stimulate or segue into inner-eye images.
5. The actors discover how repetition will uncover deeper, more complex responses.
6. The actors continue to develop their ability to trust the unexpected.

SUMMARY

Experience/Exercise 8, or "The Room," begins a rather significant stage in the actor's development. If the actor trusts his/her subconscious while setting up the exercise, meaningful investigations often take place. "The Room" exercise is also important because it is the first attempt to deal with memories of the distant past. Up until this point, the training has been to encourage the actors to respond spontaneously to their sensory conditions in-the-moment. By learning to recall responses to significant events in their past, as well as to sense kinesthetic responses to daily life, the actors are continually filling compartments in their Pandora's Box which they will be able to use as part of their sensory technique on stage. It is important to keep the emphasis on how the environment and the physical actions stimulate responses. Actors should not concern themselves with overanalysis in labeling the specific emotions they recall. In other words, at this point, the process is more important than the product.

Chapter
4

The Auditory Sense
The Psychology of Hearing

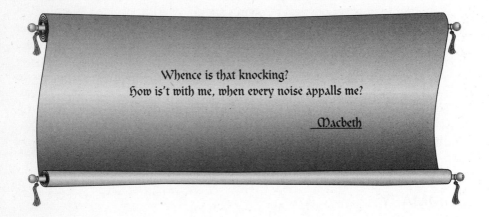

Whence is that knocking?
How is't with me, when every noise appalls me?

Macbeth

LECTURE: LISTENING TO THE SPOKEN WORD AND THE UNSPOKEN MEANING

Have you ever noticed how some people hear only what they want to hear? Sometimes, in conversation, the other person's attention seems distracted and when you ask them a question, they say "Excuse me, what was the question? I wasn't listening to what you were saying." There are other times, when our hearing is very acute. For instance, when interviewing for a job, you strain to pay attention to every question the interviewer asks, hoping to respond with just the right answer. In a relationship, especially during a fight, every word counts. Your position or his position? Who's right? Because words have different meanings to each individual, misunderstandings occur. Sometimes, we even ignore what we don't want to hear, looking for a way to misunderstand!

But if you listen closely to the way people speak, as well as watch their body language, you can often discern what's really going on in their minds.

There are three levels of hearing. The first is hearing from the periphery, not really listening to what's being said. Often, during our everyday rituals, we go on automatic pilot. For instance, I am greeted with "Hi. How are you?" I reply, "Not very well." And the person asking the question responds, "Good." out of habit. I am aware that I have not been heard. Or I say to a waiter or waitress, "Dry toast, please. No butter." or "I don't want any french fries." What do I get? Butter on my toast and a plate full of french fries. Generally, I can recognize when my order is not being heard and I cantankerously jolt the waiter out of the silent conversation he seems to be having with himself by asking, "Did you hear me?"

Unless the waiter gets angry, my question will usually move his act of hearing into the second level: to listen objectively for information. This level involves the aural process of getting directions, taking notes in a lecture, listening to the news on the television or radio, or receiving any other important, but not personally or emotionally charged, information. This level of hearing requires the listener to hear and make sense of the words and store that information for future use.

The third level of hearing is listening with the inner ear. The inner ear hears the unspoken meaning in the timbre and rhythm of the spoken word. Recently, a friend greeted me, "Hi. How are you, Bella?" I did not want to go into a problem I was having that day, so I just said, "Fine." She went on, "Something wrong? You don't feel well?" Her inner ear heard a problem in my voice. In stage vocabulary, she heard my "subtext". Subtextual listening hears more than just the dictionary sense of the spoken word; it hears the psychology. Our psychology includes our stream-of-consciousness which influences how we speak, giving our words additional meaning or multiple intentions.

In acting, all three levels of hearing are used. An actor must recognize sound before he or she can effectively use sound. I don't mean to recognize sound intellectually; I mean to recognize sound sensorially. Take time to hear the rain, thunder, wind, running water, the lake, city noises, street sounds, animal sounds, the activity in your home or apartment building, . . . everything. Most important of all, take time to listen to people. Listen to people talking, the melody of their voice or the changing rhythms of their speech. Listen to the laughing, the crying, the shouting, the silences.

Write down what you hear. In your journals, write down how the various noises stimulated you physically and psychologically. When you heard the sound, where were you? what was the environment? what did you do when the sound penetrated your body and psyche?

One of my favorite personal exercises is to identify a sound without actually seeing its source. Listening to footsteps to identify the person. Is it a man? A woman? Someone familiar? Identifying the activity in another room. Who is talking? A door is being opened. Is it a closet? A refrigerator? An exit? When answering the phone, listening to know who is on the other end of the line before you ask who is calling.

One recent morning, I called a friend, "Helen." Her daughter answered. As I waited for "Helen" to come to the phone, I could hear the heels of her shoes clicking. That sound of high heels told me she was dressed to go out. There was also a quickened speed in her walk. She was in a hurry. When Helen answered the phone, I said, "I'm glad I caught you. You must be ready to go to work." She answered, "You caught me just in time!"

To hear without some visual sense is impossible. There is a constant interplay between sound and image. For example, the sound of Helen's heels immediately conjured the picture in my mind of her shoes on the hard vestibule floor. This immediately segued into the image of Helen running to the phone. As I was listening on the phone, my visual sense was activated by all that I heard.

EXPERIENCE/EXERCISE 9: IDENTIFYING SOUND

Objective   Recognizing specific sounds and their effect on the body.

SECTION A: CATEGORIES OF SOUND

In order to help the actor specifically recognize various sounds, I have grouped them into six loose categories.

1. The Elements—Nature
    a. Water
        *   oceans, lakes, streams, rivers, the waves, the rapids
        *   rain
    b. Storms
        *   wind, thunder, hail
        *   leaves in the trees—in the barren winter, on a hot summer day
        *   tornados
    c. Fire
2. City Sounds/Traffic—Manmade or Industrial Sounds
    a. automobiles: cars, trucks, tractors, buses, emergency vehicles, horns, sirens, brakes, garbage pick-up, tire explosions
    b. trains: subways, whistles at crossings
    c. airplanes: jets, propeller planes take-offs, landings, sonic booms
    d. crime: gunshots, alarms
3. Home Environment—Dwellings
    a. openings and closings: doors, windows, closets, cupboards
    b. creaks and shifts: floor squeaks, heat expansions
    c. convenience appliances: vacuum cleaners, dishwashers, washing machines, dryers, boiling kettles, pots and pans, clocks
    d. furnaces and toilets
4. Animals—Animate Sounds
    a. pets: dogs, cats, birds
    b. livestock: chickens, roosters, cows, horses, pigs
    c. wildlife: ducks, geese, crows, sparrows, squirrels, deer, mice, rats, bats
5. People
    a. communicating: talking, laughing, screaming, shouting, crying, love-making, whispering, singing, whistling
    b. living: breathing, sneezing, coughing, sniffling, burping, belching, being sick to the stomach, and other lower possibilities

6. Music
   a. live, recorded, or via radio/TV: classical, jazz, folk, country, religious, ethnic, foreign, nationalistic, rock & roll, heavy metal, new wave
   b. ensemble: choir, band, orchestra, solo, duet, trio, quartet, etc.

SECTION B: HEARING AND SEEING

1. At various points in your daily routine, take five to ten minutes to stop and simply listen to the world.
   a. How many different sounds can you identify without actually seeing them?
   b. What effect does each sound have on you? Is it soothing? Aggravating? Pleasing? Irritating? Gentle? Hard?
2. At the end of the day, write in your journal about your listening experiences.
   a. What activities were you performing while listening?
   b. Identify the sounds. Describe them. As you describe each sound, what do you see in your mind's eye? While you were listening, did you peek to confirm what you heard?
   c. Did you have a physical response to the sound? As you recall the sound and its effect on you, is a particular part of your body energized by the memory?

After a few weeks, I begin class by asking each student to share a listening experience they might recall from their journal entries.

DODI: I was at work, waiting on tables. It was Saturday night. The restaurant was very busy and noisy, which is not unusual. Usually, I tune all that noise out, but for some reason, I thought about this listening exercise and decided to become aware of it. I listened and heard people talking, laughing, the clamor of dishes, chairs being moved and shoved about. I realized it was making my whole body anxious.

DR. BELLA: Right now, do you feel any tension in your body?

DODI: Yes, my chest feels, I don't know how to explain it, it feels high, . . . lifted. I also have a feeling of having to be very alert, to keep on top of all the orders and the quick pace of waiting tables. I want to start moving around the room, very fast.

JOHN: I was sitting in the bus, reading. From the back of the bus, I suddenly heard a woman's voice, loud and clear, laughing, talking, complaining about religion, the government, shouting obscenities. Everyone else turned around to look at her, but I tried to visualize her without turning around. I pictured a thin, old woman, with graying, stringy hair, wearing a dirty, frayed dress. When I turned around I saw a round face and the active eyes of a woman in her forties, looking very sharp. Probably some kind of radical out of the sixties.

DR. BELLA: Can you think about where in your body you were stimulated by this experience?

JOHN: When I was reading, I was pretty much in my head. Hearing the woman activated my whole body. I was listening to her, trying to imagine her. My spine, . . . I was listening to her with my spine.

LARRY: My experience also began while I was reading. I was in my living room, and I became conscious of the bathroom faucet dripping. I can't stand that sound, drip . . . drip . . . drip. I had a clear image of the faucet. Whenever I think about that sound, it's easy to recall how it unnerves me.

DR. BELLA: Do you hear the sound now?

LARRY: I sense it. My forehead can feel the pounding. My energy is centered there. In my sinuses, somehow.

MARTHA: Two weeks ago, I flew home for a cousin's wedding. When I came back late Sunday night, we arrived at O'Hare in a thunderstorm. Throughout the flight there was that constant humming sensation of the sound of the jet engines and the wind against the wings of the jet. I had been watching the clouds and the lightning underneath the plane. When we got ready to descend, the captain's voice explained we would be hitting turbulent weather and requested we buckle our seat belts. The plane began to be tossed about, and the sound of the thunder [*Martha paused for a second.*] . . . I was very scared.

DR. BELLA: What physical responses do you associate with that experience?

MARTHA: I felt sick to my stomach. I didn't want to be sick. I thought about trying to sit very still, and remain calm, but my hands were clenched on the arm rests.

DR. BELLA: Do you remember any specific sound over all the others?

MARTHA: That hum. The force of the jet. It's not only a noise, it's a sensation.

JUNE: I remember that Sunday evening thunderstorm. I was home, in my apartment. There was this sudden clap of thunder and I jumped right out of my chair and dropped the book I was reading. There was a great pelting of rain. It was pounding against my windows, hard. Then I became aware of the sound of traffic on the wet pavement. It's different on wet pavement. Initially, I was frightened. My heart was racing. Then the rain grew softer, more steady. I made myself some tea and listened to the shower. It had a kind of sizzling sound, but after the thunder and lightning passed, it was more comforting. My body relaxed.

ERIC: I have a very pleasing sound experience. About a half-mile from where I live, the railroad tracks pass before they veer out to the northwest. If the night is quiet, right about 12:20 A.M., there is a train that always blows its whistle. It reminds me of when I was a boy. I could hear the trains at night across the open fields. It's a sound that makes me feel protected. I'm under the covers and I'm being hugged. My body relaxes and I can go to sleep.

LIZ: But where is the response centered? That's what Dr. Bella will want to know.

DR. BELLA: Very good, Liz.

ERIC: In my chest. My heart.

LIZ: Dr. Bella, I enjoyed this exercise. I think I learned something. I was home on Saturday morning, learning my lines. You know I hate anything to do with memory, so a number of sounds kept interrupting my concentration. First there were fire trucks. In my imagination, I could see the front part of the fire truck, the lights, the siren. Then Don, the handyman, began to vacuum the hall carpet. I had an image of the vacuum first, then of Don. Now I was alert to all the sounds. A dog kept barking. I began to think about all the other apartments in the building and what might be going on in them.

DR. BELLA: Can you recall the sound of the fire trucks?

LIZ: Yes, easily.

DR. BELLA: Liz, that's wonderful. What makes this memory exercise easy for you, when you have been so anxious about your memory in previous work?

LIZ: I don't need to remember the details so much as the effect. I think about the sound and instantly, my body remembers a response! It's intuitive and not factual.

DR. BELLA: And for the fire trucks, where is your response centered?

LIZ: At the back of my head, or maybe at the top of my spine.

LECTURE: ENERGY CENTERS AND PHYSICAL TRANSITIONS

We don't just hear sounds intellectually. Our whole body hears and reacts. However, each of us may respond differently to the same sound. By asking each student to be aware of how his or her body responds, I have been asking them to locate where their specific physical responses have been centered. A *kinesthetic* response involves a *specific location of physical sensation.* I term this location an "energy center."

Most actors understand beats and intentions and how to mark them in a script. The difficult part is making these transitions physical. With each new intention or tactic, there is not only a change in the psychology but also in the physiology. As I have been suggesting here, all psychological intentions express themselves through behavior. Therefore, the psychological impulse for a beat change must originate out of a physical response or need. Sensory responses to sight, sound, touch, smell, and taste all have the power to effect the body in various energy centers and thereby alter the psychology or mark a transition in the physiology. By responding kinesthetically with various energy centers, actors can begin to physically realize their psychological transitions.

The next experience/exercise is designed to make the actors more aware of their various energy centers and to practice shifting from one energy center to another through kinesthetic memory.

EXPERIENCE/EXERCISE 10: RESPONDING TO MULTIPLE SOUNDS

Objective   To explore kinesthetically activating contrasting energy centers.

Format   Referring back to the six categories of sound in Experience/Exercise 9, select an experience from one category, then practice hearing it and responding kinesthetically. Then combine it with a contrasting experience from another category.

1. The kinesthetic response is to be aroused *without* the aid of furniture or props.
   a. The actor may be stimulated by his/her visual images of the sound.
   b. The actor may be stimulated by talking out his/her stream-of-consciousness about the sound.
   c. The actor should focus on sensing specific energy centers.
2. When repeating the exercise, the actor may not sit, but must physicalize his/her response through standing, walking, running, or some type of movement or gesture.

Without props or furniture, the actors will feel uncomfortable or a bit naked at first. However, when working with sound, props often tend to get in the way. The purpose of this exercise is to sense each sound and where it stimulates the body, that is, to discover the many contrasting energy centers. These energy centers may be housed at the base of the skull, the sinuses, the spine, in the chest, the heart, the diaphragm, or in the "lower regions," or "the sex," as I call it. However, for this exercise to be successful, the actors need to make their own discoveries, to determine how their physical and psychological responses to the various sounds are unique.

In real life, we hear more than one sound at a time. For instance, I am at home talking on the phone. It is an important long-distance conversation with an actor, a good friend who is seeking advice on a particular role. In the background noise, I hear fire trucks go by, an ambulance, all those sirens. They irritate me and interrupt my phone conversation. At the same time, I can hear the music on the radio in the other room. My husband is playing his favorite station. In the kitchen, I can hear the dishwasher. All these sounds are bombarding me at the same time, so that I must make an effort to focus my concentration on the phone conversation.

While exploring sensory life, actors need not jump into the most complicated or profound experiences from their lives in order to do good work. Simple choices offer a wealth of experience and are always the best way to begin. In all sensory work, the initial objective is to recognize where each sound or stimulus personally affects the body. Then the actor can identify which responses are the most potent. These will prove to be the most valuable as part of the actor's technique. A good script will provide the necessary drama. But an able sensory technique will heighten the depth of experience, serving to intensify the relationships kinesthetically. This results in believable behavior on stage.

LECTURE: RECALLING SOUNDS WITH THE INNER EAR

So far, the experience/exercises in this chapter have alerted the actors to their physical and psychological responses to sound in their everyday environments. They have been fighting sensory shutdown to revitalize their sense of hearing. They have been listening with their "inner ears" and sensing physical responses in the "energy centers" of the body. After they are able to respond spontaneously to their environments in-the-moment, then the actors are ready to focus on a deeper, more personal hearing process.

Sense memory involves hearing and remembering. Experiences are stored in the actor's Pandora's Box to be kinesthetically activated at the appropriate time. Like "The Room" exercise from the last chapter, the following work will draw on personal experiences from the actor's memory. Particulary potent experiences are often tied to strong emotional relationships, and generally this determines how strongly an actor will react to pleasant or uncomfortable sounds. An actor must firmly believe and trust both the positive and negative responses to any sensory stimulus, embracing all responses and emotions as valuable.

EXPERIENCE/EXERCISE 11: HEARING MEMORIES WITH THE INNER EAR

Objective   To uncover hearing events which consistently stimulate a kinesthetic response.

SECTION A: PRACTICING SEQUENCES OF SOUND MEMORIES TO TRAIN THE KINESTHETIC RESPONSE OF THE INNER EAR

1. Sequence #1:
   a. pleasant sounds segue into
   b. disturbing sounds which segue into
   c. silence
2. Sequence #2:
   a. frustrating or hurtful sounds segue into
   b. intimate or sensuous sounds which segue into
   c. silence

Format   Deciding on the "W" questions.

1. Where—the place where the event occurred
2. Who—the other people in the event
3. When—the time of day, year, month, week, and so on

4. What—the setting, props, furniture necessary to the event
   a. Actors may select one piece of furniture to create their setting.
   b. Actors may select an object or prop to use during the exercise. This includes using a piece of clothing such as a scarf, a hat, gloves, etc.
5. Why—why are people speaking, what is the situation?
6. Behavior
   a. How does recreating the hearing event stimulate a need, a purpose, an intention?
   b. How does the activity of that intention stimulate a psychology?

SECTION B: REPETITION

1. Repeat the sequences in Section A at least three times in succession.

Each actor must pick sounds that will always have a strong specific kinesthetic effect. The two objectives of this exercise are to recall those sounds for that effect and to develop the kinesthetic technique of being able to repeat that sensation. Rote repetition, or practice for the sake of repeating, will defeat this exercise. Good repetition discovers vital new elements in each response. Each sound must be experienced and re-experienced. Anytime we recall an experience, it is never totally the way it was in real life. Time has past and now we are using our imaginations. Spontaneously discovering subtle variations in response will enhance that sound memory's compartment within the Pandora's Box. Actively gestating and fermenting an experience makes it more useable for imaginary, creative purposes.

As I suggested previously, sometimes actors will choose particularly painful experiences for this exercise. Sometimes with more traumatic experiences, the actor will need to eliminate his/her fear of re-experiencing the event. In such cases, I suggest approaching the event through a reversal of time (realizing that more recent, pleasant experiences have allowed you to survive the event). Time is a healer. By recognizing the passage of time, the original experience can be approached and explored without the censorship of paralyzing fear. Through time, the psyche has learned to survive and we come to recognize that we were not destroyed by our more difficult experiences.

The technique being learned here is to release from the Pandora's Box what the body and the psyche know. The body and the psyche never forget. It is important, however, to emphasize that if the experience was too traumatic, it may not be useable for any creative purpose. No actor should be forced or even encouraged to explore an experience that will kill creativity. If an actor does have such an experience and he or she feels it is a block to his/her creativity, then that personal work is best left to professionally trained psychiatrists. In our work, we are looking for the most potent and useable kinesthetic reponses that will always be available to the actor. Sometimes those responses are painful, and sometimes very pleasant. As you will note, this experience/exercise attempts to employ both.

Ultimately, the real benefit of this exercise comes in the exploration of silence following the two contrasting listening experiences. After the sound has stimulated a behavior, the actor segues into sustaining the echo of the sound. The "echo of sound" is the residue of sound experienced in silence. It will tell you a lot about your energy centers.

The discussion format following presentation of this exercise in class took the format:

1. Process of selecting the listening events.
2. Relationship of the speakers or events to actor.
3. Preparation or rehearsal process. How much repetition? What new things were learned in repetition?
4. Discovery of energy centers.

JOHN: For my pleasing sound experience, I chose a memory from a year ago, when my father congratulated me on doing a good job in a play. It was the first time he ever said anything like that, and I could hear in his voice how nervous he was. But he was proud about it too. It was easy for me to recall that experience and the way it makes me kind of giddy and happy. I get this light feeling in my upper chest from it. It's almost a little like I'm choking, but it feels good.

However, working on a disturbing sound memory was more difficult. I tried to remember the time when I was seven and I overheard my father telling my mother it was time for me to know I was adopted. I can remember the event and even how I felt about it, but my emotions seemed frozen.

I remembered you talked about reversing the sequence of events leading back to the memory. I thought about an event from a year later, and another from when I was in high school. Both were memories about my father. Using those I began to think more and more about his voice during the argument with my mother. Then I was able to physicalize my actions while I was listening. You know, it's funny. I think I can remember being totally frozen when I actually heard them having the conversation, but while doing this exercise, I found myself wanting to move, to express my frustration and anger. Then when we stopped for the silence, I felt sick in my gut. My energy center for that experience is in my gut.

LARRY: When I was eight or ten, the boys in school used to pick on me. I was an easy target. I was fat. My clothes didn't fit very well. They used to call me "fatso," or say "Here comes that fat kid," or call me "sissy" because I wasn't good at sports. I can hear their voices very clearly, and I want to cry, but I don't cry. I fight the impulse so they won't see. My energy center is in my stomach. I feel this sick sensation at the pit of my stomach. Then I hear laughter, the kids calling me names and laughing at me. I'm not sure if the laughter is a real memory or something that I am afraid of hearing. From that I segued into the image of my brother, Sam. He is trying to comfort me when I come home. He's talking to me and reassuring me. It's soothing. My energy center for that is also in my stomach. It's like drinking hot chocolate and feeling warm.

JUNE: I had a difficult time doing this work. I had a particular event in mind, but I couldn't hear it. I was scared today to present it. I just kept thinking, "Should I or shouldn't I?" I don't know if it was because I am scared of the memory or scared of not being able to do the work, of hearing the event with my inner ear.

DR. BELLA: How did you practice for this session?

JUNE: My visual images were very strong. So I placed a chair in my space and imagined I was in our living room. I am studying a high school English assignment. I can see the room, the piano, and the clock. There wasn't any sound, though. I tried to hear a ticking of the clock, but. . . , so I kept time by drumming with my hands on the chair. Then I allowed my visual imagery to segue to my father. He is talking on the phone in the hallway. I remember his words, or rather I remember *the idea* of his words. He was talking to my grandmother and saying how disappointed he was in my older brother, that he was never going to amount to anything. Then he changed, and started talking about me, about how proud he was of me, his little, smart, talented June—how I was going to be a star someday. Those words were awful. They became a challenge. My body felt heavy. I felt a lump in my diaphragm. I can feel it right now as I am talking. All through the exercise, I stayed in the chair, twisting, crossing my legs, fidgeting.

For my pleasing experience, I imagined listening to the Beethoven Sixth—the Pastoral. All kinds of visual images passed through me. It's very funny, Dr. Bella. I can hear the entire orchestra clearly; every note is in my mind; but when I try to hear my father's voice and exactly what he's saying on the telephone, it's not the same, I get stronge visual images, but only an echo of his voice and tone.

DR. BELLA: June, you were very concentrated. While you were listening for your father's voice, your body told us about your discomfort. Then you re-laxed and your chest opened up as you imagined the music. I also noticed that during your times of discomfort, you were whispering something.

JUNE: I whispered three times, "I'm afraid I will disappoint Daddy." I was trying to make up for not actually hearing his voice.

DR. BELLA: What is important is that you have this experience in your Pan-dora's Box. The meaning of those words and the experience have stayed with you. It's often impossible to re-hear the exact words and sounds, but you can hear them figuratively or imaginatively. The "echo of the sound" is still in your body, and you behaved as though you heard. Your memory stimulated discomfort in your body.

LIZ: I didn't really have any specific memory to begin with. I was trying to figure out what to do. My roommate has this music box and I asked her if I could borrow it. I held it, looked at it, but decided not to play it. I kept walk-ing and looking at the music box. Then I had this visual image of my mother with one of my grade school teachers. The teacher was telling my mother I was slow. I always hear "stupid." I have no memory of that experience, but there is a feeling for it. Something is there. I feel hurt, my chest hurts and it's like some kind of trauma. But I also feel energy in my hands. Holding the box, sometimes, they feel shaky, panicked. Everytime I pick up the music box, I go back to that same imaginary memory. The music box became a catalyst for it, for me to expand on it.

DR. BELLA: Putting your energy into an object frequently focuses your concentration. Here, looking at the music box triggered your aural images. Excellent.

LIZ: I was able to contrast that experience with hearing an old boyfriend say my name. It always made me feel sexy. Of course, my energy center for that was in my sex. I'm embarrassed to talk about it. It's easier just to feel it.

MARTHA: I had some difficulty starting today. So I reversed my order. Usually I began with the disturbing experience first. Today, I decided to begin with a memory from very early in my childhood. It is my mother's voice. She is singing me to sleep. It is soothing and pleasant. My energy center is in my back. I feel like I am being petted. Sometimes, I want to stretch and relax. My other experience is also in the bedroom. My parents are in the next room. They are fighting. It is painful to listen to them. I put my scarf over my ears. I can remember my father saying "I am never going to speak to you again. I'm leaving." My mother is crying, sobbing. My center changed to my chest and it's difficult to breathe I want to cry.

DODI: I was in the bedroom, too, Dr. Bella. I find the more I go through this exercise, the closer the two memories become. They are almost interchangeable. First is my exhusband trying to propose marriage to me. I am very excited and feeling beautiful and sexy, but I also want to laugh. I feel my center is divided between my sex and my chest, especially when I laugh. But then the laugh segues into crying. It always happens suddenly. I don't have to think about making the transition. The laughter just turns to tears. I'm remembering the last thing he said to me as we were separating. It's painful.

DR. BELLA: Laughter and tears are very close together, aren't they?

ERIC: I remembered an event from my second year in high school. I wanted to be a football player. I wanted it bad. I remembered hearing my name called to come to the gym on Saturday for team tryouts. I was real excited. When I arrived at the gym, the coach looked at me and said, "You're too little. Come back when you grow up." I hated that man. I ran all the way home. In the exercise, I worked on the visual image of my father. He is telling me at breakfast that it's okay to play football. I'm really proud. Then I'm in the gym. It's brightly lit. I sense the noise. I can see the coach smiling, and then hear him speaking with that sarcastic tone. I get this panicked sensation in my gut. I want to run very hard, to get out of there as fast as I can—to run away. I feel as though I'm relying too heavily on the visual sense and not as much on my inner ears.

DR. BELLA: Don't worry about that, Eric. As with June, you have a strong memory for this event and you are able to use it creatively. Some people have stronger abilities in one sensory area over another. That's fine. And you weren't working exclusively with visual memory. Your description often included references to sound. Keep working.

SUMMARY

The most important element of this exercise is the hardest to bring across. The moment of silence that follows the two experiences is difficult because it requires simplicity. Some actors are tempted to show off or physically act out the sensation. The purpose of the silence is to *experience* the sensation and trust that others will see the residue of stimulation in the body.

As the actors repeat this experience/exercise, or explore it with other aural memories, the quick repetition of the sequence from pleasing to uncomfortable or vice versa, is also important. Such repetition practices kinesthetically stimulating energy centers. This technique is necessary for making physical transitions on stage. An ability to do this also develops the actor's sense of trust in letting his/her body do the work.

Chapter 5

The Tactile Sense

The Psychology of Touch

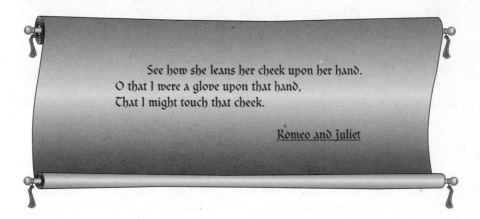

> See how she leans her cheek upon her hand.
> O that I were a glove upon that hand,
> That I might touch that cheek.
>
> <u>Romeo and Juliet</u>

LECTURE: PRIMAL DESIRE

The desire to touch and to be touched is one of the strongest primal needs in the human experience. Touch is as necessary to life as breathing and eating.

The tactile sense also includes our skin's ability to sense heat or cold (temperature), weather, climate, humidity, and physical contact with objects living and inanimate. Sometimes our skin responds with itches, allergic reactions, scratches, or various other irritating pains. When we are excited, aroused, or stimulated by something we see, the skin tingles.

The visual and tactile senses are like Siamese twins. We see something and we want to know about it: we want to touch it. We see something and we imagine how it feels to the touch.

The tactile sense is expressed in three ways:

1. Sensing the need to touch, but suppressing the impulse.
2. Sensing the need for touch and enjoying it kinesthetically, but without actually touching.
3. Sensing the need to touch by making actual physical contact.

Every person's tactile sense is active whether they respond overtly or not. Tactile human beings want to touch and be touched. However, for others, even while the impulse to touch is present, they avoid touching and being touched. Repressing their need makes them physically uncomfortable. Due to painful life experiences, the tactile sense, regretfully, has been deadened or shut down. To whatever extent the tactile sense may be active or inactive, every actor *must develop an instinct to recognize their tactile sensations in order to be kinesthetically available to a character's individual tactile needs.*

EXPERIENCE/EXERCISE 12: THE POWER OF TOUCH

Objective   To arouse the sensations of touch through the fingers, fingertips, and palms.

Format   Beginning with their eyes closed, the actors work silently, in pairs.

SECTION A: FOCUSING ON THE QUALITY OF TOUCH SENSATIONS

1. Touch only with the fingertips.
    a. easy
    b. gently
    c. firmly

      d. tapping
      e. allowing the fingertips to decide
2. Touch with the fingers and palms.
      a. smoothly
      b. harshly
      c. exploring the entire hand
3. Changing the tempo of touch.
      a. slow and sensuous
      b. fast
      c. medium
      d. explore various changes in tempo

SECTION B: SEEING EACH OTHER AS IF FOR THE FIRST TIME

1. Switch partners.
2. Create an emotional relationship by slowly approaching each other.
      a. Be aware of the impending moment of touch.
3. Repeat the format from Section A for touching, beginning with the fingertips.

SECTION C: SEGUE INTO NONVERBAL HAPPENINGS

1. Physical involvement.
      a. toes touching
      b. bodies touching
      c. physical distance, but with hands touching
      d. exploring all variations on touch
2. Pursuing emotional relationships through touch.
      a. acceptable
      b. unacceptable
      c. loving
      d. hating
      e. ambivalent
      f. the process of accepting/rejecting
3. Adding minimal dialogue
      a. "Yes"
      b. "No"
      c. short phrases: "Get away!" "Come here." "I like you." "I hate you."

The discussion following this experience/exercise went like this:

LARRY: Well, that experience/exercise certainly has a lot of sexual energy to it.

MARTHA: Standing so close, and as my toes touched Larry's, I had a strong impulse to kiss him.

DR. BELLA: Why didn't you?

MARTHA: I had ambivalent feelings. First, I was embarrassed. My concentration was on what everyone else in the room might think. Then, as Larry kept changing his touch on my hands, I got scared. It was getting too intimate. I had all these conflicting feelings.

JOHN: I was very uncomfortable with this exercise too.

DODI: I know! I felt like I was intimidating you. You would only let our fingertips touch.

JOHN: When I did the exercise with Liz, I had more success. I guess our chemistries responded to each other.

DODI: Did I do something wrong?

DR. BELLA: No, Dodi. Liz and John were able to approach each other very slowly. They began to build a sense of trust.

LIZ: When we first began to walk around each other, John would not acknowledge my presence, but I knew he sensed I was there.

JOHN: Yes, I knew we were going to have to touch and I was fighting that.

LIZ: But when we got closer, I looked in your eyes and thought I sensed from you the need to touch.

DR. BELLA: Yes, John's conflict strengthened his tactile sense.

DODI: Why didn't it work when we did it?

DR. BELLA: It did work, Dodi. John had a sensation. He rejected it. I think your natural sexuality was simply overpowering. He fought it.

JUNE: I know what you mean, when Dodi and I worked together, just touching her fingertips felt dangerous. There was definitely something sexual in it. It was difficult. Our fingers were potentially stimulating us one way, but in each other's eyes, we recognized how uncomfortable we were.

DODI: Yes. Then I took her hand more firmly and said "Can't we be friends?"

JUNE: I laughed. We had defined the relationship and that made the experience easier and, I guess I have to say, more acceptable.

ERIC: As Martha and I were approaching each other in the second part of the exercise, I couldn't decide whether she wanted me to touch her or not.

MARTHA: Yes, the longer we stood there, the more the tension grew.

DR. BELLA: You were both touching without touching.

ERIC: Finally, I had to say something, and "Forgive me" came out of my mouth.

MARTHA: He looked like such a little boy at that point, I responded with "Son." That's when I ruffled his hair. Eric has great hair! I love touching it. As with Dodi and June, speaking defined the relationship. It made it very easy for us to hug each other. My energy center changed from being in my sex to my chest. I felt very warm.

DR. BELLA: Being physically aware of your acting partner is the most potent source for sensory work. When you are working on a role, ask yourself, "Is there desire between these two characters?"

ERIC: What if I don't like my partner?

DR. BELLA: Respond to that impulse. Eventually, touch may lead to a change in the relationship.

LECTURE: ISOLATING THE TACTILE RESPONSE

Sensory work also includes responding to the touch of props or other objects on the set. The objective of this next experience/exercise is for the actors to use their hands, fingers, and fingertips to discover touch and kinesthetically rediscover that sensation by recognizing how touch activates the various energy centers.

EXPERIENCE/EXERCISE 13: EXPLORING TACTILE SENSATIONS WHILE BLINDFOLDED

Objective   To explore touch sensations without allowing the response to be visually stimulated.

Format   Working individually, actors blindfold themselves in order to explore with their hands responses to various unidentified objects. Each actor is given an object from one of two sacks I have brought to class. The actors are not allowed to see the objects.

SECTION A: EXPLORING THE FIRST OBJECT

1. Feeling the object for:
    a. size.
    b. shape.
    c. weight.
    d. texture.
    e. response.
2. Developing a response:
    a. inner-eye image of the held object—what do you think it looks like?
    b. visual memory images stimulated by the touch.
    c. aural memory images stimulated by the touch.
    d. psychological responses—the object activates which energy centers?
3. Side coaching:
    a. Do not bring the object to your face. (Everyone reverts to an infantile desire to put the object in their mouth.) The purpose of this experience is to allow the hands and fingers to explore and respond.
    b. Do not smell the object. (Again, an infantile mechanism.) Focus on touch.
    c. Put the object down. Keep your eyes closed. Continue to *touch the object without touching it*. Avoid "miming" the object; simply *have the sensation of holding it*.
    d. Are you able to kinesthetically activate an energy center in response to the imaginary touch of the object? If not, pick it up again and continue to explore its texture and shape and your responses to its character.
    e. Stimulate your kinesthetic memory of the object by talking out a stream-of-consciousness about its shape and texture, and your inner-eye and inner-ear responses.

SECTION B: USING THE SAME FORMAT AS SECTION A, EXPLORE THE SECOND OBJECT.

1. Be aware of how this second object affects you differently.
    a. What new energy centers does it stimulate?

SECTION C: EXPLORING THE CONTRASTING KINESTHETIC RESPONSES

1. After thoroughly exploring the second object, put both objects aside.
    a. Can you kinesthetically recall your physical responses to each object?
    b. How quickly can you segue from one response to the other?

The discussion following the experience/exercise went like this:

MARTHA: When I touched the quilted material, I had a visual image of my grandmother. I sensed her presence and thought I could smell her. I had images of my childhood, with my grandmother covering me with the quilt. I remembered a song she used to sing and thought I could hear the echo of her voice singing one line of that song. Of course, I started with my energy center in my fingertips, as I touched the material, but when I started remembering the song, I felt nostalgic, and my center was in my chest, my heart. I began to feel warm all over.

DR. BELLA: What about when I gave you the plastic plate?

MARTHA: I had a negative response. I recognized it immediately as a plate. It was a such a shock to my hands compared to the quilt. Goose bumps ran down my back. I don't like eating on plastic. I have a real aversion to it.

LIZ: When you gave me that piece of fur, . . . my fingers recognized fur. I loathe fur.

DR. BELLA: Liz, your kinesthetic memory of touch is very vivid. As you are sharing your response, your body and words are communicating repulsion.

LIZ: I feel a little like I'm going to throw up. I have this visual image of a dead dog and a memory of a smell. My energy centers are in my diaphragm, throat, and nose. That smell of death.

LARRY: I touched a piece of fur as well, but I enjoyed it. It was smooth and gave me a feeling of satisfaction. I got the impulse to "lick my chops."

JUNE: One of the objects you gave me elicited two different responses. It was a dagger with a wooden handle. The handle was rough. Letting my fingers rub over just the handle created the sensation of itching. I felt this itching in my legs. Touching the steel blade was dangerous. It was oddly pleasant. A relief from the itching. My lower region responded to its sharp, smooth, deadly quality.

ERIC: Having an itch sounds like a good idea. When I held the rope, I didn't feel anything, but it seems like an itch would be right.

DR. BELLA: I'm not so sure about that, for you, Eric. You had no response at all?

ERIC: I got a visual image of a monk walking. I was very uncomfortable with this exercise. I don't like touching inanimate objects. They make me feel sterile. I like touching living things. I like touching things that respond.

DR. BELLA: Why do you feel "sterile" touching inanimate objects. Do you know the reason?

ERIC: You asked that question and I remembered my hands being slapped a lot for playing with things in the house I wasn't supposed to touch, especially after coming in from the barn with my hands all covered with . . . well, dirty.

DR. BELLA: Here you can give yourself permission to touch, although your response to avoid touching is an interesting one and may be useful to you someday as an actor.

JOHN: Dr. Bella, I had a difficult time with this experience/exercise too.

DR. BELLA: I know. Please explain why.

JOHN: I felt I was forcing myself to touch the objects. Having a kinesthetic memory response after putting the object down was simply a mind game. My actions were not real, so I gave up. I don't know, I guess I'm afraid of touching. It makes me uncomfortable when someone touches me. I feel guilty. I don't know why. I'm a very private person. I avoid touching.

DR. BELLA: I was aware of your struggle and I have a suggestion. Tonight, when you go home, have your roommate put some objects on the table. Touch them. If you wish, touch them with your eyes open, perhaps that will make you feel safer. Then try repeating the kinesthetic response of touching the object without actually touching it. Give yourself permission to feel.

DODI: I had a very pleasant experience touching the silk scarf. It made me feel sexy. But the coral was prickly and sharp. It was very irritating and I didn't like it at all. I didn't want to touch it—it made me angry—so I just kept imagining the silk scarf.

DR. BELLA: You were avoiding unpleasant sensations. Don't avoid! Allow the tactile sense to penetrate you physically and psychologically. Allow yourself to touch and *not* enjoy the experience. There is a great deal to be discovered in that.

LECTURE: SKIN AND THE ENVIRONMENT

Another significant skill for actors to develop is their awareness of inner and outer skin sensations to weather, temperature, indoor and outdoor environments, or any stimulus that stimulates the skin or any part of the body. A marvelous way to develop this ability is through the imagination and recall of specific experiences.

EXPERIENCE/EXERCISE 14: DEVELOPING THE SKIN'S RESPONSE

Objective   To practice kinesthetic responses to skin sensations.

1. Select a tactile condition that stimulates your skin.
2. Think about a specific memory you have of that condition.
3. Create a physical score for reliving that memory.
   a. If necessary, talk your stream-of-consciousness about the experience.
4. Ask yourself about the psychology of your memory. How was the situation of your experience affecting your response to the tactile sensation? Is that specific memory part of your sensory recall?

The actors discuss their work:

DODI: I asked myself how weather affects my skin. I remembered walking home last winter on a particularly cold and windy night. It had been a hard shift of work at the restaurant. I imagined walking against the cold wind. My face and skin felt tight, stiff, and dry, like cardboard. Water crystals were in my nose. My forehead and skin ached. I was tired and depressed and all I wanted was to be home.

LIZ: I picked the summertime and having a sunburn. Last July, I fell asleep and had a very bad sunburn. My skin was tight and felt like it was shrinking. I didn't want to be touched. I can feel my back arching. There's this feeling of being tense, not being able to relax for fear that I'll rub up against something and the burn will really hurt me.

JOHN: I had a summer experience too. I was on the beach, walking on hot sand. My feet were burning and I was dancing around. I wanted to get down to the water. My toes really hurt. It made me want to run away, very fast.

JUNE: I sprained my ankle once in dance class. My toes hurt and began to swell. I have a visual image of all the people gathered around me and I'm very embarrassed to have been such a klutz. To avoid swelling and to relieve the pain, the instructor told me to put my feet in a bucket of ice. When I plunged my feet into the ice water, the cold shot right through my toes, ankles, and thighs. My skin got numb. It was torture to keep my feet in that bucket. I panicked a little. I felt I might wet my pants. I was so embarrassed and mad.

LARRY: I had an allergic reaction once to eating zucchini. My skin broke out in a rash and the back of my neck got prickly. I had a little difficulty breathing and felt I was going to be sick. I wanted to scratch my neck, but doing that only aggravated the itch.

MARTHA: I had a job last holiday that required me to stand on my feet all day. When I got home, my feet and legs were burning and tired. I bathed them in very hot water. When I put my feet into the boiling water, I felt a stinging pain all over. I pulled them out immediately. In order to keep my feet in the water, I concentrated on relaxing the sore muscles. I could feel my skin turning red, but I could also feel myself getting sleepy, the tension of work going away.

ERIC: I remembered walking out of the farmhouse early one morning in February. The snow gave off an eerie white glow. Even though the sun wouldn't be up for a few hours, there was light reflecting off the snow. The air snapped my face and lungs and the fresh feeling made me want to run, almost to fly. I felt twenty pounds lighter. When it's, like, twenty below zero, and I have to take off my gloves, I don't notice the cold on my hands right away. I have to keep my hands active though. Then when I put my gloves back on, my hands feel snug and I can feel the heat building up inside them. I like the winter. It's dangerous. You know death is out there. In the spring, it feels different. The morning dew makes your skin damp. It's like being washed. I can smell all the dead leaves and things from last fall, rotting. And as I slog around in the mud, it sometimes feels like I'm being sucked in. In spring, there's a feeling of damp, slow stirrings.

SUMMARY

Generally, we think that stimulating the tactile sense requires actual physical contact, but it is possible to "touch without touching." In the first experience/exercise, the desire to touch or to avoid touching stimulated the energy center in the sex, or what I sometimes call "the lower regions."

Developing an awareness of touch also means developing an awareness of how sight can stimulate the need to touch. We see something and imagine how it feels to the touch. The second experience/exercise demonstrates how touch can stimulate recall in the other sense memories, particularly sight and sound.

The tactile sense also means being aware of how our skin responds to season, weather, temperature, climate, humidity, and environment. In the last experience/exercise, the imagination recalled how the body responded to these physical conditions and their effect on our overall psychology.

LECTURE: KINESTHETIC MEMORY OF PAIN

Physical pain is a tactile response. Gentle, rough, loving, angry, hurtful, or sadistic touch can cause pain. Pain can also be caused by disease, illness, or physical impairment or disorder. Accidents can result in fractured bones or internal injuries, and while the purpose of surgery is to heal, the process is often painful. All pain is experienced involuntarily. It is a powerful sensation.

In life, extreme pain is seldom forgotten, since it stimulates nerve endings in the entire body. A specific area of pain will frequently send out tactile messages to other parts of the body.

At least thirty years ago, someone slammed my thumb in a heavy sliding door. I first felt the pain at the base of my spine, and this sent pain throughout my entire body. It gave me an awful headache. I was also very angry, "How can anyone be so stupid and not watch what he is doing!" A few moments later I realized my thumb was hurting, throbbing, and several hours later, it was swollen, discolored and feeling very hot. We frequently associate pain with temperature, from extreme heat to freezing cold.

There is another kind of pain known as psychosomatic. With this condition, physical pains are caused by emotional upheavals or stress. While the illness might not be physically inflicted, the pain is real.

When pain demands attention, it may impede the ability of the other senses. All of our attention goes to the pain. The one sense to remain acute is touch. When physically hurt, how carefully the fingers tend the wound. They are tactile and alert. The wound, too, is extremely sensitive to outside touch.

Events surrounding extreme pain are never forgotten. Pain or the memory of pain may stimulate many unexpected feelings or behavior. For instance, I had my appendix removed when I was very young. About twenty years ago, I needed another kind of surgery. As I began to anticipate the upcoming surgery, I was fright-

ened and started to feel pain throughout my entire body. My physical image was
of a truck running over me. This fear and its pain was remembered kinesthetically,
that is, involuntarily. When I think about either surgery, I can still respond with all
these sensations.

The following experience/exercises are intended to help the actor uncover
their personal sensations of pain.

EXPERIENCE/EXERCISE 15A: UNEXPECTED PHYSICAL PAIN

Objective   Recalling kinesthetic response to physical pain.

SECTION A: EXPERIENCING PHYSICAL PAIN

1. Over the period of a week, record in your journals any event of unexpect-
   ed pain.
   a. Answer all the "W" questions surrounding the event.
   b. Where did you first feel a response to your pain in the body? What
      other parts of the body were stimulated and in what order?
   c. How did the pain affect your psychology?
   d. How did the pain affect your behavior?

SECTION B: RECALLING THE EVENTS AND THE RESULTING BEHAVIOR IN CLASS

After exploring the experience/exercise, members of the class participated in the
following discussion:

JOHN: I have several black and blue toes. I bumped into a table leg last
Thursday. At first, there was a sharp, unexpected pain in my foot. I was
swearing and hopping around. I was really angry with myself, but I blamed it
on the furniture. After a few minutes, I got myself to physically calm down,
and then I rubbed my toes for a while.
DR. BELLA: Was the pain only in your toes?
JOHN: At first, but then it shot through my entire leg. After I had rubbed and
pulled on my toes for a few minutes, they felt better.
DODI: I pricked my finger on a needle as I was sewing a button. It was a
sharp sting right at the tip of my index finger. First, I put my finger in my
mouth and sucked on it; then I shook my hand. It was annoying, but the pain
was soon over.
LIZ: I was running to catch the bus and tripped. My entire body went into a
kind of shock. I was so surprised to find myself sprawled out on the pave-
ment! Then I realized I had pain in my back, neck, and head. However, the
main injury sharply became my knee. It was bleeding and the hurt smart. I

had torn my hose and this made me angry and embarrassed. I had to limp home. At first, I could hardly walk, the pain hurt so much, but the more I walked, the easier it became.

LARRY: I was walking along Michigan Avenue and daydreaming. I walked right into a lamp post. There was this thump—*bwoing*—and my head was bouncing off the post. It was a very sudden, excruciating pain. I couldn't get my eyes to focus and I had this bloody nose. Some idiot was laughing and I wanted to punch him out. I put my handkerchief on my face and leaned back. I had to walk very carefully home; my head and nose were throbbing. I didn't want to use any public transportation. I thought the movement would be too jerky and painful.

MARTHA: On Wednesday, last week, we had a particularly hard workout in dance class. I felt some cramps in my toes. That night I was watching TV and I got up to get something to drink. There was a violent seizure in my foot. I hobbled into the kitchen. I thought the cold tile floor would help. It didn't. I got some ice out of the refrigerator and put it on my toes. The muscles started to giggle. The ice seemed to help. I kept walking around to keep the toes from cramping up again.

DR. BELLA: Eric, you have a bandage on your hand.

ERIC: Yeah, I was washing the dishes and I broke a glass in the sink. As I was fishing it out of the water, I sliced my palm. Blood was pouring out of it. I turned on the cold tap and held it under. The pain was agonizing, but finally the cold water seemed to numb the pain. I took my palm out from under the tap and the pain immediately started throbbing. I put some ice in the wash cloth and held it to my palm. This felt O.K., and it helped to stop the bleeding. I still can't open my palm all the way. My girlfriend thinks I should have gotten stitches.

JUNE: I woke up last week with a dreadful toothache. As I was waking up, I opened my mouth to yawn. The air hit my tooth and the pain was unbearable. Then I took some aspirin and the cold water I drank hit the nerve of the tooth. I was crying it hurt so hard.

EXPERIENCE/EXERCISE 15B: UNEXPECTED PHYSICAL PAIN

Objective   Using the imagination to explore physical responses to pain.

Format   In-class improvisations with side-coaching.
This is an in-class exercise. I side-coach the actors through the experience by making spontaneous suggestions to discover responses to pain.

1. Wearing normal class apparel, the actors physically warm-up and shake out all tensions.
   a. See Experience/Exercise 2, Part I, "Physical Relaxation" (page 7)

2. Following their warm-up, the actors move through the neutral space.
3. In succession, the actors physically respond to the following pains as I call them out. Time is given to allow all the actors to thoroughly explore their initial reaction to the pain and their attempts at recovery.
   a. stubbing a toe
   b. sudden toothache
   c. pricking a finger
   d. falling down
   e. leg cramps
   f. walking into a post or door
   g. cutting a hand

EXPERIENCE/EXERCISE 16: KINESTHETICALLY RECALLING AN EXPERIENCED PAIN

Objective   Uncovering/discovering pain experiences lodged in the actor's Pandora's Box.

Format   In-class presentations of rehearsed event.
Students may work with or without partners in the presentation of their event.

SECTION A: PREPARATION

1. Deciding on the event.
   a. Ask all the "W" questions surrounding the event.
2. Setting up the space.
   a. Use minimum furniture and props, only enough to focus on the moments preceding, during, and recovering from the pain.
3. Apparel.
   a. Basic class apparel.
   b. Add shoes, if necessary.
   c. Add pieces of clothing that help to sustain belief.

SECTION B: PRACTICE

1. What do you discover during your rehearsals?
   a. Where is the pain located?
   b. What kind of pain is it?
   c. How did you get this pain?
   d. What other parts of the body are stimulated by your pain?
   e. How does the pain affect your psychology?
2. What activity are you performing before the pain?
3. What is your physical response to the moment of pain?

4. What is your recovery process?
   a. What activity do you perform to alleviate the pain?
   b. Do you recover from the pain?

SECTION C: PRESENTATION IN CLASS.

Following the presentation there was a discussion:

ERIC: [*The Fight*] My first step in recalling my pain was remembering my humiliation, my feelings of despair when I lost a fight back when I was fourteen. I have an image of this large, stupid classmate sitting on me. This led to my physical task of having a bloody nose and a pain in my gut. Martha, playing my mother, put a wet cold washcloth on my face. The cold soothed the pain in my nose, but made me feel clammy and I had the impulse to be sick.

LIZ: [*Boiling Hot Water*] My preparation for this experience/exercise was the activity of boiling water to take to the refrigerator so I could defrost the freezer. I picked up the empty pot, but I believed it was full of hot water. It was heavy. I saw the steam rising up and inhaled it. I shifted the pot abruptly and the boiling water spilled on my right foot. My body went into shock. My foot immediately began to sting. Dodi ran in. She saw my pain. She grabbed some ice and put it on my foot. My foot started to turn red. It had a stinging, burning sensation.

DR. BELLA: You describe the pain very well.

LIZ: That's just it. My imagination can recall all the events, but I don't really believe the pain.

DR. BELLA: How badly did you burn your foot?

LIZ: I still have some scars.

DR. BELLA: Look at your foot. Keep looking at your foot, right now. See the scars.

> *Liz starts screaming and tries to walk.*

DR. BELLA: Very good. The scars triggered a kinesthetic response to your memory of the pain.

JOHN: [*Nervous Stomach Pains*] I used preparing for an audition to aggravate a nervous stomach condition I sometimes have. I started by reading the script and studying lines. Then I had a visual image of another actor getting my role. It always puts me in a state of anxiety. My hands sweat and I get these sharp acid attacks in my stomach. I made a cup of tea and ate a little bread to calm down. It's very easy for me to get worked up in this exercise.

DR. BELLA: Do you ever feel real pain?

JOHN: At the beginning of my rehearsing, I could feel it coming on, and then maybe a few hours after, I felt a little sick. However, the more I worked on this experience/exercise, the less actual pain I felt, even though the emotions and behavior seemed to come more naturally.

DR. BELLA: Very good.

JUNE: [*At the Dentist*] For me, the sound of the drill created the pain. It stimulated my imagination to see the needle for the novocaine and I believed I was in the dentist's chair. Even before the injection, the anticipation of pain made me anxious. Anticipating the pain, I could feel the pain.

DR. BELLA: When you heard the drill, where did you feel the pain?

JUNE: Those drills have a piercing sound. Imagining that I can hear one immediately activates the sensation of having my tooth drilled. My jaw and my spine want to react. You know, Dr. Bella, I really didn't feel any pain during the experience/exercise, but I have an idea of the pain, and the behavior followed naturally.

DR. BELLA: An actor must not really feel the pain. If you did, you would not be able to perform. The circumstance is "as if" and your body did well. It communicated the pain, especially the anticipation of pain.

MARTHA: [*Gall Bladder Attack*] It didn't take any time to sense the pain kinesthetically. I had a gall bladder attack. I was not anticipating being sick. Who does? One morning, I woke up in excruciating pain. I sat up quickly, doubled over, and clutched the lower part of my stomach. Quick sharp pains shot out into my arms and chest. I was afraid I was having a heart attack. While I sat on the bed groaning, I picked up the phone, dialing with difficulty to get the doctor.

DR. BELLA: Martha, how real are your sensations of pain?

MARTHA: My groaning and fear helped me to believe my body was suffering. But to really feel pain? It was more like I felt the idea of pain. My imagination led me from one moment to the next.

DODI: [*Experiencing a Monthly Period*] Well, just before my "monthly friend" and during that time, I'm in a state of panic. I'm on edge. Then I get dreadful cramps. As I started the experience, I couldn't sit down. I kept walking. I decided to take some pain killers. I tried lying down. Eventually, I felt a little better physically. Then I picked up my script and started to cry.

DR. BELLA: Why?

DODI: I don't know how to explain it. I love working on this role. I want to be happy, but my body is still crying. During my period, I'm stressed out, then elated, then depressed. It's never logical.

DR. BELLA: Did you feel any pain during the presentation?

DODI: I know where the pain is located. I convinced myself kinesthetically to relive those physical and psychological sensations.

LARRY: [*A Bad Cold or the Flu*] I seem to be easily susceptible to the flu bug. My first physical symptoms are chills and then hot spells. My joints hurt and I feel crippled. Today, as I started the experience/exercise, I felt empty, so the beginning was not very believable.

DR. BELLA: But you did get involved. How did that happen?

LARRY: I sometimes use this lemon-flavored powder medicine that you mix with hot water. Actually, I hate the taste of it, but it seems to work. Anyway, it was easy to kinesthetically remember drinking the medicine and that aroused physical images of discomfort. Feeling weak, I also was able to imagine chills and I needed to cover myself with a blanket to get warm and to feel secure.

SUMMARY

Actors preparing for a professional career must be in good health, and they must have physical and emotional endurance. If an actor is to create a role that requires severe physical impairments, especially through the spine, s/he must have total flexibility in the back. A history of back problems should eliminate any consideration for undertaking such a role.

When working, an actor does not really feel pain or his/her performance will be destroyed. The actor's body remembers the pain imaginatively, and the kinesthetic response communicates the sensations of pain.

To find actions that will alleviate the pain is an important step. These are actions that an actor might play, so to speak.

On occasion, we can anticipate pain. Knowing that you are about to be subjected to physical abuse requires summoning up the courage to face the oncoming pain or to overcome your impending fear.

Chapter
6

The Olfactory Sense
The Psychology of Smell

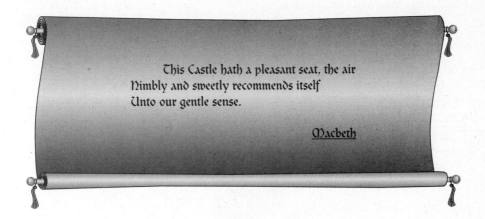

> This Castle hath a pleasant seat, the air
> Nimbly and sweetly recommends itself
> Unto our gentle sense.
>
> *Macbeth*

LECTURE: THE PRIMARY SENSE

Seeing, hearing, and touching seem obvious to creating a life on stage. They are easily indicated in a script. They can be physically scored, and, therefore, they can be communicated to the audience through activity. Smell is less obvious. In a scene, sensory conditions dealing with smell are generally inferred and do not appear to have a direct bearing on the plot.

However, smell has the power to stimulate our unconscious behavior more than any other sense. This is because it is our first sense. Our first memories go back to smell. Before babies have the ability to see and hear with distinction, they recognize their world through smell and taste.

In order to awaken the actors' understanding of the power of the olfactory sense, I ask them to make a list of events and smells over a given week.

EXPERIENCE/EXERCISE 17: INVESTIGATING SMELLS

Objective   To practice kinesthetic responses to smell.

1. Make a list of olfactory categories and your responses to them:
   a. household smells.
   b. city smells.
   c. animal smells.
   d. nature smells (include the smells of weather and the seasons).
2. Practice recalling your kinesthetic response to each smell.
   a. What is the odor?
   b. Where did you smell it?
   c. When did you smell it?
   d. Was your response to the smell unusual from previous responses? Was it affected by the weather or the season?
   e. What behavior was stimulated by this olfactory experience? Which energy centers were activated?

3. Practice alternating various smells which have opposite or contrasting physical responses.

In preparing this experience/exercise, I stress the significance of recognizing seasonal changes, of being able to recognize the "smell of spring," and of being able to distinguish one season from the next.

DODI: As I was writing down the smells in my domestic category, I recognized a trend in how I responded to the smell of garbage, detergents, and cat litter. I want to avoid smelling them, so I contract my nasal passages and hold my breath. My spontaneous response is *not* to smell. How can I use that?

DR. BELLA: The body has responded to something! You have to sense/smell it first, then react, even if negatively. What was your behavior after refusing to smell what you found disgusting?

DODI: I was a little aggravated with myself.

DR. BELLA: You can use that.

DODI: I did discover one strong kinesthetic response to the smell of the fresh air of Spring, deep, deep into my lungs! But I couldn't repeat it.

DR. BELLA: Did you have a specific time and place to remember the smell? The only way to stimulate any kinesthetic memory is to practice and to ask questions like "What is the event?" "What did I do?" "Where was I?" In the olfactory work, "How did it affect my nose?" "How does the smell stimulate responses in my eyes, my mouth, my breathing, etc.?" With weather, frequently the anticipation of rain or snow will stimulate the sense of smell. Next time it gets ready to rain or snow, make a conscious effort to smell it.

JOHN: I had difficulty remembering actual smells. But my visual images were very vivid. For example, I tried recalling the smell of rain. Instead, I saw the rain hitting the wet pavement. I love bacon. I thought it would be easy to have a kinesthetic response to the smell of frying bacon. I can hear the bacon sizzling. My mouth will water. But I cannot think of the smell. So I got hungry and actually fried some bacon. Later, I was able to remember the smell kinesthetically, but my response was stimulated through recalling the sound and the taste as well.

DR. BELLA: John, how marvelous that in trying to recall the smell of bacon, you actually got hungry! That is a kinesthetic response!

JUNE: I was in the kitchen scrubbing the sink. I spilled some ammonia on the floor. My nasal passages were instantly infected. My eyes were coming out of their sockets. I couldn't see, they were watering so much. The ammonia choked me at the back of my throat. I held my breath. There was pressure in my head and at the back of my neck. Then I had the immediate feeling of repulsion, uncontrollable, like I might vomit. I was able to contrast that experience with a pleasant smell: fresh-cut grass. I remembered a specific event from my childhood, playing in our backyard. My nostrils opened up. I wanted to breathe in deeply. My chest opened up. My auditory response was keen as well. I was able to hear the lawnmower in my imagination.

ERIC: Living on the farm most of my life, I have a strong kinesthetic memory of the seasons and the weather. Running home from school in winter, my nostrils open and close as I breathe. My breathing is short because of the cold. You know, small, quick breaths. The clean smell of snow penetrates my spine and my shoulders. It's very sharp and I feel full of energy. In the spring, I have visual images of some snow still left on the ground, the sweet air of something freshly decayed. My chest is open and free and there is energy in my pelvis. I feel loose.

DR. BELLA: The sense of smell is strongly connected to the other senses. June involuntarily hears the lawnmower as she recalls the smell of fresh grass. Eric has strong visual images, but also connects his sense of smell to the feeling of the seasons on his skin—or to his sense of touch.

LIZ: I remember the feelings instead of the odors. For rain, I have a sense of solitude and loneliness. But also for spring, happiness, sexual feelings, and anticipation. But I did spill a bottle of my boyfriend's cologne. It made my eyes sting and water. My nose burned. Then the smell became less intense and my breathing opened up. I began breathing the smell in deeply, and sexual feelings were aroused.

DR. BELLA: Liz, do you have visual images when you respond emotionally to the seasons or the weather?

LIZ: Yes. The mix of visual images and emotional responses are instantaneous.

DR. BELLA: Like John, you are already having a marvelous kinesthetic response with your other senses to the conditions we are investigating for smell, and I suspect the kinesthetic response of smell isn't far behind the rest of your senses, as you discovered with the cologne. Keep working.

MARTHA: I was going down into the subway and the smell of urine was overpowering. I thought I was going to gag. I immediately recalled my grandmother in the nursing home. She was dying of cancer. I remembered entering the hospital, the smell of disinfectant and medicine trying to cover up the smell of urine and stagnant decay. My eyes and throat hurt. I had tension in my back and stomach. It was more than just a reaction to the smell of the urine in the subway. Those odors reminded me of my grandmother's death. She died when I was ten. As I was stepping onto the train, I wanted to cry.

LARRY: I have an experience connected to the smell like that but it's kind of pleasant! I was on the bus and this woman got on with a baby. When she passed by me, it was obvious that the child needed to have its diapers changed. People were so funny in how they reacted to that smell! But then I remembered changing my cousin's diapers. Even though the smell is unpleasant initially, there is also something healthy about it. I felt physically potent, powerful, as I was taking care of my cousin. I liked it. My nose wanted to do two things at once—to smell my cousin, and yet I was holding my breath a little to avoid gagging.

DR. BELLA: Larry and Liz, you both experienced smells that aroused memories lodged in your Pandora's Box. That is the next part of your investigation, to uncover sense memory smells attached to some event from your past.

LECTURE: MEMORIES OF SMELLS PAST

Thirty years ago, or even longer, I had a dramatic experience with the sense of smell.

A student had not been able to contact her mother for almost a week. She went to her mother's apartment and found her in the bedroom, lying on the floor. Panicked, she dashed out of the apartment to call me from a pay phone. She confessed that her mother was an alcoholic and had a heart condition. As we entered her mother's apartment, an odor immediately hit me. My eyes began to sting with the impact of this smell. My mouth tasted like chalk and it was hard to swallow. I started to feel nauseated and wanted to throw up.

My student kept asking, "Do you think she might be dead?"

I went into the bedroom and saw her mother on the floor. I quickly called my doctor. After describing the smell and her mother's condition, he told me to call the police.

About ten minutes or so later, when the paramedics arrived, I greeted them by saying we were concerned whether or not the woman might still be alive. The change in their body language from urgency to quiet, careful resolve told me they recognized the smell of death before they even entered the bedroom.

In order to awaken the actors' understanding of the power of their olfactory sense memory, I ask them to recall events or smells that have had a strong influence on them. This experience/exercise can either occur in class with side-coaching, or outside through the actors' own private investigations.

EXPERIENCE/EXERCISE 18: REMEMBERING A SIGNIFICANT SMELL

Objective   To discover/uncover an olfactory event lodged in the actor's Pandora's Box.

Format   Homework investigation.

1. Asking the "W" questions:
   a. What was the odor?
   b. When did I smell it?
   c. Where was I?
   d. Who was with me?
   e. What were we doing?
2. Recreate the action:
   a. Talk out your stream-of-consciousness of the event, arousing visual, auditory, and tactile images as necessary.
   b. Use a prop if needed.
   c. What was your behavior? What did you do when you encountered the smell? Recreate that.

    d. What energy centers are stimulated by the smell experience?

    e. In silence, sustain the energy uncovered.

3. Repeat the process as many times as necessary until the discovery/uncovery of the olfactory sense memory is kinesthetic.

4. Record the process and responses in your journal for future reference.

LECTURE: PEOPLE SMELLS

Have you ever noticed how no two homes smell the same? The smell of the house is partly established by the people who live there. Think of your grandparents' home. What does it smell like? Are there different smells for each of the various rooms? What do the closets smell like? This is where their personal smell will be the strongest. What about a friend's house? What is its odor?

Recognizing "people smells" is the most potent way to develop the olfactory sense. We respond both positively and negatively to the smell of shaving lotion, perfume, cologne, soap, and other cosmetics, as well as the leftover odor of tobacco, bad breath from food, and body odor from sweat. A person's individual smell can be determined by their eating and drinking habits. Beer, liquor, coffee, onions, garlic, candies, gum, fish, or whatever a person might have been ingesting can have a direct effect not only on their breath but on their physical odor as well. A person's profession can also establish their odor. Think of gas station attendants, workers in a fish market, members of the medical professions, zookeepers or those who have any type of animal contact, carpenters, farmers, etc.

Finally, there is the smell that is unique to the individual. We each have a personal smell. To some, it is pleasing, attractive. To others, repulsive. Think of the people in your life whose smell you have always found pleasurable. Who are the people who always seem to have a slightly distasteful smell? How is your response to their smell an integral part of your relationship?

Olfactory sensations are very powerful positive or negative stimuli in intimate or sexual relationships. We can be aroused sexually by our kinesthetic memory of smell, wishing that person were near, or remembering a past contact or experience with someone we have loved. If the relationship has turned sour, a scent that was once pleasing can take on negative associations, reminding us of pain or loss.

As the actors have been developing their sensitivities to smell, they have also been uncovering many personal responses, either loving, frustrating, or ambivalent. Their emotional reactions are connected directly to a physical life, to a behavior stimulated by an involuntary physical response to each smell. As the actors become more accustomed to having spontaneous responses, that is, responses beyond their immediate control, they are ready to trust incorporating kinesthetic olfactory stimuli into improvisations or into scene study with other actors.

EXPERIENCE/EXERCISE 19A: OLFACTORY RESPONSE AND INNER MONOLOGUE

Objective   While responding involuntarily to an olfactory stimulus, to explore the inner monologue of a character in a scenario.

Format   In-class presentation of rehearsed scenarios.

1. Actors work in pairs or, if necessary, trios.
   a. Choose an event and objective to accomplish such as: saying goodbye (parting); proposing; interviewing for a job.
   b. Ask the "W" questions about your event.
   c. One actor is selected to actually establish an odor, such as: eating an onion; dousing one's self with perfume or cologne; wearing smelly clothing; or smoking a cigarette.
   d. Allow your inner monologue and behavior to be stimulated by the olfactory sense.
      • The odor should not be discussed openly during the scene. Its purpose is to stimulate the inner monologue.
      • Use the odor to heighten the stakes (either to stimulate intimate feelings or to provide an obstacle to your objective).

Following the presentations the class discussed:

DR. BELLA: June, your words were a newscast about the smell! Consequently, you did not allow yourself to fully experience the overpowering scent of the aftershave lotion.

JUNE: What did I *do?*

DR. BELLA: You talked about it.

JUNE: What should I have done?

DR. BELLA: First, let me say there are a lot of possibilities in the event of saying goodbye to your boyfriend. However, you destroyed them by shouting at Eric "Oh, that awful aftershave lotion!" That is your inner monologue. It is private. How will it affect your behavior without being stated directly?

June, Eric, I would like to make some private suggestions to each of you and have you perform the exercise again. First, Eric.

June exits, and I talk quietly to Eric.

You've come to say goodbye. Why?

ERIC: I have been called to serve in the war. I must report for duty today.

DR. BELLA: Is this a serious relationship?

ERIC: Yes. I want to ask June if she'll marry me when I get back.

DR. BELLA: Where are you coming from?

ERIC: My parents. My mom made me a huge breakfast.

DR. BELLA: Eric, I can smell something in your backpack. Did you bring your usual lunch with you today?

ERIC: You mean my liver sausage sandwich with raw onions?

DR. BELLA: Yes. Would you please go out and wash off the aftershave lotion and then eat some of your sandwich, especially the onion.

June, come back in and let's talk. How do you feel about Eric having to go to war.

JUNE: I don't like it. I love Eric and I'm frightened he won't return.

DR. BELLA: Marvelous. That is a strong decision, remember it!

The following is a physical score and record of the dialogue that resulted.

> *June begins with the activity of touching up her make-up and brushing her hair. When Eric enters, she runs to greet him. They kiss, but June breaks the kiss and gently pushes him away. She crosses over to the couch and sits down. Eric, startled, looks at her and then crosses to sit down next to her.*

ERIC: What's wrong?

> *June does not answer. Eric feels rejected, but puts his arm around her. June continues to face forward.*

JUNE: I'm worried.

> *They sit in silence.*

ERIC: Are you angry?

> *June kisses him gently on the lips. Eric stands up and lifts June off the couch. He kisses her passionately. He looks into June's eyes with a question. She goes over to her purse and pulls out some gum, unwrapping and handing a stick to Eric.*

ERIC: What's this for?

> *June starts laughing.*

JUNE: You fool!

> *They both laugh and go out together.*

DR. BELLA: That was marvelous! Your behavior was very spontaneous, you were seeing, hearing, and sensing each other in the moment. But now, can you repeat the experience? And to make it even more challenging, can you repeat it without actually wearing cheap cologne or eating a liver and onion sandwich during the scene?

EXPERIENCE/EXERCISE 19B: KINESTHETIC OLFACTORY RESPONSE AND INNER MONOLOGUE

Objective   To respond to the kinesthetic memory of an olfactory stimulus while exploring the subtext of a scenario.

Format   Repeat the scenario set up in Experience/Exercise 19a, but *without using an actual scent*.

Class discussion followed the presentations:

DR. BELLA: Liz, where was your attention at the beginning of the scene? It seemed scattered.

LIZ: I was preparing my kinesthetic memory of John's body odor.

DR. BELLA: What do you mean"preparing"?

LIZ: I was trying to remember how my body responded the last time. We had a really good rehearsal yesterday. I was trying to activate the same energy centers.

DR. BELLA: You were doing your homework in class and therefore anticipating the event. You knew the imaginary circumstances, but you did not trust yourself to use them, or even to trust yesterday's rehearsal. You allowed your personal fear of performance to interfere with your kinesthetic ability to communicate.

LIZ: What can I do?

DR. BELLA: Trust your homework. Concentrate on your activity and scene partner. Start there. You have to see John before you can react to John.

John, you also anticipated the events of the scenario. You knew Liz was going to reject you, therefore, I did not feel you were really fighting for this secretarial position in the interview.However, Liz, your response to Dodi when she came in was very believable.

LIZ: I hate the smell of smoke on people's breath and clothes. It's such an awful stink. It's easy for me to have a kinesthetic response. Even just talking about it now, my body is having an ugly response.

DR. BELLA: Keep working, Liz. Trust that your body will have a response to all sensory conditions, not only real, but imaginary ones as well.

SUMMARY

The sense of smell is our most primal means of identifying and reacting to our environment and our relationships. It can arouse us sexually or provoke an immediate, involuntary sense of disgust.

Some smells have a stronger degree of potency. They release responses more easily from our Pandora's Box. Olfactory responses can also be stimulated by sight, sound, and taste. Generally, the most difficult olfactory awarenesses to develop are of the weather and of the seasons. These responses are closely tied to the sense of touch.

More than any other sense, smell has the ability to alter our psychology. It can play a major role in determining attraction or repulsion, directly affecting our behavior and psychology.

Chapter
7

The Gustatory Sense

The Psychology of Taste

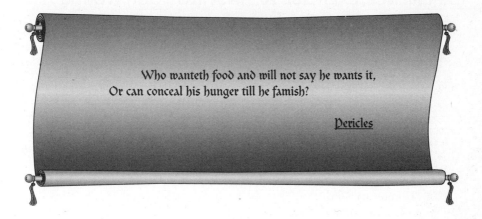

Who wanteth food and will not say he wants it,
Or can conceal his hunger till he famish?

Pericles

LECTURE: SUSTENANCE

Taste buds are active when we eat, drink, smoke, chew gum, brush our teeth, use mouthwash, and take medicine, among other things. Our sense of taste can be stimulated by what we smell, see, and hear. Think of bacon sizzling in the pan. The sight and sound activate your sense memory of bacon and its taste. However, before you can actually experience the taste, you must be able to smell. Taste and smell are inseparable.

The relationship between smell and taste is so powerful that smell has the power to arouse our hunger. Imagine entering a movie theater. The olfactory sense is attracted to the smell of popcorn. Perhaps you've just eaten a very satisfying meal. You have no desire to eat any more. The smell of popcorn makes you salivate anyway. You need to eat! As you get closer to the concession stand, the sound of popping kernels and that smell overpower you and against all common sense you indulge your impulses.

The act of eating involves more than the senses of taste and smell. There are tactile responses from the lips, the teeth, the tongue, the back of the throat, the esophagus, and the stomach. When eating something crunchy, like a carrot or a celery stalk, the lips moisten with saliva, the teeth chomp down, and we hear the vegetable snap off in a healthy bite. As we chew, the mouth continues to salivate. Then we swallow and feel the food travel down to the stomach.

Another very popular activity for the mouth is kissing! The organ for chewing, tasting, and digesting food (which sustains daily life), is also intimately related to the act of sex (which ultimately sustains life by creating new life).

We also use our mouths for breathing. If we did not have this capability, then the vocal cavity's other important function—speech—would be impossible. Actors tend to forget that speaking is a sensorial process too. It involves not only the auditory sense, but the tactile sense as well.

EXPERIENCE/EXERCISE 20: TASTING YOUR WORDS

Objective   To experience the sensory power of speech.

SECTION A: MAKE A LIST OF WORDS FOR EACH OF THE FOLLOWING CATEGORIES. ADD ANY OTHER CATEGORIES YOU CAN THINK OF.

1. Vulgar phrases: Include gutteral sounds.
2. Slang: Include sayings your parents use, or ones you know from past generations.
3. Scientific words
4. Humorous words
5. Sensuous sounds

SECTION B: SAY THE WORDS OUT LOUD.

1. What is the physical response to speaking the word or phrase?
   a. Is it difficult to say the word? Easy? Pleasing? Hard?
   b. Chew the words. How are you stimulated by speaking the sounds?
   c. Listen to others speak the words. What are your responses to these sounds?

LECTURE: DEVELOPING TASTE

Many roles and scenes involve the activity of eating. There is the famous tea scene between Cecily and Gwendolyn in Oscar Wilde's *The Importance of Being Earnest*. Classical drama as well relies heavily on oral gratification. Falstaff is probably the theatrical epitome of gustatory study, although he has close competition in the figure of Henry VIII. Much contemporary drama also takes place in the kitchen.

Actors can easily recall the particular taste of different foods, but the anticipation of eating is as important as the actual activity. The following experience/exer-

cise will alert the actor's awareness to how *all* the senses influence the anticipation of, as well as the actual process of taste.

EXPERIENCE/EXERCISE 21A: THE ANTICIPATION OF TASTE

Objective   To discover/uncover the sense of taste.

Format   Eating an apple and then a tomato.

SECTION A: THE APPLE

1. Place the apple on a small dish on a table.
   a. See the plate.
   b. See the apple.
   c. Pay attention to:

- size
- shape
- weight
- color
- texture
- smell

2. Pick the apple up and slowly bring it to your lips.
   a. How does it feel to the touch?
   b. What is its smell?
   c. How does the body anticipate eating the apple?
3. Eat the entire apple.
   a. What does it sound like to eat an apple?
   b. What is the process of biting and chewing the apple?
   c. How does it stimulate your tongue, inner cheeks, teeth, and throat (when swallowing)?
   d. What is the aftertaste? How does the mouth respond after swallowing?
   e. What do you remember about the process?

SECTION B: EATING A TOMATO

1. Use the same process as Section A. However, eat the tomato without cutting it.

SUMMARY OF EXPERIENCE/EXERCISE 21A

While tasting the apple and then the tomato, the actors discover that touch, smell, sight, and sound all contribute to the sense of taste. The apple and the tomato have unique smells which are very different from each other. Each contains a juice of a different quality. With the anticipation of taste, the mouth begins to salivate in preparation for the taste experience. The anticipation of taste can actually inspire the kinesthetic response of taste.

As I noted at the beginning of this chapter, the lips, teeth, tongue, inner cheeks, throat, and stomach are all a part of tactile response in taste. Biting and chewing these two fruits stimulates unique responses in all those physical areas.

EXPERIENCE/EXERCISE 21B: THE ANTICIPATION OF TASTE

Objective   To become aware of the vast range of taste experiences.

Format   Same process as Experience/Exercise 21a.

SECTION A: CATEGORIZING TASTE

1. Discovering kinesthetic responses to the taste of food and drink that is:

      a. raw
      b. fresh
      c. frozen
      d. canned
      e. cooked/hot

2. Discovering kinesthetic responses to the taste of food and drink that is:
      a. sweet
      b. sour
      c. bitter
      d. salty
      e. bland
      f. spicy
      g. tangy

3. Associating food and drink with particular physical/psychological conditions:
      a. medicine
      b. caffeine
      c. alcohol

LECTURE: THE PSYCHOLOGY OF TASTE

We each have foods we like and foods we dislike. Sometimes the foods we prefer are determined by our culture, or by what's available. It's very easy today to have the choice of Mexican, Japanese, Chinese, Indian, Greek, Italian, Polish, French, German, Cajun, or any other ethnic food by traveling a short distance to a restaurant that specializes in that particular cuisine. Citizens of these regions probably have an affinity for their native foods.

What foods do you like to eat? What foods do you dislike? What are your images of those foods? Are there any particular experiences that you associate with these foods? Sometimes the psychology associated with particular foods can be unpleasant, even though the initial response to the taste of that food might have been pleasing. An unpleasant response to a particular taste can develop, if as a child you were forced to eat something you didn't want to eat.

Health concerns can also play an influencing role in taste. Colds, because they block the sense of smell, dull our sense of taste and bring pain to the back of the throat, making it difficult to swallow. Taking medicine or eating according to the restrictions of a specified diet can also influence the psychology associated with those tastes.

EXPERIENCE/EXERCISE 22: ALERTING AND REPEATING
                          VARIOUS TASTE
                          SENSATIONS

Objective   To identify the psychology associated with a kinesthetic response to taste.

SECTION A: MAKING LISTS

1. Make a list of pleasant or delectable food and drink that arouses your sense of taste.
2. Make a list of unpleasant or detestable food and drink that stimulates your sense of taste.
3. In both categories, note those responses which are particularly strong. How does that response stimulate your behavior? How does it influence your psychology?
4. Is there a specific event in your memory related to a particular food or drink which heightens your response positively or negatively to that food?

SECTION B: PRACTICING KINESTHETIC RESPONSES TO TASTE

1. Choose a pleasing taste and a revolting taste for which you have strong responses.
2. Recreate an event associated with each taste.
   a. Use as many objects—plates, cups, glasses, knives, forks, spoons, or whatever else you might need to inspire believability in your event.
   b. Do not use the actual food or drink.
   c. If you choose a taste for which you have no specific memory of an event, create an imaginary event.
3. Practice your events to show in class.
   a. When practicing and showing your events, take as much or as little time as necessary to enable you to *believe* and *sustain* your memory of the taste.

SUMMARY OF EXPERIENCE/EXERCISE 22

Almost everyone finds their psychology lifted by exploring the kinesthetic responses to pleasurable foods. As actors work on more than one response, they discover that the texture of each food becomes important to sustain believability for that kinesthetic response.

Unpleasant responses can stimulate other energy centers in the body. For instance, responses to cough medicine not only include the foul aftertaste, but also the psychology of being sick. This might recall a physical queasiness in the stomach, as well as an emotional feeling of inadequacy or dependency.

LECTURE: THE PSYCHOLOGY OF HUNGER

There are various kinds of hunger that people must satisfy. We talk about a hunger for knowledge, to know all you can. There is a physical hunger—that is, sexual desire. But the most obvious hunger is for that which sustains life—food and drink. This is the hunger for survival.

Most of the time, we take our diet for granted; however, when our ability to satisfy hunger is threatened, the results can be devastating. Poor eating habits, either through abuse, neglect, poverty, or famine can result in disease and death. When poverty threatens our basic instinct to satisfy hunger, the result is often criminal.

A simple experience/exercise for the effect of hunger would be to fast for one day, only allowing yourself to drink plenty of water. How does your energy change? What do you do to compensate for not being able to eat? Are your emotions affected positively or negatively by this experiment? What is your response to eating when you allow yourself to break the fast? In some religions, fasting is a healthy part of the diet ritual.

I remember when I was a child in Communist Russia in the middle of the 1920s. Food was at a premium. Lately, as I watch the news or read the newspapers, things have not changed much. Russian people are still standing in line, fighting for food.

As a child, I stood in very long lines for bread. The only kind of bread to purchase was black bread. The first time I had white bread was in Paris, when I was twelve years old. I was served white rolls and steaming hot chocolate. Today, I can pig out on white bread. It is a comfort food for me. If I allowed myself, I could pig out on hot chocolate or any kind of chocolate.

This behavior is a different kind of hunger. It is hunger stimulated by emotional needs. It is compulsive hunger. Normally, we feel content and relaxed after a large, very good meal. However, compulsive behavior stimulated by emotional needs such as loneliness, fear, anger, deprivation, and/or sexual desire often results in over-eating, bulimia, anorexia, or alcoholism.

EXPERIENCE/EXERCISE 23: THE VULNERABILITY OF HUNGER

Objective   Recognizing eating habits.

SECTION A: WHAT STIMULATES YOUR HUNGER?

1. Think about your eating habits.
   a. Do you have a regular eating routine?
   b. What makes you deviate from that routine?
   c. What behavior is associated with hunger?
      - Especially note the changes in behavior when your eating routine changes.
      - What energy centers does hunger activate?

SECTION B: KINESTHETICALLY RECALLING HUNGER

1. Talk about what makes you hungry.
   a. How does the body respond?
   b. Can you kinesthetically taste the food?
   c. How does talking about hunger arouse your psychology?

Following the presentations, the class discussed their work:

LARRY: Since I only eat when I'm hungry, I very seldom focus my attention on what I'm tasting. It was difficult at first to do this experience/exercise. But I did remember an experience at home. The one meal I enjoy and taste is at Thanksgiving. When I arrive at my folk's home, the smell of roasting turkey and pumpkin pie gives me a very secure feeling. I am warm and content. My physical center is in my stomach and in my heart. As I am speaking now, I have very specific visual, sound, smell, and taste images of home at Thanksgiving.

MARTHA: My grandmother always had a box of chocolate in the dining room. When I got good grades or did something nice, Grandma would reward me with chocolate. I love chocolate. Unfortunately, eating chocolate, craving chocolate, has become an addiction. Particularly when I am afraid or I have failed an audition or have some other emotional upheaval, I yearn to feel comforted as I did when I was a child. My hunger for chocolate is very powerful. What drives me crazy is the smell and the soft texture of chocolate. However, when I eat chocolate, I stuff myself so much, that I don't remember the specific taste. After binging, I surge on a sugar high with all kinds of nervous energy, then bottom out. I feel physically and emotionally guilty. While the desire to be comforted is very strong, I know that chocolate is an addiction and not the answer to my feelings of inadequacy. Still, it's always a struggle.

DODI: I eat two sensible, sparing meals a day. Generally, these meals include rice, pasta, some greens, chicken or fish, if it is not too expensive. I'm never starving, but it seems like I'm always mildly hungry. I work, but with tuition, rent, and everything else, I don't have a lot of money. Sometimes on payday, I get cravings, especially for ice cream. I love the soft, luscious texture in my mouth. Eating ice cream is very sensuous. I love the taste of vanilla and strawberry. It's a little crazy, but I stock up on it unnecessarily, even if I already have some in the freezer. It makes me feel secure to know it's in there.

JUNE: Every once in a while, when I felt fat, I used go on a week-long crash diet. I generally survived three to five days, then I would get physically weak and be emotionally on edge. Often I was battling a headache and feeling very tired, but sleeping didn't help, it only made matters worse. Also, I found myself very sexually frustrated. My body would have a lot of cravings. One way or another, I would give in to my cravings and binge myself. I especially liked bread, crackers, pasta, but I would eat so fast and so much, I never really tasted any of it. I knew this was unhealthy and that was very frustrating. Now I try to eat sensibly every day. By exercising, I've kept my weight down, but I also take the time to taste my food while I'm eating it. This makes the eating last longer. Meals can really be pleasurable experiences. If I am still craving food after a meal, I will allow myself to eat a rice cake. The crunch of one of those is very satisfying.

LIZ: In the late afternoons, I teach an aerobics class. I enjoy working up a healthy appetite. After class, I feel like I've cleansed my whole body of all the day's tensions and I am hungry for food that will give me energy. A good Chinese meal or Italian pasta always tastes great. I love broccoli, it's a crunchy vegetable, chewing it is very satisfying. Fortunately, it's popular in both these cuisines.

ERIC: Liz, sometimes you make me sick. Health food, healthy bodies, healthy minds, it's too much trouble. I'm used to big meals. On the farm, coming in from chores in the morning, my mom would make us a big plate of eggs and bacon, and there would be toast and lots of coffee. And so what if we ate all the greasy cholesterol, we worked it off! My girlfriend has got me eating all these health foods, like Liz. It's like bird food, no weight. I crave a good, juicy, thick, red hamburger. It just sits there in my stomach after I'm done. It's great! And a nice big pile of baked beans and frankfurters, ohhhh, with some good beer and then a ball game, and I just spread out on the couch and start snoring. That's what life's all about.

JOHN: Some people here know, . . . I am an alcholic. When I was drinking, seeing something alcoholic or smelling it would drive me crazy. The taste pinches the tongue, but that didn't stop me from being greedy for the sensations of liquor inside my mouth, on my tongue and down my throat. The desire to drink was overpowering. After swallowing, the feeling in my stomach was great. My relationship with alcohol was the most personal relationship I ever had. Eventually, I would drink anything put in front of me. I stopped drinking before I began studying acting, but the urge is still there. Coffee has become my substitute. The smell of strong coffee and its taste arouses my hunger. One thing I have noticed since I stopped drinking, food tastes better to me. When I get anxious, like when I know I have an audition or something important coming up, I have the old urges, but coffee or a coke boosts me up. The caffeine gets me going.

LECTURE: DRINKING AND ALCOHOL

Of all the taste sensations to explore, alcoholic beverages are by far the most complex. Generally, students easily respond to the idea of drinking beer or wine at a social event. A class, recalling the smell of malt, or visualizing a sudsy foam in a mug, will spontaneously jump into an improvisation of party relationships. Frequently, however, dramatic situations require a response to alcohol that explores a more complicated side of our psyche.

Every class has at least one or two students who border dangerously near an alcoholic problem or who are recognizing a multigenerational heritage as adult children of alcoholics. All the experience/exercises, because they encourage the actors to develop their abilities to respond spontaneously and without prejudice, have the potential to release psychological conflicts. However, when the work begins to explore the psychologically disturbing behavior of drugs and their related psychologies of abuse and disorientation, the personal risk becomes much greater. The process of uncovering kinesthestic responses is a sensitive one and requires an individual approach and pace. Each actor must choose what will work best for him or her. No actor should be pushed into psychological areas they do not wish to explore.

I repeat, I do not recommend these experience/exercises as forms of therapy. That is for another kind of professional. On the other hand, members of our profession must have respect for the work being explored by other actors. It is not our job to sit in judgment of another's experience, either positive or negative. However, it is to our advantage to embrace our experience when we can and to include it in our work, as well as to support the attempts of our colleagues to do the same.

Some actors, for religious or personal reasons, have never tasted alcohol. They should not be required to do so for the sake of "art." We have imagination. An actor's responsibility is to create believable behavior. Actual alcoholic drinks are not served on stage. Whiskey is cold tea. Wine is colored water. Vodka is plain water. Actors should explore their kinesthetic responses to beverages which simulate the qualities of beer, wine, or whiskey for how they stimulate the mouth, nose, and eyes. For whiskey, try a shot of mouth wash, for red wine—concentrated grape juice, for white wine—lemonade, or for champagne—ginger ale or club soda. All these stimulate the oral cavity. Also, there is nonalcoholic beer on the market, which approximates the malt taste of real beer.

Alcoholic behavior also extends itself into the physical life. If an actor has never been drunk, s/he might adopt the actions of someone they have observed. Often drunks complain of dizziness. Spin around several times and try to walk. What is the behavior?

In exploring the need for a drink, what complusive/obsessive actions are personal to each actor? Each of us has habits which can be compulsive and which we sometimes keep secret. How does this behavior reveal a psychology? How does it reveal vulnerability?

EXPERIENCE/EXERCISE 24: ALCOHOLIC BEVERAGES

Objective   Exploring the physical/psychological behavior of alcoholic beverages.

Format: Solo preparation and presentation of an event dealing with alcohol.

PART I: PREPARATION

Section A: Choose an Event

1. Personal experience
2. Observed experience
3. "As if" experience based on scripted material

Section B: Score the Event

1. Ask and answer the "W" questions.
2. Outline a physical score including the:
    a. beginning.
    b. middle.
    c. end.

Section C: Objects (Washed and Clean)

1. Any drinking objects or props that will help the actor believe in the event.
2. Transfer liquids or substances may be used if necessary.

PART II: PRACTICE

Section A: Rehearse the Event Outside of Class

1. As you work on experiencing the event, continue to ask yourself:
    a. What do I do when I'm under the influence of an alcoholic substance?
    b. What does my body feel like?
    c. How does the kinesthetic memory stimulate my behavior and my feelings?
    d. How do I behave with other people? How are my responses heightened or suppressed?
2. Especially in this experience/exercise, an actor should feel free to use any approach s/he desires in order to allow the kinesthetic response to taste and smell.
    a. The experience/exercise may be performed silently or by speaking an inner monologue.

PART III: PERFORMANCE OF EXPERIENCE/EXERCISE 24 IN CLASS AND DISCUSSION FOLLOWING

John's Physical Score as Observed by the Class

John, asleep on the floor, is surrounded by empty beer cans. He wakes up and grabs his head. He moans. He sits up and for a few moments looks at the room, focusing on the empty beer cans. He picks up each can, smelling to see if there is any beer left. They are empty. He finds one still full. He smells and drinks. John quickly gets up and runs out of the room. The sound of throwing up. He returns. He sits down, very sick, holding his head. Slowly he gets up and proceeds to clean up the room, throwing all the beer cans into a trash bag.

> **DR. BELLA:** John, you have told the class that you are an alcoholic. Was this a difficult experience/exercise for you to do?
>
> **JOHN:** Yes. I didn't want to repeat my self-destructive behavior, but remembering the "morning after" always reminds me how destructive drinking is for me.

DR. BELLA: The physicalization of the event was very convincing. Your concentration was right on and your kinesthetic response of needing the drink when you picked up the full beer can was very vivid. Your negative experiences with alcohol have had enough passage of time for you to deal with them in a creative way! Good for you.

June's Physical Score as Observed by the Class

June dances into the kitchen after a party. She feels happy and energetic. She carries an empty martini glass. She picks up a gin bottle in order to pour another drink, but it is empty. She starts looking for another bottle, . . . any bottle. After searching and finding nothing, she sits down. The happy high is starting to wear off. June undergoes a physical transformation. She gets up, feeling very shaky. She walks around the kitchen checking dirty glasses. No luck. June sits down, her body shaking. She starts to cry.

DR. BELLA: Very riveting. What did you use for your preparation?
JUNE: When I had to audition for Kirsten in J.P. Miller's *Days of Wine and Roses*, I panicked. I have never been that drunk. Kirsten is an alcoholic who can't and won't dry out. I remembered taking diet pills to help me suppress my hunger in order to lose weight. Right after taking the pills, I felt happy and emotionally high, but when the effect wore off, I would be jumpy, very hungry, and depressed. I started taking two a day and then I couldn't sleep. My doctor found out and told me to stop taking the pills. I was addicted. The withdrawal was awful. I was depressed, angry, listless, shaky, and on edge. In this experience/exercise, I combined the high/low effect for my transitions. I also checked with a friend who is a recovering alcoholic to see if my responses were similar to a drinker's.
DR. BELLA: This was a good preparation. As I recall, there are several accounts about playing drunk in the author's notes to that play. I would suggest you also look those up. I also wanted to comment on your transition from being happy to being depressed when you got up. That was particularly convincing.
JUNE: I used the experience of having a runny nose at that point, and then once, while I was rehearsing, my hands started to itch. As I got closer to the performance, I also included the sensation of itchy feet. It gave me a restless feeling.

Larry's Physical Score as Observed by the Class

Larry stumbles into the room carrying a bottle. He looks around and then takes a large swig from a bottle. He puts the bottle down. He mumbles and then stumbles over to a washstand. He washes his hands, wiping them on his sleeve. He walks back to the bottle and takes another swig. He starts sobbing. He stumbles out.

DR. BELLA: Larry, you were trying too hard to be drunk.
LARRY: But the Doctor is drunk.

DR. BELLA: The Doctor?

LARRY: I based my score on Chebutykin in Act III of Chekhov's *The Three Sisters*.

DR. BELLA: Don't Chekhov's directions say that he enters without staggering and acts as if he were perfectly sober? How did you prepare?

LARRY: Before I came in, I was spinning in place to get dizzy.

DR. BELLA: That's fine, but next time, try to control the dizziness. Also, where has the doctor been? Why does he need to wash his hands? Why is he drinking? What does he want to get away from? These are important questions which will make the sensory work in the scene about more than being drunk.

Liz's Physical Score as Observed by the Class

Liz enters with a plain brown paper bag. She sets the bag on the table and goes to get a glass. She returns and slowly opens the bag. In the bag is a bottle of scotch. She takes it out of the bag and carefully breaks the seal to open it. She sniffs the bottle. She pours a large amount into the glass. She looks at the glass and then smells it. She can't decide whether or not she wants to drink it. She downs a large gulp and starts gagging and coughing. She touches her chest and stomach in pain. She quickly pours a glass of water and drinks it. She takes slow deep breaths of air.

> LIZ: I like wine on occasion, but have never tried hard liquor. I decided for this experience/exercise I would actually go out and try scotch. Today, of course, for the presentation, I used iced tea.
>
> DR. BELLA: What do you remember most vividly about your first experience?
>
> LIZ: Coughing, almost gagging on the scotch, and then my eyes burning. My throat was on fire.
>
> DR. BELLA: How did you feel about those responses today in your presentation?
>
> LIZ: For some reason I felt rushed. I didn't allow myself to remember kinesthetically the sensations.
>
> DR. BELLA: I think you knew drinking the scotch would effect you that way before you even tasted it. Even though you were taking this from an actual experience, when it becomes an exercise, it must be "as if" for the first time.

Dodi's Physical Score as Observed by the Class

Dodi walks around the room with a paper cup and a bottle of champagne (ginger ale). She is drinking and giggling and singing. She pours more champagne into the cup. She tries to walk very straight and then falls into the chair giggling.

> DR. BELLA: Well, Dodi, you seemed to be having a very good time.
>
> DODI: The experience was at my wedding. I began by enjoying the tactile sense of the bubbles in my nose and on my face. It tickled. Then I kinestheti-

cally recalled the sweet taste of the champagne. In the presentation, sustaining the tickling sensation made me a little drunk and very happy.

DR. BELLA: And yet you were very successful in combining the sensation of taste with the experience because the taste didn't stand out like "Now I'm tasting." It was simple and not over-done.

Eric's Physical Score as Observed by the Class

Eric clutches a brown paper bag tenderly to his chest. He has bent shoulders and looks down at the floor. He begins walking. He cases the surroundings, making sure no one is near or watching. He quickly steps into the doorway. His hands become nervous and have difficulty getting the whisky bottle open. He quickly gulps from the bottle. He seems not to taste the liquid. He straightens himself up. He checks the street. He drinks again, this time more slowly, enjoying the taste of the whisky. He sees a friend. He grins. He offers the friend a drink. The friend walks away. Eric feels rejected. He starts swearing, muttering to himself, then walks away quickly.

> **DR. BELLA:** Detailed physical behavior, Eric. Share your preparation with the class.
>
> **ERIC:** Last Sunday at about 8:00 A.M., I saw this friend of mine across the street. I watched him. There were some other drunks around and he was leery of them. This guy had been with alcohol long term. I decided first to explore his behavior more than his response to being drunk, but his need for the drink was pretty intense.
>
> **DR. BELLA:** Your relationship to the bottle was very specific. You held it tenderly. But then your hands had difficulty opening the bottle and it was very convincing. How did you prepare for that?
>
> **ERIC:** In winter, when working outside on the farm, my fingers would be almost frozen. For this experience, I practiced opening the bottle "as if" my hands were almost frozen. I also had a conversation with John. He shared with me that his relationship with the bottle was very personal, almost like having a lover. So when I clutched the bottle, I clutched it possessively, lovingly.

Martha's Physical Score as Observed by the Class

Martha enters gently carrying a small paper cup full of a dark red liquid. She has endowed the cup, as though it were crystal or fine glass. She moves slowly and serenely, . . . very satisfied. She places her hand on her stomach. She is stuffed from food. She moves to the chair and sits. Martha smells the sweet aroma of the wine and slowly sips some of it, holding it in her mouth and then slowly swallowing it. She sips some more and proceeds to stretch and relax into the chair. With her hand, she feels the flush on her neck and cheek. Finishing the wine, she puts the glass down on the end table. She leans back and begins to fall asleep.

DR. BELLA: Your treatment of the paper cup as a glass of wine was very clear.

MARTHA: I enjoyed this experience/exercise. I was using the personal experience of having a sweet after-dinner wine at Thanksgiving.

SUMMARY

Eating and drinking are as necessary to life as breathing. The arousal of the gustatory sense can often be a very pleasing and stimulating experience, activated by and activating the other senses as well.

However, in moments of insecurity or in lives of desperation, these activities can become compulsive. There is drama in this conflict between the compulsive need for gratification and the desire to be accepted by others. What makes the work challenging both on and off stage is that this kind of vulnerability is often hidden from the public view. Characters who have compulsive eating or drinking habits require actors who have a thorough and totally accessible awareness of their own tendencies.

Chapter
8

Body Language

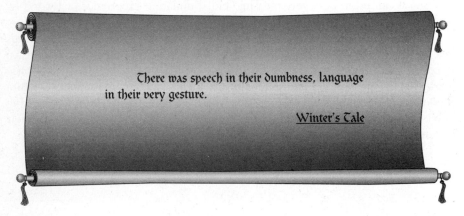

There was speech in their dumbness, language in their very gesture.

Winter's Tale

LECTURE: RHYTHM AND TEMPO

The gestures of posture, of face, of gait, of arm, or of any part of the body which signals a need or desire, communicates a "body language." Recognizing one's own body language is a complicated process. So far in the training we have focused on recognizing kinesthetic responses through each of the five senses and built a technique for repeating those responses. Beginning with Chapter 4 on hearing, the actors began to discover that sensorial responses often locate themselves in specific parts of the body. These locations of response we termed "energy centers." Activating these energy centers stimulates a behavior/psychology unique to each individual actor.

In preparing to play a character for the stage, the actors must now learn to extend themselves more fully into body language. It is a demanding procedure that requires both intuition and objectivity.

Objectively, actors need the ability to recognize when certain energy centers have been activated and to know why. With some awareness, actors need to know their own process for re-activating their energy centers. This is how they will explore a full sensorial/psychological life in rehearsal and on stage.

By trusting their intuition, actors need to *allow* this physical process to take place, without trying to control it.

There are times when a body language can contradict the meaning of what a person is saying. An actor must develop an uncanny perception (an intuition) of what people really mean with their physical and verbal gestures.

Think about your best friend. What is his/her favorite gesture? If you were to imitate your friend, how would you do it? The repetition of a particular gesture tells us something about a person's individuality and gives their body language a unique *rhythm*. Each of us has a distinct rhythm to our personality.

Three things contribute to make our gestures unique, our physiology, our sociology, and our psychology. [Please refer to Egri's "Tri-Dimensional Chart," in Chapter 10, page 130.]

> *Physiology* is the physical make-up; a person's sex, height, weight, physical deformities, age, skin color, eye color, sight (near/far sightedness), quality of voice (bass/soprano), etc. For example, in determining a physical gesture, physiologically speaking, a short person would have a different gait in his/her walk than a tall person; a heavy-set person is generally slower in their movements than a thin person.

> *Sociology* is a person's environment; his/her ethnic heritage, culture, education, language, dialect, class, profession, etc. Sociologically speaking, an actor accepts an audience's gratitude with a bow that is quite distinct from the way a football player acknowledges approval when scoring a touchdown. A professor addresses an audience in quite a different fashion from a rap singer on the street.

> *Psychology* is our physical/emotional response to our physiology and sociology. Each person's psychology is unique. That is, two people may share the same physical and social conditions, but will respond to these conditions with totally different psychologies.

Physiology, sociology, and psychology are intertwined in an extremely complex history of personal experience and response. For instance, a black person is black because of his physiology, that is, his genetic make-up. However, sociologically speaking, the cultural bias against or for skin color will put this individual into situations that are going to develop his psychology. The repetition of those experiences, as well as the repetition of his/her responses, will be responsible for creating a unique body language. This repetition of responses (or habitual behavior) creates a kind of psychological rhythm, as well as a physical rhythm.

Rhythm, as defined by Webster, includes the phrase "procedure characterized by basically regular recurrence." Physically, this implies a repeated pattern of gesture in the walk, posture, vocal inflection, lexicon (word choice), and body movement, among other things. Psychologically, rhythmic patterns are the repeated behaviors or responses to sociological conditions. Hives may be the result of a physical allergic reaction or they may be a response to the psychological condition of anxiety or fear. What invariable response does your body have when faced with overwhelming fear? How do you respond physically to alleviate your fear? With what physical action? With what type of behavior? This pattern is part of your psychological rhythm.

In addition to rhythm, there is tempo. Tempo is the speed at which a rhythm is played. Think of your favorite song. You can sing it fast or slow. The rhythmic pattern of the song remains the same, only the tempo has changed. The intensity of a person's emotional state from moment to moment determines the *tempo* of their rhythm. You can perform the gesture slowly or quickly and it will still be the same gesture. However, in acting, changes in tempo will influence the feeling of the gesture.

In order to become sensitive to physical and emotional rhythms and tempi (that is, to body language), I recommend that actors first observe and become sensitive to the body language of others.

EXPERIENCE/EXERCISE 25: OBSERVING BODY LANGUAGE

Objective   Recognizing energy centers in the body language of others.

Format   Observe and become sensitive to the rhythm/tempo of someone you encounter on a regular basis. It need not be someone you know intimately.

PART I: POINTS OF OBSERVATION

Section A: Physical

1. Sex
2. Height
3. Weight
4. Posture
5. Walk
6. Gesture
7. Age

Section B: Behavior—Natural Rhythm

1. Physical—recurring patterns in gesture, in facial expressions, in walk.
2. Vocal—patterns of speech, inflections, favorite words, melody of accent.

Section C: Tempo Changes Through Physical Stimuli

1. Pain
    a. Headache
    b. Toothache
    c. Stomachache
    d. Sore muscles
    e. Broken limb
    f. Bodily discomforts or illness (itch, sunburn, rash, fever)

2. Environmental conditions
    a. Heat of day/cool of evening
    b. Rainstorm, snowstorm
    c. Smog, exhaust fumes, rotting garbage.

Section D: Tempo Changes Through Psychological Stimuli

1. Work
    a. Deadlines
    b. Heavy demands/workload
    c. Strained relationship with boss or co-workers
2. Personal relationships
    a. Illness of mate or child
    b. Argument with significant other
    c. Relationship crisis

PART II: WRITE OUT ALL YOU OBSERVE AND HAND IT IN.

PART III: ISOLATE ONE OF THE BEHAVIORAL PATTERNS YOU HAVE OBSERVED AND APPLY IT TO YOUR OWN BODY.

1. How does it change your psychology?
2. How does it change your own natural rhythm?
3. Does it activate any particular energy centers in the body?

EXPERIENCE/EXERCISE 26: DISCOVERING NATURAL RHYTHMS

Objective   To discover physical rhythms and psychological energy centers through wearing a variety of apparel and footwear.

Format   In-class exercise with side coaching.

SECTION A: EXPLORATION OF PHYSICAL ACTIVITY IN BARE FEET

1. Cross the room, with an intention of your own choosing
    a. in a slow tempo,
    b. in a medium tempo,
    c. in a fast tempo.
2. Stand a few seconds.
3. Sit a few seconds.
4. Repeat motions of standing and sitting
    a. in a slow tempo,
    b. in a fast tempo,

   c. in a medium tempo.
5. Repeat crossing the room in various tempi.

SECTION B: EXPLORATION OF PHYSICAL ACTIVITY IN EVERYDAY
APPAREL AND STREET SHOES

1. Follow the same format as Section A.
2. Notice and feel how your rhythm changes.
3. Observe changes in your classmates.

SECTION C: EXPLORATION OF PHYSICAL ACTIVITY IN SHORT
SKIRTS, ATTRACTIVE BLOUSES, AND HEELS FOR
THE WOMEN, AND IN TIGHT PANTS, JACKETS, AND
BOOTS FOR THE MEN

1. Follow the same format as before. Ask yourself how this costume changes
your rhythm and energy centers.

SECTION D: EXPLORATION OF GESTURES AND RHYTHMS OF
SOMEONE YOU HAVE BEEN OBSERVING USING THE
SUGGESTED FORMAT ABOVE

1. Ask yourself how this role-playing alters your natural energy centers.
2. What new things do you perceive about your own body language?

Some helpful hints to explore during the exercise:

1. Energize your spine as you walk, sit, and stand.
2. Think of your chest as a hot creative volcano.
3. Walk with a purpose. Sustain that purpose when you sit. (This is similar
   to the "echo of silence" as discussed in Chapter 4, Experience/Exercise
   11.)
4. Take larger steps.
5. Feel taller.
6. Feel stronger.
7. Energize the lower regions—communicate your sexuality.

After exploring Experience/Exercise 26 the actors had the following discussion:

LARRY: I know I have a staccato rhythm. I visualize things and think very
fast. My brain always seems to lead me. While doing this exercise, I inten-
tionally focused on being nosey. This influenced my posture and put my
energy center into my nose and chin. I also concentrated on putting energy
into my eyes, as if to discover people's secrets. When I changed clothes, into
my dress pants and boots, I felt handsome and masculine. I segued into a

smoother, somewhat legato walk. I was stimulated sexually. I gave myself the intention of going to see my girlfriend. This also helped to sustain the energy center in my sex. Consequently, I was not leading with my head and chin like I usually do.

DR. BELLA: Yes, there were two distinct Larrys here. One was funny and the other, an attractive young man.

LIZ: It may be a stereotype, but being from the South, I feel my tempo is generally slower than that of most Northerners. It takes a lot of emotional stimulation to change my tempo. I know I have sensitive hands. They express most of my rhythms. I was brought up to behave and walk like a lady.

DR. BELLA: When I suggested during the side coaching that you "Brush your hair, since you are getting ready to see your boyfriend." your tempo changed.

LIZ: Yes, I was still expressing myself with my hands, and they are a natural energy center for me, but getting ready to feel attractive also stimulated my sexuality, even though I was still expressing that with my hands.

ERIC: I have this tendency to take small steps.

LARRY: It's very strange, when I first met you Eric, I thought you were very shy, not sure of yourself. After awhile, I realized that's not the case at all. Sometimes, you walk like a little boy, but your gestures are always like a strong man.

DR. BELLA: When Eric had his suit and boots on, his rhythm changed. He took longer strides in his steps.

ERIC: It was easy to imagine being outdoors, in the field. I felt my energy going further down in my body and in the back of my spine. In formal situations, like school, I think generally I keep my energy in the upper part of my chest.

JUNE: I've been told I look like I'm suspended from a hanger. I often hide my bosom with my gestures. Having to wear high heels and a short skirt forced me to attempt a better alignment. I felt embarrassed. I know I hide my sexual feelings.

DR. BELLA: Many of us have a difficult time learning to trust our sexuality. This goes for our everyday life, as well as on stage. As you challenge yourself with exploring various body languages, you will overcome this!

DODI: I think my body language is sensuous. Changing footwear, clothing, or the tempo did not change my feelings or rhythm.

DR. BELLA: You have been living with this body language for some time!

DODI: But that's me.

DR. BELLA: But that's not all of you! Try taking longer steps, pretending you are in the military, marching in a parade. Or what about a business administrator? Someone who is very precise, has a sense of authority, and must maintain a professional dignity in a legato tempo. What will happen to your energy center then?

JOHN: I don't think it mattered what clothes I wore or what tempo I used, I generally slouch and usually when I am in front of people, I want to disappear.

JUNE: That's not true! When you were wearing your suit and boots, your posture was still a little sloppy, but I had the feeling you wanted people to look at you, that you felt attractive. At least, I noticed you looked pretty good in a suit!

JOHN: Yes, I felt dressed up. I knew I looked good, but I still felt self-conscious about it.

DR. BELLA: Keep working. Keep working.

MARTHA: Even though I have lost a lot of weight, I still feel fat. I plow through space. While wearing the short skirt, I allowed myself to feel thin and attractive. My tempo changed. It perked up. I think I even got taller! My rhythm changed too. Generally, my energy center is in my stomach. I feel weighted down. But when I was thin, my energy went into my hands and eyes. I felt light. My gestures were sharper.

LECTURE: THE HEAD, THE HEART, AND THE SEX

When the word "psychological" is used in the acting process it refers to behavior. Emotions energize physical centers in the body and the result is a certain kind of behavior. There are three basic psychological centers, the head (i.e., the brain, the intellect), the heart (emotions), and the sex (physical desires). The gift of thought, the gift of feeling, and the gift of life.

These three psychological centers are motivating forces developed by our physiology, sociology, and psychology. They are influenced by an individual's past, his/her sensorial response to the present, and a perception of the future. The psychological centers influence conscious and unconscious decisions. They motivate a person's rhythmical behavioral patterns and tempi. They are the basic areas of need which result in an active body language.

Often, the psychological centers conflict with each other, one dominating another, two trying to overcome the third. This causes emotional crisis or conflicts within a person's feelings, needs, and relationships. In communicating these conflicts, the three basic psychological centers direct the flow of energy into other physical centers such as the diaphragm or the gut. Often, the diaphragm becomes an emotional thermometer in our life, or of a role. However, this does not exclude other physical energy centers such as the eyes, face, shoulders, arms, hands, legs, feet, toes, and voice from being active. All these areas are at one time or another, a physical energy center, contributing to the communication of a body's psychology. All of these energy centers originate in one of the three basic psychological centers.

Each of us is housed primarily in one of these three centers, the head, the heart, or the sex. Think about yourself and people you know. In the academic world, one often meets people who are primarily intellectual. Their center is in the brain. Working with artists, one often encounters individuals whose center is housed in the heart. They are emotional. Others have their center in their sex. Everything they do bespeaks a sexuality. I have purposely omitted any exercise work in investigating or determining each actor's psychological center. This is highly personal work, and besides, while we may be primarily in one center, there are needs which push us into other areas. The well-rounded individual is comfortable with expressing himself/herself in all three centers. And life constantly asks us to participate with all three. Sometimes we are very rational, until some event touches the heart and a different behavior and rhythm results. Psychological centers tend to interchange frequently.

A character's rhythm can be stimulated by an actor's choice of a basic psychological center and how that will inspire the flow into other physical energy centers. In preparing a role, actors must make physical/psychological choices, discoveries, and adjustments while in rehearsal. Often, actors will make physical choices suggested by the writer. But it is an actor's instinct in interpreting this behavior psychologically that will communicate skillfully to an audience.

"The body never lies!" The sound, look, voice, speech patterns, gesture, and movement between the physiology and psychology of the character must make sense. Marilyn Monroe's physiology communicated a sensuous woman whose basic psychological center was sexual. This was her great strength as an actress. Geraldine Page exhibited a variety of body languages in her characters. Alexandra du Lago, the Princess Kosmonopolis in Tennessee Williams' *Sweet Bird of Youth*, had her basic psychological center in the sex. Carrie in *A Trip to Bountiful* had her basic psychological center in her heart. The mother in *The Pope of Greenwich Village* shrewdly had her center in her head. Of course, Laurence Olivier was another master of this craft and any actor would do well to study and compare the many characterizations of his film career.

The art of characterization/transformation was explored indirectly in Experience/Exercise 25. By observing others, and extracting a physicalization in order to explore a different rhythm and tempo, the actors had the opportunity to not only practice transformation, to "try on" new emotional experiences, but by comparison, to find out more about their own rhythms and tempi. This led to Experience/Exercise 26 which consciously investigated each actor's own rhythm and tempo. They were practicing, adjusting, and transforming their energy centers to expand their own body language. These two exercises have prepared the actors to work on the technique of uncovering the basic psychological center of a character. However, this skill requires an awareness of the actor's own centers in order to adjust and transform their body language to serve the variety of roles they will play.

Discovering and exploiting one of the three psychological centers while working on a role is a complex process. Centers tend to interchange. Body language in life is frequently subtle and sometimes deceiving. Interpreting body language is a difficult phenomenon. It requires more intuition than logic.

We are at a point where the work can no longer be pinned down rationally and that is the point. In good dramatic literature, characters that change their psychological centers and behavior are exciting. An actor has a responsibility to make sure his/her technique is up to the task.

Preparation begins with discovering similarities and differences between the role and the actor's own instrument. Physical requirements may be similar to the actor's (as is well known by all working actors who have been "typed" in or out of an audition), but often the behavior and temperament are not. At the deepest level, understanding how the character responds to his/her psychological centers (although the character does not have a conscious knowledge of this as the actor does!) will help the actor to discover and uncover a new body language with rhythms different from his/her own.

The following considerations may be helpful in uncovering which psychological center to use and in what way.

1. What is the source of the deepest emotional conflict for the character in the play? Which psychological center does it stimulate—the head, the heart, or the sex?
2. What are the sensorial demands within the script? Which energy centers do they stimulate? During rehearsal, do these energy centers tend to activate one of the three psychological centers?
3. How are the three psychological centers in conflict with each other? In life, the conjunction of the head, the heart, and the sex can work together to bring us to our happiest moments. Drama, however, depends on conflict. How are the three psychological centers in conflict? Do they have opposite needs? Is the head overpowered by the sex? Does the intellect rule the heart?
4. What are the energy centers of this character? Are they primarily in one area? Does the character express him/herself primarily with the hands, voice, feet, etc.? What is the relationship between these energy centers and the ruling psychological center of the character?
5. While I have not tried to emphasize it, I find that the diaphragm or the gut and the back of the spine are the two areas that respond readily to each of the psychological centers. Consequently, they can become emotional thermometers for the character and are effective when used to stimulate body language. (The voice is related to the diaphragm. When speech is affected by a psychological center, it's frequently activated through a response from the gut.)
6. Invisible energy centers can change the rhythms of a character's body language. This in turn can lead to a transition in the character's basic psychological center.
7. The deeper the unexpected feeling in a character, the deeper its connection to a psychological center. This connection will influence the tempo of the character's rhythm.

SUMMARY

The actor has achieved a successful transformation from him/herself when a rhythm different from the actor's own has been discovered through the character's kinesthetic responses stimulated not only from the imaginary sensory conditions, but also in relation to one of the three basic psychological centers. Please note that a psychological center is not a manifestation in itself. It inspires a body language, a sensory life, a behavior that is unique to the character.

I would like to re-emphasize that although it is presented here as a seemingly logical set of tasks to undertake in order to produce a character, the work is much more intuitive than that. If an actor simply "produces" the effect of this material, the acting won't be believable. The body finds the answers to these questions more surely than the intellect. Discover the rhythms of a character through the sensory work prescribed in the script. Remember that words have sensory weight. Respond to your partner. Even if you don't agree with your partner's "interpretation" don't judge it, simply respond. You might discover something you didn't expect. This is especially true when allowing the sense of touch to arouse the psychological centers. Of course, the physical demands of the role, such as posture, weight, gestures, age, deformities, speech (including dialect), and costuming will all have their immediate effect on the interpretation of a role. Nothing is more effective in this last category than wearing the shoes of the character. Shoes will inform an actor about the rhythm of the character more than any other piece of costuming.

Uncovering rhythms of behavior, energy centers, and the psychological center of a role is not a simple task. It has no set method of being accomplished. But it offers the supreme challenge for an actor—to trust all that he/she has learned about how the senses inform the body—to allow the psyche to respond to what the body has learned in order to communicate a full, living, breathing human being on stage.

Chapter
9

The Sensory Life of Emotional Relationships

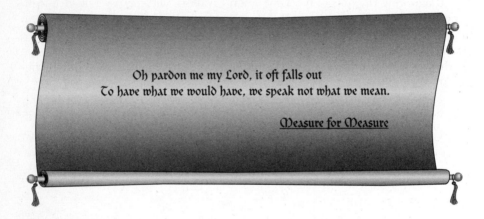

Oh pardon me my Lord, it oft falls out
To have what we would have, we speak not what we mean.

Measure for Measure

LECTURE: USING THE POWER OF SENSORY RESPONSES TO STIMULATE BEHAVIOR AND DEVELOP RELATIONSHIPS

Behavior is how we go about getting what we want. It is what we say and do. All behavior includes a psychology. This psychology expresses itself through our physical and verbal responses to life. A complete sensorial life is a psychologically rich life.

An integral part of any life includes the moment-to-moment awareness of and response to other people. The most powerful sensory responses we have are stimulated by our relationships with other human beings. It is through our desire to see, to hear, to touch, even to smell and to taste one another, or by the repulsion of these senses, that relationships develop.

A complete sensorial life is a language; in particular, a "body language" that receives and sends out these messages. Sometimes the language can be direct, through both the words and the actions. At other times, it is inferred in a "subtext." All too often, the subtext of "No!" is "Yes!" and when someone says "I hate you!" they really want to say "I love you."

The process of exploring sensory responses naturally begins to reveal personal vulnerabilities. In other words, advanced sensory work can be scary because it will begin to touch on private issues. However, developing vulnerability is a necessary part of developing sensory skills and of becoming an actor. It is important to honor your vulnerability, as well as to respect it in others.

In scene work, intuitive vulnerability leads to an open, exciting *exchange* of creative impulses. The work has an "edge" to it. There is a sense of the unknown. What will happen next? Part of this quality comes from being on the "edge" of your vulnerability. Even though the scene has been rehearsed many times, good actors risk anticipating their *unknown* response, instead of a rehearsed response. In order to do this, they continually remain aware of and respond to their scene partners. Two phrases I frequently use in class and rehearsal are: "Sense each other," and "Take your impulses off each other."

In order for actors to become more physically aware of their responses in relationships, that is to "take their impulses off each other," I suggest working with an unspoken need or intention in an improvisation. A need that is kept secret becomes a *subtext* in the scene. In the following experience/exercise, each actor keeps his/her subtext a secret, not telling it to his/her partner. They remain aware of how the verbal and physical messages are stimulated by their subtext. Subtext (or keeping a secret) is the springboard of this improvisation; therefore, as little dialogue as possible is encouraged.

EXPERIENCE/EXERCISE 27: USING SUBTEXT TO SENSORIALLY STIMULATE EMOTIONAL RELATIONSHIPS

Objective   To stimulate and be stimulated in-the-moment by the behavior of another person. In this case, behavior includes silence, physical action, and nonverbal sounds such as laughing, sighs, gasps, crying, etc.

Format   Improvisation with subtext.

Setting   Any public place.

SECTION A: PREPARATION

1. Working in pairs, the actors decide on a relationship.
   a. The relationship may be long term and intimate or the actors may begin the improvisation as total strangers.
   b. Actors establish both personal and mutual histories. I encourage the actors to write out their histories as a monologue in the first person.

2. Actors mutually decide on an event.
   a. The actors agree on the where, the location of the scene.
3. The Floater
   a. If desired, or if there are an odd number of people in the class, the Floater is the third party to enter the improvisation. In setting up a personal history and intention, the floater listens to all of the decisions discussed by the two actors in establishing their relationship and in deciding on the location of the improvisation. The Floater then operates as an independent agent, entering the scene at his/her own discretion.
4. Each actor (including the Floater) decides on his/her secret subtext.
   a. Some suggested subtextual phrases:
      • I have a secret (each actor creates his/her own).
      • I don't trust you.
      • I love you.
      • I'm scared of you.
      • You betrayed me.
      • I want to renew our relationship/get back together.
      • I want to kiss you.
      • I am jealous of your relationship with _____.
      • I can't stand you.
   b. Each actor submits a written secret as their subtext for the scene.

SECTION B: THE IMPROVISATION

The development of the plot of the improvisation (that is the development of the relationship) is determined by the subtext, that is, by how each actor observes and responds to the physical life of his/her partner. However, the subtext should not be revealed or spoken during the improvisation.
Some questions for discussion:

1. What was your need/challenge in the given circumstances of the scene?
2. When you began the improvisation, where was your energy centered?
3. How well did you meet the challenge of the scene?
4. How well did you pursue your need?
5. During the improvisation, which of the three psychological centers (the head, the heart, or the sex) became most activated by your partner?
6. How did this psychological/sensorial response intensify the relationship?

The actors submit their personal histories and secret subtexts, followed by a discussion of the questions posed above after the presentation of their improvisation.

Martha/Eric

I. Their *mutually* decided history, relationship, and event:

MARTHA: I am a professional stage manager. Today finished the last of three days of grueling auditions for Sam Shepard's *True West*. The director and I are good friends. We have worked together often. She trusts and depends on me. Often confiding in me, she knows I will keep all information about casting and other production matters, as well as personal issues, private.

In order to relax, to relieve the tension of the last three days of work, I am going for a walk in the park. It is around sunset, 7 or 8 o'clock on a nice spring evening.

ERIC: I am an actor. For the last three days I have read and re-read for the role of Lee in *True West*. I know I am physically and psychologically right for the role, but because I was read so many times, I'm worried that the director won't cast me. I know that Martha was in on the casting decisions. I am very anxious and angry about the whole process. I decide to take a walk in the park.

II. Martha and Eric submit their *secretly* and independently decided subtexts:

MARTHA: I am in love with Eric. Not only is he talented, I am very attracted to him sexually as well. I cover up my vulnerable feelings for him by maintaining my professional role as stage manager. I also know he has been cast as Lee.

ERIC: I am infatuated with the director and I would really like having more than a professional relationship with her. I know Martha and she are close and that Martha would know whether or not the director likes me. I must charm Martha into revealing what the director really thinks about me.

III. Discussion following the scene of their responses during the improvisation:

ERIC: When I started the improvisation, I was certain I had not been cast. I was tired and miserable. I began with pacing and then I slumped onto the park bench. My psychological center was in my heart. I was depressed. But I was also anxious. I could feel this ache in my gut.

MARTHA: As I was walking, I felt very exhausted. My inner eye images were of the audition process. My back was in pain. That was my energy center to start, in my spine. When I saw Eric sitting there looking like he was going to cry, I thought, "What am I going to do?" I wanted to put my arms around him, but knew I must behave professionally. I felt myself straighten up a bit.

ERIC: When she adjusted like that, I thought "Oh, I didn't get the part, she's uncomfortable to have discovered me here." But that's when she told me what a good audition I had given. I got very confused. So I decided to charm her a bit to see if she would reveal anything to me.

MARTHA: When Eric smiled with that evil little grin he has, I immediately felt myself respond sexually and wanted him to touch me.

ERIC: I saw her smile for just a minute, and sensed something open about her. I asked, "You really thought so, huh?"

MARTHA: This became difficult for me. I wanted to let Eric know that I liked his work, but I didn't want to drop my professional guard.

ERIC: I knew she was being sincere. We had that long pause.

MARTHA: I was so embarrassed. I thought I was sending out the silent message "I love you. I want to touch you."

ERIC: I put my arm around her and said, "Let's go have coffee and talk." I felt a little sleezy. I was doing it because I knew I could take advantage of the fact that she seemed attracted to me.

MARTHA: His touch was electric. I looked into his eyes and didn't trust him. I felt hurt. I knew he was using me.

ERIC: When Martha pushed me away, my face got hot. I suddenly clenched my fists and without realizing it said, "Go to hell! You think you're so important." That frightened me. I had so much rage, I thought I was going to lose control. I didn't know where it came from. That's why I stopped the improvisation.

DR. BELLA: When that happened, Eric, where was your energy centered?

ERIC: In my groin. I was ready for a fight.

DR. BELLA: You discovered a powerful emotion. Your stance also became more masculine, not shy. You had real sexual energy. Eric, you must learn to use that in your acting.

John/Dodi

I. Their *mutually* decided history, relationship, and event:

DODI: We have been married for three years. The first year of our marriage was a honeymoon. Then John started drinking. He lost his job and continued drinking. We love each other, but keep hurting each other. John's drinking is out of control. We are fighting too much and I am getting scared of his violence. After our last fight, I told him I was leaving and went home to see my parents.

JOHN: Last night, Dodi called to say she wanted to meet me and talk. We are meeting at the train station. It is 6:00 P.M.

II. Dodi and John submit their *secretly* and independently decided subtexts:

JOHN: For several days after Dodi left, I kept drinking, heavily, and feeling sorry for myself. I missed her and wanted her back. I wanted her to love me again and to be proud of me. I decided I had to do something. But I got scared and really drunk. Then I called Alcoholics Anonymous and someone came over to help me dry out. Last night, when Dodi called, I had just returned from my first meeting at A.A. All night, I couldn't sleep. I was afraid to see her again. My secret is that I have joined A.A., but I'm not ready to tell her I'm an alcoholic. I need to make her believe everything is under control and that I did it all myself.

DODI: While I was at home, I found out I was pregnant. I called John to tell him we have to talk and that I am coming back. I have decided not to tell him I am pregnant until he promises to stop drinking. If he stops and joins A.A., I will have the baby, if not, I will have an abortion.

III. Discussion following the scene of their responses during the improvisation.

> **DODI:** When I first saw John, he looked awful.
> **JOHN:** I was shaky and weak from not having slept. I'd been drinking a lot of coffee, which gave me a nervous energy. My center was in my stomach, which felt a little queazy.
> **DODI:** I sensed his condition was not from being drunk and I was so happy. He had missed me. We hugged each other, but then I smelled the mint on his breath. That was a dead giveaway he had been drinking. I started crying.
> **JOHN:** I was embarrassed by her crying. I believed we were in a train station and people were watching. I didn't know what to do or say. I thought, "She still believes I'm drinking." I wanted to tell her, but I could not bring myself to say I had joined A.A. I felt like a failure.
> **DODI:** I felt betrayed. John didn't say anything. He kept looking away guilty. I was terrified and kept thinking "This means I have to get rid of our baby."
> **DR. BELLA:** The silence at the end was wonderful. Your bodies were full of energy and different conflicting feelings. Your obstacles energized you both totally. The subtextual secret was a powerful tool. It kept the tension and suspense going. Each moment was unexpected and so we had no idea what was going to happen next.

Larry/June and Liz (the Floater)

I. Larry and June's *mutually* decided history, relationship, and event:

> **JUNE:** Larry and I have been engaged to be married for two years. He is a musician and has been gone on tour for six months.
> **LARRY:** I have been composing and playing in a band. I have had a difficult time making a commitment to get married.
> **JUNE:** Larry called me and said he was going to be home in several days and was very anxious to see me. I thought "Good, we are going to get married." We arranged to meet at our favorite outdoor cafe. I am very anxious and happy to see him. I missed him a lot. It is 8:00 p.m., on a pleasant fall evening.

II. Larry, June, and Liz submit their *secretly* and independently decided subtexts:

> **LARRY:** I lied to June. I was kicked out of the band. For the last six months, I have been in a drug rehabilitation program. While there, I tested HIV positive. June is not only ignorant of my drug problem, she doesn't know anything about the disease either. I have been home for several days, trying to decide how to break our engagement. I don't want her to know the real rea-

son. My intention is to break the engagement. My secret is that I have AIDS.
JUNE: My intention is to persuade/force Larry to set a wedding date. My secret is that I have already picked one for the end of next month and made arrangements with the church and for the reception. I also have travel brochures and have purchased air tickets for our honeymoon to Hawaii.
LIZ: Larry and I met secretly and decided that I was from his past. He told me about his drug problem and about having AIDS. I decided we had shared needles and I am sure he is responsible for infecting me. I have not seen Larry for a long time. I came to the cafe to turn a trick and get some money for more drugs. When I see Larry with June, I decide to blackmail him for the money.

III. Discussion following the scene of their responses during the improvisation:

JUNE: When I began the improvisation, my psychological center was in my heart. I was anxious, nervous to see him after such a long time away. I had ordered a glass of wine. Sipping it made me warm. As I looked over the brochures and plane tickets I had purchased, I had inner eye images of Larry, the wedding, and our honeymoon. My whole body felt energized in anticipation.
LARRY: I entered the cafe from behind June. First I just stood there looking at her. I had a buzzing sensation in my head and ears. My internal monologue was "How am I going to tell her?" Finally, I made the decision to go to the table and sit down. Her happy greeting hurt, especially when I avoided kissing her. I didn't want her to touch me, I felt dirty. My skin felt clammy. June's love and need for me really played against my intention. It made me feel even more guilty and dirty. My center was in my heart, but I kept having to keep my head straight. I wanted to say "I love you, but I had AIDS. Please, I don't want to hurt you."
JUNE: Larry's guilty actions hurt me. I didn't want to make myself any more vulnerable, so I tried to calmly put the Hawaii brochures and tickets back in my purse.
LARRY: Watching June try to maintain her composure, I knew I had to be honest with her, but then Liz entered the cafe. I recognized her right away.
LIZ: In the beginning of the improvisation, I was using a sensory condition of nausea, being sick and needing more drugs. My energy centers were my stomach and my sinuses.
JUNE: I saw Larry recognize someone and thought "It's another woman and she's come in here!" But when I turned around, Liz looked so sick and disgusting, I couldn't imagine what was going on. That's when I said to Larry "You're not being honest with me." I felt myself get tight in my lower region and in my legs and feet.
LARRY: Liz came over to the table. I felt my body wanting to shake, I was so frightened of what might happen. I couldn't say anything. Then she put her hand on my shoulder. I was disgusted. Then June started to cry. I wanted to run out of the room as fast as I could.

LIZ: When I said, "It's your fault. I need money and you have to give it to me," I thought June was going to hit me. I got ready to defend myself.
LARRY: That's when I finally did it. I stood up and said "I'm sick. I can't marry you. I have to leave."
JUNE: When Larry left, I stopped crying. I was totally numb. All I could do was sit and stare into space.
LIZ: I felt so awkward standing there. I hadn't gotten any money. June wasn't going to do anything. What was I going to do next?
DR. BELLA: A loaded event for all of you. Each of you was involved in the suspense of what would happen next which kept us involved in the suspense of what would happen next.

LECTURE: USING SENSORY CONDITIONS TO STIMULATE BEHAVIOR AND RELATIONSHIPS

In Experience/Exercise 27, the actors discovered that choosing a secret subtext added an element of the unexpected to a scene, keeping their acting fresh and in-the-moment. Concentration was on observing partners in order to develop the relationship and tell the story of the improvisation. Often, the subtext initiated a sensory condition within the context of the scene - Martha felt fatigue; Dodi worked with being pregnant; John had alcoholic withdrawal, etc. Consequently, each actor was filled with a total sensory life, so that their energy was simultaneously physical and psychological.

In Experience/Exercise 28, this same ability for spontaneous behavior and relationship can be achieved by choosing a sensory condition (in place of a subtext) and allowing that condition to stimulate a psychology. In addition, the exercise adds the challenge of scripted material. This moves us one step closer to scene work and in fact, the exercise can be altered if desired by using a single beat from a scene the actors might be working on (a cutting from the scene of approximately ten to fifteen lines).

EXPERIENCE/EXERCISE 28: OPEN-ENDED SCENES

Objective Choosing a sensory condition that will organically stimulate the actor's throughline of physical/verbal action in order to intensify the need in an emotional relationship.

Format The actors work with one of three "open-ended" scenes, provided below.

Setting Any public place.

SECTION A: PREPARATION

1. Working in pairs, the actors decide on a relationship.
   a. The relationship may be long term and intimate or the actors may begin the scene as total strangers.
   b. Actors establish both personal and mutual histories.
2. Actors mutually decide on an event.
   a. The actors agree on the where, the location of the scene.
3. Three-character scene.
   a. See Open-Ended Scene III (page 119).
4. Each actor decides secretly on his/her sensory condition.
   a. Some suggested sensory conditions:
      - an itch
      - hives
      - sunburn
      - temperature: fever; chills
      - foul body odor (of scene partner)
      - nausea
      - stomachache
      - extreme hunger
      - toothache
      - cramps
      - walking barefoot on blistering hot sand
5. Suggestions for using a sensory condition to develop behavior and relationship:
   a. Sense the condition. Feel it, but don't show it. Don't make the scene about the sensory condition. In fact, the condition should remain unknown to your scene partner.
   b. Integrate the essence of the sensory condition into your verbal action.
   c. Integrate the essence of the sensory condition into your need (or possibly allow it to act as a conflict).

OPEN-ENDED SCENE I

A: Oh.
B: Yes.
A: Please.
B: Why are you doing this to me?
A: It's the best thing.
B: You can't mean it.
A: No, I'm serious.
B: Please.
A: What?
B: Listen.
A: No.
B: So different.

A: Not really.
B: Oh?
A: You're good.
B: What?
A: Forget it.
B: [???]
A: Go on! Go!
B: I will.

OPEN-ENDED SCENE II

A: Is it time?
B: Yes.
A: Shouldn't we. . . . Could we try later?
B: How?
A: [!!!]
B: Why?
A: I'm unhappy.
B: God.
A: All right.
B: How?
A: You can't mean it.
B: No, I'm serious.
A: Please.
B: What?
A: Listen.
B: No.
A: Oh?
B: Look. You're good.
A: You must help.
B: I know.
A: It's awful.
B: What.
A: I can't stay.
B: God.
A: Goodbye.
B: Wait.

OPEN-ENDED SCENE III

A: Hi.
B: Oh?
A: Oh, . . . yes.
B: Go away.
A: Come on.
B: I must?

A: What?

B: Forget it.

"C" enters.

A: Imagine that.

B: I know.

A: Go on.

C: Leave it alone.

A: Maybe.

B: O.K.

C: Listen.

A: Oh?

B: I will.

A: Oh, no.

B: Great.

C: Why?

A: Please, don't.

C: You don't mean that.

A: I can't help that.

C: Help me?

B: No.

A: Goodbye.

C: Wait.

B: It's over.

A: We could try.

B: No.

A: Goodbye.

C: Wait.

SECTION B: QUESTIONS FOR DISCUSSION FOLLOWING THE SCENE PRESENTATIONS

1. Did the sensory condition strengthen your intention or need?
   a. Did the sensory condition create an obstacle in achieving your need?
2. How did your sensory condition and its effect on the verbal action or "story" of the scene stimulate your psychological centers?
   a. Which center was the most active?
3. Was the behavior both verbally and physically spontaneous?
   a. Did the sensory condition strengthen your ability to respond unexpectedly to your partner's verbal and physical action?
   b. Did the sensory condition yield any surprises in your verbal action, . . . meanings that were unexpected?
   c. How did the sensory condition stimulate the development of the relationship physically?
4. Did your sensory condition remain a secret and not become obvious?

SUMMARY

The two experience/exercises in this chapter begin to explore how to do more than merely play an intention or a beat. By using a secret subtext or a sensory condition, the actors are developing their technique for expressing a *complete* sensory life on stage.

The technique for expressing a complete sensory life has been the object of the text thus far. With each chapter, the actors have developed and acquired the skills to trust their imagination; to be possessed by visual images, to communicate those images both verbally and through a life filled with physical sensation; to be stimulated by sound, the spoken word, as well as the echo of silence which is derived from sustaining the sensation of sound (as well as the residue of other sensory responses) in the body; and to be stimulated by smell and taste, realizing that taste is an integral part of smell. The actors have recognized intellectual, emotional, physical, and sexual hunger. The actors have learned to allow their senses to kinesthetically activate physical/sensorial pain and pleasure, uneasiness and comfort. Finally, a physical life communicates a set of needs or intentions and these needs are directly connected to a psychological life.

The ability to sustain and connect all the various sensorial demands in a role creates a *Kinesthetic Sensorial Throughline* for the actor. This technique provides the actor with moment-to-moment, unexpected giving and taking. It merges the sensorial, emotional, verbal, and nonverbal (body language) responses into one organic, that is believable, behavior. A Kinesthetic Sensorial Throughline gives substance to an actor's beat/intention throughline, making it more potent.

In the final analysis, actors in performance have time only for a kinesthetic sensorial response. They must always stay in the moment. As a kinesthetic sensorial throughline is an involuntary phenomenon, the rehearsal process must include a means for the actor to explore the character's journey from the beginning of his/her first scene to the end of the play.

PART
Two

PREPARING A ROLE AND REHEARSING A SCENE USING SENSORY TECHNIQUE

Chapter
10

Working on a Role

Preparation

In working on the experience/exercises in the first section of this book, the actors have been building a psychological foundation for their physical technique. They have been developing an ability for kinesthetic responses. From their other fundamental acting classes, I hope they have learned how to do their basic script work, to break down beats, find appropriate motivations, and think about appearance and posture. I recommend Charles McGaw's *Acting Is Believing*, the Third Edition as an excellent text for any student who has not been introduced to this process.

In addition to their physical/sensorial training, the actors' vocal instruction should have also provided a technique for their speech work, so that it has become natural and does not appear conscious or intrusive. This means that the actors have discovered that language too can be experienced viscerally, that is, sensorially and spontaneously. Sensory work combines a physical life with a vocal life.

Good vocal work is sensorial! Actors *taste* their words and their words stimulate the body. They *experience* words. Again, it is sometimes hard to say which comes first, the physical or the vocal expression. Certainly, a good actor doesn't rush the impulse to speak, but he doesn't waste a lifetime waiting for the motivation either. In the best acting, the physical life and the vocal life merge into a complete sensory life and speaking is as much a part of the experience as breathing.

There are traditional ways by which actors prepare a role. I suppose I am a traditionalist. I strongly believe that actors must know the play. They must read and re-read the entire play. During their readings, actors must continually ask questions. These questions often demand research into the playwright's other works, as well as an investigation of the playwright's life. In a professional undertaking, a thorough actor will ask many questions about the author's sociology, psychology, and philosophy. Additionally, these same questions will be put to the world of the play, especially if it represents a period foreign to our own.

After the basic readings and research, many actors believe they are ready to begin the rehearsal process. Perhaps these actors have worked primarily with directors/teachers who give blocking, stage business, or line readings early in the rehearsal process. However, that kind of approach (especially for the young actor) is destructive. It restricts actors to lifeless, cardboard characterizations, lacking any human depth. The inexperienced actor turns in "results" and not moments of discovery.

The best rehearsal process encourages the discovery of as many spontaneous moments in the play as possibile. This process must be respected by the director and claimed by the actor. The following outline of activities and questions can be used by both actors and directors, although their methods for arriving at some of the answers will, of course, be different.

HOMEWORK: A WORKING OUTLINE

Questions for *before, during,* and *after* the rehearsal process.

BASIC READING REQUIREMENTS

Section A: Reading the Play

1. Read the entire play in one sitting.
   a. Make notes about your first responses:
   - What stimulated you the most?
   - What disturbed you the most? Why?
   - What pleased you the most?
   - Where was the play the most intriguing?
   - Where were you confused?
2. Re-read the play often.
3. Read and re-read the scene to be rehearsed several times.
   a. Find opportunities to read the scene with your partner.
   b. Give each scene a title.
   - Discovering the title through the action of the scene
   - Discovering the title through emotional relationships
   - Discovering the title as part of the rehearsal process

Section B: Research

1. Read the playwright's other works.
   a. What themes recur in his/her work? Does he/she have a primary concern?

2. Investigate the history of the period:
   a. morals of the period
   b. behavior of the period
   c. architecture of the period
   d. music of the period
   e. art of the period
   f. any primary resource material from the period
   g. costuming of the period
   h. historical research on the period
3. Compare the play's world with today's.
   a. In what ways was society significantly different from today?
      • What were the social customs in the relationships between men and women?
      • What was the social structure like?
      • Who ruled and how?

WHO AM I IN THIS ROLE?

Section A: What's Before?

1. Speaking or writing in the first person, give a descriptive analysis of your character.
   a. Refer to Egri's "Tri-Dimensional Chart" [see page 130].
   b. What is my relationship to each of the other characters at the beginning of the play? What is our prior history together?
2. What has happened to me before the play starts?
   a. Draft a time-line of events in the character's life.

Section B: For Each Scene, Ask the Following Questions:

1. Where am I?
2. What do I want?
3. Why do I want it?
4. Who do I want it from?
   a. a blood relationship?
   b. an emotional relationship?
   c. an enemy?
   d. a friend?
5. What action do I take to get what I want? [What is my behavior?]
   a. actions = beat intentions
   b. the doing of each action = my "tactic"
      • Each change in a tactic represents a new mini-beat.
6. What is in my way?
   a. obstacles/conflicts
      • with whom?
      • with what?
7. What actions [including verbal arguments] do I take to overcome my obstacles/conflicts?
   a. actions = beat intentions

b. the doing of each action = my tactic

c. how is each action influenced by my sensorial life?

Section C: What Is My Journey?

1. Where do I start physically/emotionally? With what relationships?
2. Refer back to Section A, questions 1 and 2, and your work on the Egri chart.
3. How do I change during the course of the play?
   a. Where are the major turning points in the script?
   b. How does each change alter my behavior?
      * physically
        age
        health
        energy = changes of tempo in my physical rhythms
      * psychologically
        emotional/physical relationships
        needs, behavior, actions
        modulations in psychological centers
4. What is my central conflict in this play?
   a. Where does my conflict begin?
   b. How is my conflict resolved?
   c. How do I personally [as an actor/artist] relate to this conflict?
      * Does it have any relationship to my real life?
      * What was my gut response to this conflict when I first read the script?

Section D: What Are the Physical/Sensorial Requirements of Each Scene?

1. The voice and the text.
   a. Paraphrase the text to understand the *exact* meaning of the words.
   b. Learn the lines in relationship to the needs/actions of the scenes *while in rehearsal.*
      * Early memorization sometimes limits the possibilities for spontaneous discovery in a scene.
2. Specific vocal demands—how do they influence my sensory life?
   a. foreign languages, accents, dialects
      * Am I a stranger in a strange land?
   b. speech impediments
      * Am I an outsider?
   c. the effect of speaking verse and/or prose
      * Do I love language?
3. Investigating the relationship between the text and the subtext
   a. There is no text without subtext.
      * What do I really want, but cannot say?
      * How will the subtext be inferred by my behavior? For the actor, this is discovered in rehearsal.

4. Sensory tasks stated in the script
   a. climate/weather
   b. season
   c. time of day/night
   d. geography: outdoor terrain or interior?
   e. costuming
   f. physical impairments—alcohol; health/physical deformities
5. Sensory tasks discovered through relationships
   a. uncovered in the rehearsal process
6. Relationship between the sensory life and the psychological life of the character
   a. discovering active energy centers in rehearsal
   b. discovering physical/psychological centers in rehearsal
7. Marking the transitions or beats
   a. Are my beat changes realized by shifts in my energy centers?
      • How is the transition marked by a change in my sensory life?
      • Are there shifts in psychological centers?
      • Do these affect the rhythms of my character?
      • Do these affect the tempo of my character?

Section E: Personalizing the Role

1. What are the physical and emotional similiarities between the role and myself?
2. What are the physical and emotional differences between the role and myself?
3. What are the weaknesses of the role vs. myself?
4. What are the strengths of the role vs. myself?
5. What do I learn about myself:
   a. in how the conditions of the period of the play alter or restrict my behavior?
   b. in how I effectively use my imagination?
   c. in the similarities/differences between the role and myself?
   d. while rehearsing the role with other cast members?
   e. after the performances have finished?

Discovering My Kinesthetic Throughline

The kinesthetic throughline is the involuntary flow of behavior from moment to moment in the character's life. The actor is "in-the-moment," responding organically to all sensory elements, which in turn stimulates the shifts in his/her tactics. The kinesthetic throughline can be discovered only in rehearsal. It is not predetermined through analysis, but experienced and recognized as behavior. Uncovering the kinesthetic throughline begins with the discovery of one particular moment in the behavior and then strings that moment with other sensory responses found in rehearsal. Eventually, all the moments are connected into one continu-

A TRIDIMENSIONAL-CHARACTER BONE STRUCTURE

PHYSIOLOGY

1. *Sex*
2. *Age*
3. *Height and weight*
4. *Color of hair, eyes, skin*
5. *Posture*
6. *Appearance:* good-looking, over- or underweight, clean, neat, pleasant, untidy; shape of head, face, limbs
7. *Defects:* deformities, abnormalities, birthmarks; diseases
8. *Heredity*

SOCIOLOGY

1. *Class:* lower, middle, upper
2. *Occupation:* type of work, hours of work, income, condition of work, union or non-union, attitude toward organization, suitability for work
3. *Education:* amount, kind of schools, marks, favorite subjects, poorest subjects, aptitudes
4. *Home life:* parents living, earning power, orphan, parents separated or divorced, parents' habits, parents' mental developments, parents' vices, neglect; character's marital status
5. *Religion*
6. *Race, nationality*
7. *Place in community:* leader among friends, clubs, sports
8. *Political affiliations*
9. *Amusements, hobbies:* books, newspapers, magazines read

PSYCHOLOGY

1. *Sex life, moral standards*
2. *Personal premise, ambition*
3. *Frustrations, chief disappointments*
4. *Temperament:* choleric, easygoing, pessimistic, optimistic
5. *Attitude toward life:* resigned, militant, defeatist
6. *Complexes:* obsessions, inhibitions, superstitions, phobias
7. *Extrovert, introvert, ambivert*
8. *Abilities:* languages, talents
9. *Qualities:* imagination, judgment, taste, poise
10. *I.Q.*

Source: From *The Art of Dramatic Writing* by Lajos Egri. Reprinted by permission.

ous flow of living/doing. The action never stops. The actor's attention is one hundred percent on the activity of his/her role. When scenes or even entire acts are rehearsed, I do not call them "run-throughs". Such a rehearsal needs to be thought of as an *"experience-through"*.

In order to uncover a kinesthetic throughline in rehearsal, the actor must make choices about the action or the beat intentions and his/her tactics for carrying out those intentions. However, how a character carries out his/her intentions is also influenced by the given sensory conditions in the script, as well as by the sensory tasks the actor discovers while in rehearsal.

A *given sensory life* is one stipulated by the text. Eating, drinking, the weather, taking a shower, all these are examples of sensory requirements which might be given in the text. They involve seeing, hearing, touching, smelling, and tasting. A *sensory task* is personal, inferred by the behavior discovered in rehearsal through the character's relationships with others. It involves subtext. It is imaginatively invented by the actor. While given sensory conditions are important in discovering the kinesthetic throughline, ultimately, relationships with other human beings predominately determine the course of the throughline.

Getting to Know Your Acting Partner

I have watched many marvelous actors in the midst of large casts giving great solo performances, but they have been just that, *solo* performances. These actors have considered all the necessary questions of the play. They have created a full and interesting physical life for themselves. But they have left out, from the very beginning of the rehearsal process, the most important element—their partner.

The following improvisation is one way for the actors to begin exploring the sensory demands of the role, while also working to establish a relationship with their fellow actors. Its purpose is to help the actors know each other, to trust each other, as well as to provide the initial step in personalizing the role through rehearsal.

SECTION A: PREREQUISITES

1. The actors have read the play.
2. The actors have researched their roles.
   a. They are aware to some extent of the character's action, needs, motivations, and throughline.
   b. They are aware of the sensory conditions in each scene.
   c. They are aware, to some extent of possible costuming considerations or other physical requirements of the role.
3. The actors have read the scene to be rehearsed.
   a. They've gone over it separately in preparation for rehearsal.
   b. They have read the scene together.

SECTION B: SETTING UP THE IMPROVISATION

1. The actors are dressed in leotards, tights, bare feet, neutral clothing.
2. The actors select a few pieces of appropriate clothing for the character (most especially, this might include the type of shoes the character will wear).
3. One prop or personal object may be used if needed.
4. Two chairs are placed at the periphery of the acting area facing each other:
    a. for the actors to begin with by facing each other.
    b. to house the clothing and personal objects.

SECTION C: BEGINNING THE IMPROVISATION

Objective   To discover each other.

1. See your partner in the neutral, open space.
    a. The actors begin simply with each other.
2. Listen to your partner.
    a. Hear your partner's breathing.
    b. Hear any noise created by your partner's movement.
3. Approach each other simply.
    a. Be aware of the natural physical energies between you.
    b. Explore intuitively your tactile sensations.
        • Are there positive feelings, negative feelings, ambivalent feelings?

SECTION D: TRANSFORMATION (PHYSICAL/PSYCHOLOGICAL)

1. Segue into one aspect of the body language of the role.
    a. The actors put on a few pieces of costume and/or footwear.
    b. Pick up and handle your personal object.
2. Through movement, explore your new relationship to your acting partner.
    a. How is it influenced by the change in costuming?
3. Through movement, explore one of the sensory conditions of the scene.
4. Begin to improvise some dialogue.
    a. Base the conversation on the relationship and desires of the scene.
    b. Attempt to use your own words and not the playwright's.
    c. Use character names.

SECTION E: SOME QUESTIONS FOR THE ACTORS TO ASK THEMSELVES *PRIVATELY,* FOLLOWING THE IMPROVISATION

1. What is this emotional relationship?
    a. Where did it establish itself in the improvisation?
2. How well did my sensory condition communicate my need or relationship to my partner?

SUMMARY

This text is devoted to stimulating the actor's sensory skills and finding a practical application for that technique in discovering a kinesthetic throughline for any character. The following chapters provide examples of the procedures outlined in this chapter as applied to the works of David Feldshuh, Tennessee Williams, Bernard Pomerance, Anton Chekhov, and William Shakespeare. For instance, beginning with John Merrick in *The Elephant Man,* and with every character thereafter, a biography is presented in the first person, as it might be spoken by an actor playing the role (Section II, "Who Am I in This Role?" page 127). In Chapters 12 and 14, I suggest an improvisation similar to the one outlined in "Getting to Know Your Acting Partner" from above; followed by a physical score of how that improvisation might actually occur between the two actors playing the roles. Chapters 12 and 14 also include historical background and suggested readings for the study of Chekhov and Williams, as asked for in Section I, "Basic Reading Requirements".

In order to suggest how an actor might arrive at a "Kinesthetic Throughline", the last three chapters end with a breakdown of the scene into "action/subtext/intention", and "sensory tasks". The process whereby an actor or a director might themselves arrive at a breakdown such as this is no simple, logical homework assignment. Especially for the actor, the discoveries noted in the breakdown would be made mostly in rehearsal (and of course, could very well be different from the discoveries I have made). A good director needs to be ahead of this process in order to provide a creative environment that will subtly "direct" the actors into thinking they are making these discoveries on their own.

The outlines presented in this chapter contain sections which might not be significant to every character or play. Therefore, the starting point with each role will probably be different. As such, I have focused each of the following chapters on one aspect of sensory work and how the actor might realize its importance and application to developing a fully believable human being on stage, or that is, a character who does not o'erstep "the modesty of nature. "

Chapter
11

Physical and Emotional Pain

Physical pain is something each of us has endured to some extent or other. Sometimes our pain is met with compassion, sometimes with indifference. How an individual afflicted with physical problems struggles and copes for survival often makes interesting drama. In comedy, there is almost always some kind of emotional pain hidden under the surface of the motives for a character's actions. The physical challenge of presenting pain on stage can range from pratfalls to unbearable torture. While the playwright may have many motives for including pain in a drama, plays are not about disease, physical impairment, or pain. Relationships are always the primary focus of any good dramatic writing. How we respond to pain can often depend on who is near us at the time.

An actor facing the challenge of a role that includes physical disability, abuse, or pain must be sensitive to the world that confronts his/her character. All of the research suggested in Chapter 10 remains important. In addition, after reviewing Experience/Exercises 15 and 16 in Chapter 5, there are a few extra questions the actor might want to consider.

1. How was the pain created?
   a. disease/illness
   b. physical impairment
   c. inflicted by others
   d. inflicted by emotional disorder

2. Where is the pain specifically located?
   a. How does it stimulate responses in other parts of the body?
   b. How does it affect the other senses' abilities to respond?
3. What is the nature of the discomfort?
   a. dull
   b. itching
   c. aching
   d. throbbing
   e. hot
   f. sharp prick
   g. unbearable
   h. fatal
4. If the pain is anticipated, what action does the character take to prepare him/herself for the impending abuse?
   a. What is the physical response when the pain is a surprise?
5. How does the character deal with the moment of most severe pain? Does he or she have a desire to behave in a certain manner?
   a. Are there character relationships to consider, motivations which might alter a response?
6. What action does the character take to relieve the pain?
7. What are the playwright's suggestions in communicating the pain?
   a. How does the playwright make the pain more specific through stage directions or by dialogue, either what your character has to say, or what others say about the pain?
8. If necessary, contact a doctor, nurse, or patient afflicted with a similar condition to research the specifics of your character's adversity.

SECTION I: PHYSICAL PAIN

I recently saw an excellent production of David Feldshuh's *Miss Evers' Boys*. In Act I, scene v, the character of Caleb Humphries receives a spinal tap to determine the extent of his syphilitic infection. Caleb is one of four characters who represent well over 400 black men used during the thirties and forties in a government study of the effects of syphilis in the black male.

In those days, spinal taps were performed without any anesthetic and they were very painful. In order to soften the idea of the impending pain, the doctors in this study decided to call these spinal taps "back shots."

As Nurse Evers readies Caleb for his first "back shot" by having him dress in a hospital gown and then by applying antiseptic to his lower back, Caleb begins to emotionally prepare himself for the impending pain. He tells a story about his youth wherein he recalls a lashing and says "This back shot can't hurt worse than that day." He is afraid of the pain and tries to reassure himself.

The actor playing Caleb finds the script filled with physical and sensorial suggestions:

MISS EVERS' BOYS BY DAVID FELDSHUH

Douglas enters rapidly, wearing a gown, mask and gloves.

DOUGLAS: Sorry to keep you waiting, Nurse Evers. Good morning,
CALEB: Nice to see you.

Caleb starts to stand. Evers helps Douglas adjust his mask.

DOUGLAS: Now just keep sitting the way you are. I'm going to locate that spot between the vertebrae in your lower back and make a small needle puncture. Not much to it really.
CALEB: Good.
DOUGLAS: Bend your head over. Further. Further, I said. But you're going to have to sit very still. Nurse Evers will help you. Especially once that needle is inside your spinal canal; don't move then or that needle might injure the nerves to your legs.
CALEB: To my legs?
DOUGLAS: That's right. That's why we don't want you to move.
CALEB: Don't worry, I'm not movin'.
DOUGLAS: All right; here we go. I'll just take that needle, Nurse Evers.
CALEB: Let me see it.—It's big. . . .
DOUGLAS: Only a little part will go in.
CALEB: What's it made out of?
DOUGLAS: Gold.
CALEB: Well, that's good.
DOUGLAS: Here we go.

Douglas is sitting or standing behind the table focused on Caleb's lower back; each time the needle goes in or comes out, it is searingly painful.

CALEB: [*Controlling the pain*]: Aah. You goin' too far.
DOUGLAS: I have to try to find the spinal canal. [*Calmly repositioning the needle*] All right, here we go now. [*He focuses intently; he doesn't want to miss again.*]
CALEB: [*He resists moving and, trying to ignore the intermittent bursts of pain, automatically falls into the preaching voice*]: That needle is the work of the devil . . . ahhhhhh . . . it's sharp and burning and greedy gold in color . . . ahhh . . . [*A catechism*] What color was Job? Black. What color was Jeremiah? Black. Who was Moses' wife? An Ethiopian. David said he became like a bottle in the smoke. What's natural? It's as natural to be black as the leopard to be spotted . . . Ahhhh . . .
DOUGLAS: [*Stopped for a moment*]: What in the world are you saying, Caleb?
CALEB: [*In pain*]: Catechism of the Church of the Living God founded by William Christian in Wrightsville, Arkansas, in 1889.
DOUGLAS: Does it help?
CALEB: It keeps my mind from violence, Dr. Douglas.

DOUGLAS: Then just keep saying it . . . One more time now. Hold it. [*Needle in suddenly*]

EVERS: Dr. Douglas—

DOUGLAS: Be quiet, Nurse Evers.

CALEB: Ahh, no more, I'm getting off this here table now.

DOUGLAS: [*Alarmed*]: No.

EVERS:[*Taking charge*]: Caleb Humphries don't you move, you hear me; you sit there and don't move; you gotta be a walkin' man, not a cripple man; now you sit there and don't move. Stop moving.

CALEB: Ahhhh.

EVERS: Dr. Douglas—

DOUGLAS: [*Over her, triumphant*]: Got it. There we go. We're all set. [*Carefully*] Now I'll just collect some fluid if you will be so kind as to give me the test tube, Nurse Evers.

EVERS: Don't move.

> *Douglas puts tube under the needle and collects a small amount of fluid.*

DOUGLAS: There we are.

> *He pulls out the needle. The removal of the needle stings.*

CALEB: What you doing?

DOUGLAS: Just removing the needle.

> *In slight discomfort, Caleb moves to get off the table.*

DOUGLAS: If you don't want a bad headache, Caleb, take my advice and sit there for a while.

CALEB: Why'd you do that to me?

DOUGLAS: I didn't do anything to you, Caleb. It's not uncommon that the exact entrance to the spinal canal can't be found the first time. Unfortunately, that can cause some pain. Let's get ready for the next patient, Nurse Evers.

CALEB: Dr. Douglas?

DOUGLAS: Yes, Caleb?

CALEB: Practice.

DOUGLAS: I beg your pardon.

CALEB: I said practice, sir, 'cause you're not gonna have a next patient if you go stickin' them the way you stickin' me. How many patients you think'll come here when they find out what you're doin' feels like getting a hot screwdriver twisted in your back.

Scene 5 from *Miss Evers' Boys* by David Feldshuh. Reprinted by permission.

Earlier in the scene, when Nurse Evers applies the antiseptic to Caleb's lower back, he responds with the exclamation "That's cold."

Caleb asks to see the needle for his "back shot" and comments "It's big. . . ." In those days, the needles were very large.

Dr. Douglas has difficulty finding the correct position for the spinal tap. Each
time the needle goes in or out "it is searingly painful" according to the
stage directions.

Each time the needle is injected or extracted, the script gives Caleb an
"Aaahhh" to attempt to control his pain.

To resist moving and "trying to ignore the intermittent bursts of pain," Caleb
"automatically falls into the preaching voice." When Dr. Douglas asks
Caleb if his spontaneous preaching helps him overcome the pain, he
replies: "It keeps my mind from violence, Dr. Douglas." The script sug-
gests therefore that Caleb uses images of his "catechism" to avoid the im-
ages of pain and the desire to commit violence.

Caleb decides to end the pain by "getting off this here table now." He is com-
manded by Nurse Evers to sit still or risk the danger that he will not walk
again; given this motivation and perhaps since he has flirted with her ear-
lier in the scene, he remains on the table for the final successful probe of
the needle.

Mr. Feldshuh provides one final tactile image of the excruciating pain caused by
the injection of the needle. Caleb tells Dr. Douglas that he needs "prac-
tice", "cause you're not gonna have a next patient if you go stickin' them the
way you stickin' me." He then describes the pain saying, "How many
patients you think'll come here when they find out what you're doin' feels
like getting a hot screwdriver twisted in your back." This is a very vivid
image for the actor to work with.

The actor playing Caleb must be able to communicate the pain circumstances
in this play. He has several choices: (1) He can find a way to transform pain cir-
cumstances from his life to the imaginary reality of the play. In other words, he
must be familiar with physical pain. (2) He can use his imagination to stimulate
physical responses as called for in the script. (3) Finally, he can rely on Mr. Feld-
shuh's stage directions and the character's relationships to communicate motiva-
tions for believable behavior.

SECTION II: A PSYCHOSOMATIC CONDITION INFLICTING PHYSICAL DISORDER, PAIN, AND ILLNESS

Alma in Tennessee Williams' *Summer and Smoke:* A Brief Discussion of Her Rhythmic and Psychological Throughline

Who is Alma? Why is she susceptible to emotional disorder? Why does her emo-
tional disorder cause physical discomfort and illness?

Alma Winemiller was born in the small town of Glorious Hill, Mississippi
somewhere between 1891 and 1892. The residents of this community are narrow-
minded; it is an inert society. Her father is the Reverend Winemiller, the town's
minister. He maintains a strict moral ethic. Her child-like mother is mentally un-

stable, or at least she gives that impression to Alma. While still in high school, Alma had to assume her mother's responsibilities for taking care of the social and household duties, as well as managing the rectory.

Alma is a music teacher. She gives singing lessons and also sings at public functions. There is something poetic about her nature. She is a super-sensitive young lady in her mid-twenties.

From the time she was ten years old, she has been in love with her neighbor, now the young Dr. John Buchanan. He was the town's bad boy. When the play begins, Alma is desperately in love with John. Her journey through the play begins with a sexual need for John that is overpowering. However, Alma does not admit these sensations. Tennessee Williams is writing about Alma's struggle between Puritanism and sexual desire, about what a strict religious code of sexual behavior does to a young, attractive, sensuous, and talented woman. Alma has the power to love, but she must repress her desires and cannot admit her feelings.

Consequently, Alma's sexual repression manifests itself in a variety of physical/emotional disorders. She has convinced herself that she has a heart condition, as well as a past malaria illness which causes her occasional physical discomfort. When Alma sees John in Scene One of Part One of the play, the summer weather is extremely hot, but her hands and fingers are cold. They feel paralyzed. She is dizzy. The casual (but intentional) knee touch that John playfully inflicts on Alma sends cold shivers through her body. Her kinesthetic responses to these impulses are part of her physical rhythm.

Another example of Alma's physical rhythm is her habit of twisting her ring and hurting her finger when she is in a state of emotional stress.

The only relief Alma experiences is in taking sleeping pills. They act as a sedative, relaxing her for a time, but they do not make her sleep. However, by the end of the play, they have aided in relaxing her sexual fears.

There are two Almas, the proper social lady and the inner passionate, sexual woman. (Dr. John recognizes the sexual woman in Alma as her *"Doppelgänger."*) In the first part of the play, Alma represses her sexual desires. As those feelings come to the surface, she has a difficult time coping with them.

Part Two of the play takes place during the fall and winter. Alma has spent the hot summer in her room, only going out for walks in the early morning hours. She endures a long illness, but by Scene Eleven, although still weak, she is recovering and has arrived at a decision—she must tell John that she loves him and that she wants to have sexual intercourse with him. However, the reformed and now successful Dr. John is in love and engaged to be married to Nellie, Alma's former singing pupil. John must reject Alma's proposal. He explains that he could have never made love to her as he respects and admires her purity and beauty too much.

This heart-breaking rejection pushes Alma to the Stone Angel Fountain where she meets and picks up a young shoe salesman passing through town. Alma finally recognizes her sexual needs, but as Tennessee Williams suggests by the tragedy of her late recognition, perhaps in order to satisfy this hunger, she will become the town prostitute.

Process in Discovering Physical Pain/Discomfort Inflicted by an Emotional Disorder

1. Read and re-read the play.
2. Answer all questions outlined in Chapter 10.
3. Explore Experience/Exercises 15 and 16 from Chapter 5.
4. List all the physical actions and conditions Alma performs or experiences during the play.
   a. The actor wearing period clothes is bound by a corset.
      • This means that Alma must have good alignment.
      • Figuratively speaking, Alma is bound by an emotional girdle, but as a physical rehearsal technique, the actor will want to use a corset as early as possible. Initially, the corset will feel tight. When the actor is able to depend on her kinesthetic memory, it can be loosened.

[NOTE: Frankly, if I were acting Alma, I would want to depend on my kinesthetic memory of being bound and not have my body constricted. It's necessary to maintain the silhouette of the costume, but not good to impede the actor physically.]

   b. Alma has difficulty breathing.
      • She takes air in through her mouth. This causes her dizziness and in turn her chest pains.

[NOTE: It is important to remember to perform this activity kinesthetically. Actually overdoing this kind of breathing might cause the actor to hyperventilate.]

   c. Alma has convinced herself that she has a heart condition.
      • The activity of holding her breath and the involuntary taking in of air through her mouth increases the sensation of the heartbeat.
   d. The only thing that calms Alma are the taking of sleeping pills. They act as a mild sedative on her emotional constraints. Following this activity, the actor will discover relaxed moments in Alma's kinesthetic throughline.
   e. Alma is very sensitive to cold and heat.
      • Frequently, Alma's hands and fingers are freezing. They are so cold that they are stiff. She has difficulty unfolding and using them.
   f. When Alma is excited, she puts her energy into her hands and fingers in a "fluttering gesture."
   g. Williams' suggestions of turning her ring is a very important activity. Alma does so when she is:
      • frightened
      • frustrated
      • unhappy
      • humiliated
   h. The violent turning of the ring hurts her finger.
   i. Alma avoids close physical contact, especially with John. However, she has an intense desire to touch John.

- In Scene One, John's knee touches Alma's knee and she responds with a chill, a slight shake of her body. She tenses her spine, keeping her knees together, and her hands feel cold.

j. In Scene Nine, Alma gets dizzy when she sees the reformed Dr. John and almost loses her balance.

- A quick rise from a chair might create this sensation, or spinning in place. When playing the scene, the sensation is experienced kinesthetically. However, it is probably even more helpful to understand that Alma is having a private orgasm. She may not understand this, but the actor playing the role certainly can.

k. In Scene Eleven, Alma finally touches John's face. It is a pleasing tactile sensation.

l. In Scene Eleven, Alma's sense of smell is also acute. She smells the ether in Dr. John's office and it makes her dizzy.

m. In Scene Eleven, Tennessee Williams provides sensorial stimuli in light, sound, wind, and weather to aid in Alma's tactile response of cold hands as she is rejected by John.

n. In Scene Twelve, taking sleeping pills relaxes Alma and gives her the confidence to pick up the shoe salesman.

Psychological Centers and Rhythm

The actor playing Alma must be familiar with sexual frustration and rejection. If this is a problem, the woman creating this role should focus her attention on that time of the month when sexual anxiety, urges, and frustrations are experienced. Frequently, irrational behavior either takes over or is fantasized during this time. Early in the rehearsal process, the actor should consider how these sensations influence the physical and psychological centers of the heart and the sex. In Part One of the play, both these centers are suffocating Alma. The actor might want to consider an activity or an improvisation in which she has difficulty in showing love.

Finally, the actor will want to explore in rehearsal how the repression of Alma's psychological centers of the heart and sex affects her rhythm and tempo. During the first part of the play, her rhythm is frequently very staccato and she has sudden changes in her tempo. As she begins to recognize her emotional needs, her rhythm is more legatto and her tempo changes are not so abrupt. She starts to allow herself to be more physically free.

The actor creating Alma must discover various ways to establish her physical/emotional disorders. If some of Tennessee Williams' suggestions are foreign to the actor, she must discover personal sensorial conditions to transfer. The goal is always to find a workable sensorial, kinesthetic throughline for the character's journey. Most importantly, remember, it is the actor's imagination that is used. It is always "as if!"

SECTION III: PHYSICAL PAIN OR DISCOMFORT
CAUSED BY CONGENITAL DEFORMITY

John Merrick in Bernard Pomerance's *The Elephant Man*
[An Actor's Interpretation of John Merrick's Life and Self-Perceptions, As Told in the First Person]

I am John Merrick. I was born in 1863 or 1864. My death occurred in 1890. I lived during the Victorian period in England.

When Dr. Frederick Treves discovers me, I am twenty-one or twenty-two years old. I am being used as an animal. I am called "The Elephant Man." My keeper/manager, Ross, exhibits me to the public for a fee. I am tormented, ridiculed, stared at, and physically attacked by the crowds and police. I have no hope for anything better than being exhibited as an animal. I know of nothing better. My purpose in life is to endure physical and mental pain.

My memories of kindness and love are very faint. I had a beautiful mother whose miniature portrait I carry with me. I was physically deformed from birth. My mother was knocked down by an elephant in a circus before I was born. I believe she must have been a performer in the circus. I don't remember all the facts about her, only that she loved me. She didn't have much money and she needed her job in the circus. I am sure she was forced to give me up, to put me in the workhouses. I was so ugly, I must have been a burden. My mother died when I was very young.

I never knew my father. He deserted my mother when I was born.

The workhouse is a hell devised for the poor, the insane, and the crippled. I remember the cruelty, the dirt, and the loathsome work I had to perform. The fear of being returned to the workhouse has haunted me all the rest of my life. My manager Ross, rescued me from that miserable torment, only to plunge me into another kind of inhumane existence, as a freak of nature. Ross is cruel. He uses my gross deformity to make a profit and then he even steals my share of the money. Everyone hates me.

I am discovered by Dr. Frederick Treves of the London Hospital. He is a "lecturer in anatomy at London Hospital Medical College." My first visit to hospital is in 1884. Dr. Treves pays Ross in order to study my unusual physical disorder. After this first lecture, he returns me to Ross; however, in parting, Dr. Treves gives me his card.

Two more dreadful years pass. The London authorities do not permit Ross to exhibit me. Consequently, we end up at a Brussels Fair. The authorities throw us out. Exhibiting me is an "indecent act." Since Ross cannot earn any more money off me, he deserts me, but only after stealing my money. He leaves me enough to get a ticket to London.

I am lost and frightened. The police find me. They rescue me from a mob beating. The police cannot understand me when I try to speak. Because of my deformed lips, I cannot talk clearly. I can only make sounds and weep. A policeman finds Dr. Treves' card in my coat pocket and delivers me to the Doctor.

When I arrive, I frighten the people because I am so ugly. Because I do not

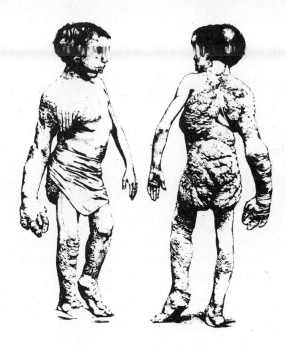

bathe, my sickening odor makes them nauseous. My first activity in the hospital is to bathe.

It is 1886, and I am twenty-four years old. I have found a home in Dr. Treves' hospital. I am cared for. I learn to talk more properly. I learn to read. I become human. For the next few years I know comfort. I am educated in religion. I am able to communicate with men and women in the outside world. I come to know dignity.

Who Am I/What Am I?

1. I know I am ugly and deformed.
   a. I have a congenital deformity. My face is misshapen, so I cannot smile or show emotion. However, even if my face is incapable of expressing emotion, my voice can.
2. I have been humiliated.
   a. Ross put me on public display. People are revolted when they see me.
   b. I am always afraid I'm going to be sent back to the workhouse.
   c. I wish I could live in an institution for the blind, so that people, especially women, could not see me.
3. I am a man of intense feelings.

a. I am frightened by the world.
b. I cry when I am frightened.
c. I am shy.
d. I am lonely.
e. I cry when I am happy
f. I weep when I see beauty.
g. I am romantic.
h. I like reading *Romeo and Juliet*.
4. I have the instincts and desires of a normal heterosexual male.
a. My male organ is intact.
b. I want desperately to see a naked woman.
c. I hate sleeping alone.
5. I am religious.
a. I enjoy making a paper model of the beautiful St. Philip's Church.
b. I like reading the Bible.
6. I want to be like everyone else.
a. I want to be able to dream the dreams other people have when they sleep. I would like to be able to sleep in the same physical position and not to be propped up.

Finding the Physical Life of John Merrick, Through the Text and Through Resource Material of the Period

In scene iii, "Who Has Seen the Like of This?", Treves addresses a medical group, detailing the physical deformities of John Merrick. His speech is a catalogue of the sensorial tasks facing the actor who portrays this role. Since the playwright has suggested that re-creating the literal physicality of John Merrick would be distracting as well as unbelievable to most audiences, it is up to the actor to accept the challenge of stimulating the audience's imagination through his sensorial and physical skills.

SCENE III, *WHO HAS SEEN THE LIKE OF THIS?*

Treves lectures. Merrick contorts himself to approximate projected slides of the real Merrick.

TREVES: The most striking feature about him was his enormous head. Its circumference was about that of a man's waist.

My job as an actor is to believe sensorially in the largeness and heaviness of my head. In order to believe in the large head, I need to deal with weight on my entire body. In preparation, I put heavy objects on my head and then kinesthetically recall the experience.

From the brow there projected a huge bony mass like a loaf, while from the back of his head hung a bag of spongy fungous-looking skin, the surface of which was comparable to brown cauliflower. On the top of the skull were a few long lank hairs.

I must believe in the tactile sensation of loose skin. This is skin that could easily be pulled. It is a personal sensation, as most of my skin is covered by clothing, but it effects the way I stand and especially the way I sit. It controls my physical activity.

The osseous growth on the forehead, at this stage about the size of a tangerine, almost occluded one eye.

Bone growth covers some of my vision. By closing my right eye a little, I give the appearance of seeing only with the left eye. This alters the way I shift my head to see. Consequently, it becomes very usable in rehearsal and performance for suggesting John Merrick's rhythm.

From the upper jaw there projected another mass of bone. It protruded from the mouth like a pink stump, turning the upper lip inside out, and making the mouth a wide slobbering aperture.

It is difficult to turn the lip inside out. However, distorting the lips is possible. At the start of the play, when Merrick is frightened and hurt, he lets some saliva run out of his mouth. This suggests how his muscular coordination is deformed. As Merrick learns to speak and the speech becomes clearer, I still retain the physical effort it takes to speak.

The nose was merely a lump of flesh, only recognizable as a nose from its position.

Nothing can really be done with the nose itself. The suggestion would be that there is difficulty in breathing. On occasion, it can become obvious that I am having to take air in through my mouth.

The deformities rendered the face utterly incapable of the expression of any emotion whatsoever.

As Merrick, I feel things deeply. However, I cannot smile or express any emotion facially. I weep when I am frightened, am hurt, or when I see beauty and experience happiness. The sound of crying, as well as an awareness of how emotion is expressed by my entire body is necessary in order to communicate my feelings effectively (both to my fellow actors and to the audience).

The back was horrible because from it hung, as far down as the middle of the thigh, huge sack-like masses of flesh covered by the same loathsome cauliflower stain.

Having had these physical appendages for as long as I can remember, I am used to the tactile sensation of this extra skin, however, in rehearsal, I hang a material that has some weight to it in long patches from my back in order to acquire a natural sense of how it effects my movement and rhythm. As with using a heavy object to weigh down my head, this rehearsal technique helps me to understand how Merrick is weighed down.

The right arm was of enormous size and shapeless. It suggested but was not elephantiasis, and was overgrown also with pendant masses of the same cauliflower-like skin. The right hand was large and clumsy—a fin or paddle rather than a hand. No distinction existed between the palm and back, the thumb was like a radish, the fingers like thick tuberous roots. As a limb it was useless.

My right arm is heavy. To get the feeling that it is large and nearly useless, I wear a boxing glove in rehearsal.

The other arm was remarkable by contrast. It was not only normal, but was moreover a delicately shaped limb covered with a fine skin and provided with a beautiful hand which any woman might have envied.

This is my arm of gesture. Sometimes I look at how beautiful my arm and hand are. Why are they beautiful and the rest of me deformed?

From the chest hung a bag of the same repulsive flesh. It was like a dewlap suspended from the neck of a lizard.

Using the same technique as the loose skin which hangs from my back, I construct a bag of material which hangs from my neck and chest for rehearsal.

The lower limbs had the characters of the deformed arm. They were unwieldy, dropsical-looking, and grossly mis-shapen.

My hips, legs, and feet are heavy. This effects the way I sit and walk. By looking at the pictures of Merrick, I see that my legs are slightly turned in. This effects my physical rhythm.

There arose form the fungous skin growths a very sickening stench which was hard to tolerate.

I observe the physical response of those around me to my smell. It overpowers them. It makes me feel dirty. The activity of bathing is especially enjoyable for me. It makes me feel more human. It is my first step in becoming like others.

To add a further burden to his trouble, the wretched man when a boy developed hip disease which left him permanently lame, so that he could only walk with a stick. [*To Merrick*] Please. [*Merrick walks.*] He was thus denied all means of escape.

In studying the pictures, I see that it is the left hip which is crippled. The entire physical weight of the head, the hanging flesh, the deformed hip, and the large legs and feet leads to working with a curvature in my spine. I am being pulled down. The cane is very effective in keeping myself pushed up.

Psychological Centers

Dr. Treves recognizes that Merrick has a weakened heart which "won't sustain him much longer." Merrick is not aware of this condition, but the actor must be. In the early part of the play, physical pain has been inflicted on "The Elephant Man". He has also been humiliated emotionally. The actor must retain an awareness of that source of pain. Perhaps the sensorial condition of a weakened heart can be communicated in the source of John's early emotional pain. In addition, even though he is living in a hospital and has been relieved of most of his physical pain, there is still the opportunity to capitalize on the shortness of breath and fatigue that results from his heavy labor of movement. John Merrick's head is full of dreams. He desires to be like everyone else. He is, however, lonely. Even though he wants to sleep like a normal human being, horizontally, with his head on the pillow, to have dreams that he might accomplish, as other people are allowed to do with their dreams, the physical weight of his head is too much. As he lays down to sleep, he is weighed down. He dies from the weight of his physicality.

SUMMARY

Theatre is an imaginative situation which must be sensorially real. This chapter has explored examples of dramatic situations which involve physical or emotional pain. The actor is not really in pain or deformed, but must skillfully communicate the behavior of pain and/or deformity. In order to do this, the actor's physical and emotional condition must be healthy. Only then can s/he create and communicate all the elements, physical and psychological, of a character. As has been the procedure for all of the exercises explored in Part One, the first step is to determine the physical action and sensorial demands of the scene or character. The actor can then allow for the psychology of the character (as well as his/her throughline) to be revealed through the kinesthetic responses discovered in rehearsal.

Chapter
12

Subtext and Sensory Life in Chekhov's *The Three Sisters*

The accepted use of the term "subtext" refers to the hidden meaning in the words or to what is *not* said, but meant. This definition can limit subtext to an intellectual interpretation of meaning. Subtext is more complex than that. In Chapter 9, Experience/Exercise 27, the actors explored how a secret held by one or more of the improvisation partners affected the physical relationship between them. Experience/Exercise 28 (using the text of the "Open-Ended Scenes") extended this process of "subtextual" exploration into sensory work. In doing those experience/exercises, the actors uncovered spontaneous meanings in the words. More importantly, they practiced listening to their bodies' impulses in order to play a scene. They did not rehearse a sequence of line interpretations.

When we speak, there is always a subtext operating underneath the meaning of our words. *There is no text without subtext.* In accordance, each of us possesses a daily physical life which is the culmination of our history of spoken and unspoken, realized and unrealized needs. We hear the inner voice of that history, sometimes consciously, sometimes unconsciously, and it affects how we behave. Therefore, any definition of subtext must also include physical behavior, as well as unspoken meaning. By extension, this means that silence can also have a subtext,

since there is behavior and unspoken meaning in a silence. A main objective of Part One of this book has been to train the actor to hear the inner voice and recognize its affect on the subtext of his/her physical life.

A character also possesses a physical life which is the culmination of his/her history. This is why it is important for an actor to complete as much as possible Egri's Tri-Dimensional chart, as well as attempt to answer the many other questions asked about a character in Chapter 10. With this knowledge, an actor might then dig into the private world of his/her Pandora's Box, using some secret or some sensory response to stimulate the relationships in a scene. A good script often provides sensory requirements that will complement this work. But, of course, rehearsing is what really informs the actor about his/her character's silent needs, feelings, and conflicts. Exploring the sensory requirements of a scene while rehearsing always frees an actor from that rather dangerous outside activity of playing head games with the psychological reasonings behind a character's behavior. It is a fortunate actor who trusts his/her technique to allow sensory work to uncover the relationship in rehearsal. Then the actor discovers his/her physical responses and subtext by *doing* and *experiencing* (and not by discussing).

A great play enjoys the miracle of outliving its playwright. As I indicated above, even though a play's themes and concerns have direct significance to our contemporary world, understanding the environment of the play, the daily habits of the characters, and their political and social relationships, always benefits the actor with information necessary to creating a fully believable life on stage. This is especially true of Anton Chekhov, a playwright whose work depends on the ability of the actors to explore and use subtext.

The Three Sisters takes place in a Russian provincial town around the turn of this century. This was the same time in which Chekhov actually wrote the play and in which it received its first performances through the direction of Stanislavsky and the Moscow Arts Theatre. A lot of primary resource material is available about that first production. The process of rehearsal and production is discussed in the letters of Chekhov to his wife Olga Knipper (she played the original Masha), as well as in his correspondence with Stanislavsky (who not only directed the production, but created the role of Vershinin). Additionally, there is Stanislavsky's account, most notably found in his autobiography *My Life in Art* (required reading for any student of the theatre for his contribution to the technique of acting, as well as for its information on his collaboration in Chekhov's plays).

In coming to understand this period in Russia, I have also found Henri Trozat's *Daily Life in Russia Under the Last Tsar* a particularly informative text, as well as reproductions of original photographs from the period in such books as *Russia in Original Photographs: 1860–1920,* by Marvin Lyons, and *A Portrait in Photographs,* by Chloe Obolensky, with an Introduction by Max Haynard.

Of course, every student should be thoroughly familiar with Chekhov's three other great plays, *The Seagull, Uncle Vanya,* and *The Cherry Orchard.* While Chekhov's profession was medicine, his avocation (he used to say his "mistress") was writing. Indeed, he put himself through medical school and helped to support his family by writing short stories. In the beginning, these were mostly very short comic pieces which he published under a pseudonym. It is fascinating to trace Chekhov's development as a writer from these very simple early pieces to his last years and his final four plays. Many characters and themes can be uncovered in their various stages of development in his stories. I recommend that anyone preparing for a role in *The Three Sisters* take a look at several of his stories such as "The Lady with the Dog," "The Kiss," "On Official Duty," "In the Ravine," "The Schoolmistress," "An Attack of Nerves," and "A Dreary Story."

Olga, Masha, and Irina, the three sisters of the play, are highly educated, energetic, bright, and talented. They are able to speak French, German, and English, and Irina also knows Italian. But they are suffocating in this small town. There is no one to appreciate and share their standard of class and education. In addition, the three sisters are dependent on the men in their family. Women had not acquired the freedom or independence realized today. When their father was alive, they enjoyed an active social life. His prominent standing as general and commander of a brigade in the military brought many sophisticated young men into their home. Sadly, the beginning of the play recalls the anniversary of his funeral exactly one year ago. Now Olga and Irina look to their brother Andrey as the man of the family and Masha must rely on her position as the wife of the school teacher Kuligan for respectability. Her lack of personal freedom is emphasized in the Act III discussion between Tuzenbach and Kuligan over whether or not she should play the piano in public as part of a benefit for the fire victims. Since Kuligin's headmaster might disapprove, her talent continues to go to waste.

The sisters still live in the dream of an old aristocratic Russia. Part of their dream is to return to Moscow, where they were born, and where their mother died. Moscow is a symbol of the glittering city with its exciting life of restaurants, theatre, universities, and opportunity. They remember the Moscow of their youth. Moscow is their hope for being able to re-attain that innocent happiness. Having been protected from the world by their father, the sisters are not prepared to adapt to the violent social changes taking place.

At the turn of the century, the rumblings of revolution were being heard in Moscow and other large cities. Stories circulated of literary censorship, rioting in the streets, starvation, poverty, and chaos. Political and social changes were about to erupt. Even though the urban turmoil is not a direct part of the rural life depicted in *The Three Sisters,* social changes are beginning to be felt. The new, but ambitious bourgeoisie is rising in Russia. Natasha and the unseen city council, Michael Ivanovitch Protopopof, represent this ambitious lower class. During the course of the play, Natasha marries Andrey, and then she and Protopopof slowly evict the sisters from their home and destroy their brother. Andrey's hope for a professorship dies and with it, the sisters' ability to get to Moscow. Instead, he becomes a servant of the city councilman Michael Protopopof (who is also Natasha's lover). Andrey gambles and loses the family's money, and finally their home to Protopopof. The sisters are trapped.

But Chekhov does not leave his audience without some hope for a better future. At the end of the play, the sisters Olga and Irina are not in search of happiness or escape. They have matured. They are realizing they must educate the next generation of the Russian illiterate youth. The action running through the play is the preparation of the women to be strong enough to fight for their independence in this world of cruelty and social change.

ACT II OF *THE THREE SISTERS:* MASHA AND VERSHININ

Preparation   Masha and Vershinin talk about their histories and relationships leading up to this scene.

Masha

I am Masha. At the beginning of the play, I am twenty-two years old. I am of the intelligentsia, well-educated in languages, literature, music, and history, as well as in the socially accepted behavior of a lady. I have been brought up in the Russian Orthodox Church.

I am trapped in a marriage. My husband dotes on me, but I do not love him. I was married at eighteen. My husband, Kuligan, is much older than I. He is a teacher of Latin, a dead, classical language. When I first knew him and married him, I respected his knowledge, but my feelings for him are now dead. He irritates me, and he overprotects me. I can't stand it when he touches me. I am stagnating in a boring environment. I want to escape, to go to Moscow, where I was born. I remember my childhood joys. Moscow is where I knew my mother. She died and is buried there.

At the beginning of the play, my main escape is in the reading of romantic novels and poetry. My primary psychological center is in my head, with frequent pangs in my heart. I am dressed in black (as is the Masha in *The Seagull*). In a sense, "I am in mourning for my life." But I have an independent streak in me. I want to live. At the end of Act I, I bang my fork on the table and announce that I intend to "eat, drink, and be merry." I say what's on my mind. Well-behaved ladies do not act in that fashion in public. I rebel in other ways. I whistle and indulge myself in singing bits of poetry. I use Pushkin's poem, "Ruslan and Lyudmilla" during Act I (and Act IV) to underscore my emotional state.

By the curved seashore, a green oak,
and round that oak, a chain of gold,
and round that oak, a chain of gold.

I ask myself why I keep repeating the phrase. I think Masha feels trapped, "chained". I sense that I am the "green oak". I want to break the chain.

I meet Colonel Vershinin. He remembers me as a little girl in Moscow. He fascinates me. He talks about life and how the world can be magnificently better. I am attracted to him. I become revitalized.

Act II is twenty-one months later. By now I am in love with Vershinin. He has aroused passions in me that I have never felt before. There is a new energy. Now my psychological center is in my sex. I cannot think clearly. Tonight, I am dressed in an attractive white blouse, but I still wear a black skirt. I have agreed to meet Vershinin and I hope to have some time alone with him before the other people arrive for tea. I want to give in to my emotions.

I am in terrible confusion. I am in love with Vershinin. I want him, but I am afraid. I am a married woman. To have a love affair with him would be committing a mortal sin. But when I am with him, I feel happy. I find the courage to defy conventions. For a time, I will have happiness.

Vershinin

I am Lieutenant-Colonel Vershinin, a battery commander in the Russian military. I arrived in this provincial town nineteen months ago to command an army battalion of soldiers who fight with field artillery. We are not presently at war. There is nothing to do in this small town but wait for orders. I am bored.

I dress in the standard army uniform. I am forty-two years old at the beginning of the play. I am trapped in a loveless marriage to my second wife. She is a hysterical woman, always threatening to commit suicide if ever I leave her. I am the father of our two little daughters, ages six and eight. I love my children. At one time, I must have loved my wife. However, we no longer have a sexual relationship. I feel trapped and frustrated by my wife. I am very lonely.

I knew the Prozorov family in Moscow. I went to school there, began my military service and was stationed in Moscow for many years. I remember the three sisters as young girls. They used to tease me, calling me the "love-sick major". I enjoy being in love.

Shortly after my arrival, I met Masha. I fell in love with her. I desire her. She is beautiful. She listens to my unhappy life. I love to talk, to share my unhappiness with her. I hope she will want me to be happy. I frequently announce my hope for a happy future. I believe it is possible that there will be a new order.

I sense an obstacle in Masha's uncertainty. She is afraid. I must make love to her. I want her to want me. I cannot restrain myself any longer. I must persuade her to have an affair with me. This evening is very important. I am consumed with passion.

Uncovering and Using the Sensory Conditions and Tasks for Masha and Vershinin in Their Scene from Act II of *The Three Sisters*

In Act II, the primary sensorial task for Vershinin and Masha is the desire to touch. This desire to make love has been slowly building and overpowering them since their first meeting twenty-one months ago. This desire is expressed through the subtext, not through what they say, but in what they want to say. The strain of wanting to touch is revealed in their physical behavior. It is expressed in the silences between them. Finally, at the end of the scene, they touch. Their kiss is interrupted by Irina and Tusenbach's entrance. However, Masha and Vershinin sustain the feelings and sensations they have uncovered into the rest of the act.

A valuable way to prepare for this scene is a combination on Experience/Exercise 12 from Chapter 5, which explored touch and the desire to touch, and Experience/Exercise 26 from Chapter 8, which explored physical rhythm through costuming. The improvisation begins with the act of dressing in the clothes of the period. During this activity, the actors may speak out their inner monologue. The second part of the improvisation explores their outdoor meeting in the cold and walk to the Prozorov house. This improvisation prepares the actors for "What's Before?" the scene and enables them to carry the energies and relationship they discover into the play.

Improvisation: "What's Before?"

Two chairs upstage left and right represent Masha's and Vershinin's private rooms. They may have mirrors for dressing if desired. The actors may begin with their undergarments on. The objective of the exercise is to ready themselves for their imminent and exciting meeting. While they are dressing, the actors are free to express their inner monologues out loud. I encourage the actors to use this time to actively vocalize their subtext for the scene to follow.

The final score for this improvisation might follow these actions:

I. Preparing for Their Meeting
    A. Masha in period corset and long slip.
      1. Activity
        a. Puts on long black skirt.
        b. Puts on white blouse.
        c. Arranges hair. Looking in the mirror, is pleased with appearance.
        d. Puts on hat, coat, and gloves.
      2. Inner monologue topics:
        a. "I love Vershinin."
        b. "Should I or should I not meet Vershinin?"
        c "I am a married woman."
        d. "I am trapped in a dull, boring marriage."
        e. "I'm afraid I am going to give in to my feelings."

    B. Vershinin in military pants and t-shirt.
      1. Activity
        a. Puts on shirt.
        b. Puts on military jacket/tunic.
        c. Puts on boots.
        d. Combs hair.
        e. Puts on coat, hat, and gloves.
      2. Inner monologue topics:
        a. "I am stationed in a dull boring town."
        b. "I can't stand my wife."
        c. "I am trapped in a chaotic, loveless marriage."
        d. "Masha understands me."
        e. "I love Masha. I must have her."

II. The Meeting
Vershinin enters first and paces to keep warm. When Masha enters, she sees Vershinin. She wants to run to him, to touch him, but doesn't. They greet each other politely. Appropriate to the period, Vershinin kisses Masha's gloved hand. Masha tenderly pulls her hand away. The kiss intensifies their need to touch. In silence, they begin to walk. They talk about the weather. They talk about the dull town. Masha laughs unexpectedly (she has a private joke). They enter the Prozorov house.

III. Beginning the Scene
On entering the room, Masha and Vershinin brush off the snow from their coats. Masha goes to the fireplace and takes off her gloves. She warms her hands over the fire. Vershinin takes off his hat. He watches her at the fire. She is aware that he is watching her. Masha begins to take off her coat. Vershinin approaches

her and helps her with her coat. He hangs up both their coats. The actors approach each other, sensing their need to touch. They touch each other without really touching. They touch each other with their eyes.

IV. The Actors Begin the Scene

Title chosen for scene: "Unspoken Illicit Intimacy."

Some Final Sensory Considerations

Finally, there are several sensory conditions inherent in the scene, which the actors should consider and include in the rehearsal process as early as possible.

Time: 8:30 P.M. in late January

Outside it is very cold—a snowy, black Russian winter. However, it is also Carnival time, the week before Lent. There are public celebrations. Street sounds are heard in the distance. Guests are expected for tea. There is music from outdoors. An accordian is faintly heard.

Place: The Prozorov Living Room

The room is darkly lit. A fire in the hearth provides warmth. The nurse sings a lullaby offstage. A wind whistles in the chimney. For Masha, the room represents her home before she was married. It is an intimate space, filled with memories of her father. Vershinin feels comfortable in this room. He was warmly welcomed here by the sisters on his first arrival.

Table 12.1 is a breakdown of the scene between Masha and Vershinin. The first column is the text of the play. In the second column are notes on the physical action of the characters, the subtext of their lines, and their intentions. In the third column are notes about the sensory or physical tasks suggested by the environmental conditions of the scene or the psychological condition of either character. The breakdown gathers together all of the work investigated during this chapter and applies it directly to the scene. The process whereby actors might arrive at playing a scene to these specific suggestions could not be as mechanical as the breakdown might suggest. A kinesthetic throughline must be discovered intuitively. My hope in presenting such an exhaustive outline as this (and as those which follow in later chapters) is to make the actors aware of how rich the possibilities are for sensory work in a scene.

Table 12.1 *THE THREE SISTERS*, ACT II, BY ANTON CHEKHOV

Text	Action/Subtext/Intention	Sensory Tasks
MASHA: I don't know.	Must get warm	Cold.
[*Pause.*]		Hearing the lullaby.
Of course, habit is important. But aside from habit, I believe it's only fair to say, of course, this may not hold true for other places, but in this town the nicest, best bred and best educated people are in the military.	Wanting to continue conversation; not knowing how to talk about the real subject *Subtext:* "You are wonderful."	Looking at Vershinin, wanting to touch him
VERSHININ: I'm thirsty. May I have some tea?	Removing coats *Subtext:* "You are beautiful."	Shaking off snow (cold).
MASHA: [*Looks at watch.*]		
They'll bring it soon. My marriage was arranged when I was eighteen. I was afraid of my husband, because he was a teacher and I'd only just finished school. Then he seemed to me very intelligent, clever, and important. But now it's not the same, I'm sorry to say.	Not much time till the others arrive. Masha wants Vershinin to know she doesn't love her husband.	Image of Kuligan.
		Looking at Vershinin.
VERSHININ: Oh, well, . . . Yes.	Understanding Masha's intention	Desire to touch Masha.
MASHA: Of course, I'm not talking about my husband, I'm	Changing subject: desire to express subtext,	

(continued)

157

Table 12.1 (Cont'd)

Text	Action/Subtext/Intention	Sensory Tasks
used to him—but civilians as a rule are such vulgar, unpleasant, uneducated people. Vulgarity offends me, it upsets me. I can't bear to see a person who lacks refinement, lacks good manners, good breeding. When I find myself with a group of teachers, my husband's collleagues, I'm simply miserable.	"You are wonderful." "I cannot stand my husband." Waiting for Masha to say "I need you."	Image of Natasha. Chills. Image of husband and friends; feeling of restlessness.
VERSHININ: Yes, . . . But it seems to me whether civilian or military, they're all exactly the same, at least they are in this place—exactly. If you listen to one of the leading citizens, civilian or military, what you hear is that he's sick to death of his home, sick to death of his horses, . . . the most completely typical thing about a Russian is his lofty way of thinking. But, then, his way of behaving is anything but lofty. Why is this? Can you tell me?	Complaining about the town. Subtext: "I need you to make me happy." Physically closer to Masha.	Both physically closer. Hearing, seeing, and smelling all becoming very acute.
MASHA: Why indeed?		
VERSHININ: Why is he sick to death of his children and his wife, and why are the wife and children sick to death of him?	Wants Masha to know he is also miserable.	Image of wife and daughters.
MASHA: You're out of sorts today!	Trying to comfort Vershinin.	

Dialogue		
VERSHININ: Maybe so. My daughter's not very well, and when my girls are sick, I get so anxious; my conscience bothers me because their mother is what she is. We began to quarrel at seven this morning and at nine I left, slamming the door behind me.	Wanting Masha to know he is constricted by his life.	Image of daughter.
		Image of wife and quarrel.
[*Pause.*]	*Subtext:* "Please love me."	
I never talk about this. It's odd, but you're the only person I tell.	Wants to tell Masha how intimately he feels about her, wants to be more intimate with Masha.	Each aware of physical presence of the other smell.
[*Kisses her hand.*]		Touching Masha.
Don't be angry with me. Except for you, I have nobody, . . . nobody.	*Subtext:* "I hope I have won Masha's love."	Both are physically aware/aroused.
[*Pause.*]	*Subtext:* for Masha: "I want to make him happy."	
MASHA: Just listen to the wind! . . . When Father was dying, the wind was moaning, just like it is now.		Masha hears the whistling wind, memory of her father. She becomes afraid.
VERSHININ: Are you superstitious?	Trying to comfort Masha. *Tactic:* A joke.	
MASHA: Yes, I am.		Masha continues to touch Vershinin.

(*continued*)

Table 12.1 (Cont'd)

Text	Action/Subtext/Intention	Sensory Tasks
VERSHININ: How strange.		Intimate touch.
[Kisses her hand.]		
You are a wonderful, extraordinary woman. I love, love, love . . . your eyes, the way you move; I dream about. Wonderful! Extraordinary woman!	Declaring his love for Masha	Seeing Masha, images of touching her in his inner eye; wanting to touch her now.
MASHA: [Laughing softly.]		Smell, touch, and sound of Vershinin is overpowering. Physically wanting Vershinin.
When you talk like that, I can't help laughing, even though it frightens me. . . . Don't talk like that again, please. [Sotto voce.] And yet,—I don't mind if you do.	Declaring her love for Vershinin.	
[Covers her face with her hands.]		Embarrassed.
I don't mind. Someone is coming. Talk about something else.		Hearing Irina and Tusenbach. Physical separation.

Chapter
13

Discovering a Sensorial Life Through Language and Imagery in Shakespeare's *Romeo and Juliet*

Body language is an actor's most valuable and exciting skill. However, in everyday life our primary method of communicating is speech. We rely on the spoken word to share information, as well as to indicate our needs and desires more openly and readily. Words are also the primary tools of a playwright. Plays are primarily scripted dialogue. And dialogue—spoken language through its images and meanings personal to each actor—has the power to stimulate body language, and ultimately our behavior.

When an actor begins to think more specifically about words, s/he realizes that each one possesses within its meaning the potential of personal experience. That is to say, the wealth of each word's meaning is tied to specific memories. Words, therefore, have the power to stimulate the actor's sensorial energies through the specific sense memory they carry. Think of the words "mom" and "dad." Instantly your mind floods with an image for each word, or even an image for these two words together. Emotions associated with your images are also stimulated. Each person's response will be unique.

In everyday speech, we often ignore these deeper associations for the sake of expediency. But poets know how to arouse through their craft, deeply-seated subconscious memories. Therefore, for sensorially trained actors, poetry can be a very physical, as well as psychological experience.

The greatest poet, as recognized by literary scholars and students of the theatre alike, is William Shakespeare. His plays, because of their poetry (which extends itself even into the prose speeches through his use of imagery) are language experiences which stimulate a sensorial life. Actors must not only develop an appreciation for the imagery, but a *taste* for Shakespeare's words as well. Speaking his words is a sensory experience much like taste. With Shakespeare, actors learn to experience language viscerally and sensorially, and therefore, psychologically.

Since Shakespeare dictates so much of the behavior and psychological life of his characters through language, it is necessary for actors to begin their creative process by focusing on his language. In order to understand how rich the meaning of Shakespeare's language is, the actor must paraphrase (or in other words "translate") Shakespeare's dialogue into contemporary speech. This can be a tedious process, but often, if the work is thorough, the benefits are great. Besides being able to understand specifically what is being said, paraphrasing personalizes an actor's physical responses to the text. This process makes the words themselves a potent stimulant for need, behavior, and emotional relationships.

I strongly urge actors to consult the *Oxford English Dictionary* in order to write a word-for-word paraphrase of all speeches. Language is constantly changing. Since the Renaissance, English has undergone many changes. Words which had a particular meaning during Shakespeare's day may have lost that meaning over the years or even gone out of our language altogether. The *OED* provides the most complete history and list of definitions of any dictionary available.

To illustrate the specificity required in understanding the meaning of a Shakespearean scene, I have supplied an example of a paraphrase of the "Palmer's Sonnet" from Act I, scene v, of *Romeo and Juliet.* I have retained the spelling, capitalization, and punctuation of the First Folio for this paraphrase to emphasize how different Shakespeare's English was from our contemporary language. It is important for young actors to realize that with Shakespeare, it is almost as though they are speaking another language.

Paraphrases of speeches and scenes follow throughout the chapter. While the paraphrase of the "Palmer's Sonnet" is fairly literal, later paraphrases tend to be a little looser, allowing for slang, subtext, and acting vocabulary established in previous chapters. When looking the individual words up in the dictionary, the actor will discover that there are often multiple meanings playing underneath the surface of the text, therefore, every actor's paraphrase of a scene will be different. Each actor must come up with the most comprehensive meaning personal to him/herself.

Act I, scene v, "The Palmer's Sonnet"*

ROMEO: If I prophane with my unworthiest hand,
Should I violate by my most meritless palm,
This holy shrine, the gentle fin is this,
Your divine image, the honorable penalty becomes that
My lips to blushing Pilgrims did ready stand,
The two edges of my mouth—most modest, religious travellers—
willingly offer themselves.
To smooth that rough touch, with a tender kisse.
To refine the harsh contact through a gentle caress.

JULIET: Good Pilgrime, You do wrong your hand too much,
Courteous wayfarer, you mistreat your palm in excess.
Which mannerly devotion shewes in this,
As modest religious observance makes plain by the following action
For Saints have hands, that Pilgrims hands do tuch,
Because statues of holy persons possess praying palms for
worshippers palms to stroke
And palme to palme, is holy Palmers kisse.
Therefore, hand touching hand represents the sacred Pilgrim's act
of affection.

ROMEO: Have not Saints lips, and holy Palmers too?
Don't the canonized have mouths, as well as reverend worshippers?

JULIET: I Pilgrim, lips that they must use in prayer.
Yes, traveller, mouths that are required for speaking devotions.

ROMEO: O then dear Saint, let lips do what hands do,
Ah, in that case precious deity, allow mouths to perform that
which palms perform.
They pray (grant thou) least faith turne to dispaire.
Consent that hands make earnest petitions to prevent confidence
from changing into hopelessness.

JULIET: Saints do not move,
Holy statues remain motionless,
Though grant for prayers sake.
Even if they bestow requests to a holy petition.

ROMEO: Then move not while my prayers
In that case, do not stir, during which time my holy request's
fulfillment I obtain.

[*They kiss.*]
Thus from my lips, by thine my sin is purg'd.
In the way we just kissed, out of my mouth through yours, my
transgression has been freed.

JULIET: Then have my lips the sin that they have tooke.
If that is so, my mouth retains the transgression it consumed.

ROMEO: Sin from my lips? O trespasse sweetly urg'd:
Transgression out of my mouth? Ah sin, pleasingly provoked.

163

Act I, scene v, (Cont'd)

> Give me my sin again.
>   *Render back the transgression as before.*
> **JULIET:** You kisse by'th'booke.°
>   *You act affectionately by rote.*

°This is a transcription of the scene as it appears in the First Folio.
°Also a play on words, as Romeo has kissed a book separating their mouths, and not Juliet's actual mouth—as was the Renaissance practice when boy actors played women's roles.

The Imagery Pattern Stimulating Romeo and Juliet's First Encounter

The Palmer's Sonnet is a complex acting assignment. During the dance that precedes this passage in the play, Romeo has watched Juliet, along with her other guests, engage in a formal ritual for communicating sexual feelings. They have been dancing. Now Romeo engages Juliet's wit, and their mouths spontaneously dance with iambic feet in poetry. A game of improvised speech, . . . the very act of speaking has been exciting! As we learn in the paraphrase, the sonnet is a clever play on saintly worship and sexual stimulation. The religious imagery demands innocence. However, the tactile sensation of "paddling palms" is physically potent. The public setting demands restraint. However, the initial attraction of two young and healthy teenagers arouses desire.

When Romeo first sees Juliet, he does not know her identity, but he immediately begins to feel the heat. The room is warm. Earlier in the scene, Capulet (Juliet's father) stirs up the dancing by calling for more space in the hall. During this speech, he also lets us know how hot it has become in the room.

> **CAPULET:** A hall, hall, give room, and foot it girls,
>   More light you knaves, and turn the tables up:
>   And quench the fire, the room is grown too hot.

The lights already burning are augmented, so now it is not only hot, but very bright. This is quite a contrast from the night scene of Mercutio's "Queen Mab" speech which immediately precedes this one.

When Romeo first sees Juliet, he says:

> O she doth teach the torches to burn bright.

Romeo is aware of the blazing fire all around him. However, he is also scorched by the instantaneous heat of love and experiences a passion which stimulates tactile sensations of desire. The first tactile response for any Romeo, while gazing on the beautiful Juliet, is to respond to the warmth both physical and sexual in the room.

As he watches, he yearns to know this beautiful creature.

It seems she hangs upon the cheek of night,
As a rich jewel in an Ethiop's ear;
Beauty too rich for use, for earth too dear.

There is a luxurious contrast between dark and light which communicates Romeo's passion. In these lines, the visual imagery of Juliet glistens so beautifully to Romeo that she makes the already bright room seem dark as night by contrast.

So shows a snowy dove trooping with crows,
A beautiful white bird dancing with clumsy,ugly birds,
As yonder lady o'er her fellows shows:
Stands out in the same way as that beautiful young girl above the other dancers here.
The measure done, I'll watch her place of stand,
When the dance is over, I will see where she goes
And touching hers, make blessed my rude hand.
And by touching her hand I will bless my own coarse one.

Juliet's beauty is too pure for his rough hands. By touching Juliet's hand, Romeo hopes to purify himself. Purification comes by fire. The room is filled with fire. (In Greek, the word for fire means "pure.") The actor can use this sensory condition to physicalize the psychology of the scene.

However, before Romeo has a chance to speak to Juliet, the play's heated mood of love changes to the fire of hate. Tybalt recognizes Romeo's voice.

This by his voice, should be a Montague.
I recognize the voice as Montague.
Fetch me my rapier, boy, what dares the slave
Get my sword, servant. How can that low life
Come hither cover'd with an antique face,
Enter here, disguised in a grotesque mask
To fleer and scorn at our solemnity?
To jeer and make fun of our celebration?
Now by the stock and honor of my kin,
Here, with my forefathers and the reputation of my relatives,
To strike him dead I hold it not a sin.
I believe it is not a moral offense to kill him.

This threat of hate and death sounds in the play before Romeo can speak to Juliet. Shakespeare has foreshadowed doom for these young lovers. Under this threat, their innocent game of passion is played out in the Palmer's Sonnet. As we have already discussed, the love game has a virginal innocence, but the tactile sensations of touching fingers ("in prayer") are overpowering, and the game ends with a kiss. It is the first culmination of their joy in each other. It is a joy which is fleeting, however, when Romeo discovers that Juliet is a Capulet and when she learns he is Montague.

ROMEO: Is she a Capulet?
Can she be the enemy?
O dear account! My life is my foe's debt.
What an expensive reckoning! I owe my life to my enemy.
JULIET: Go ask his name: if he be married,
Find out who he is.should he be already wed,
My grave is like to be my wedded bed.
It is likely I will marry and lie with death.

A literary analysis would say that as they each learn the identity of the other, both Romeo and Juliet foreshadow their deaths. But an actor cannot play that. However, death is still a part of this scene. Romeo and Juliet come from opposing families. Revealing their new love could bring about their death. Also, when we fall in love we know that if we cannot have that love, we feel as though we might as well die. So when Romeo says his life is in debt and Juliet evokes the grave, the *subtext* of their speech is the *fear of death.*

The rhythm of the scene becomes that of (1) passion (Romeo's first sighting of Juliet), (2) hate (Tybalt's recognition of Romeo), (3) passion (the Palmer's Sonnet), (4) fear (discovery of the beloved's identity and its consequences), and (5) death. This rhythm is played over and over again in the play's swift tempo. Romeo and Juliet's whirlwind journey of hate, love, and fear is four days and a few hours long. The Prologue sets that pace as "two hours traffic of our stage." The swiftness and secrecy of their love is entangled by passion and fear. Juliet already understands the immensity of their problem by the end of this, their first meeting.

Hate and fear are two powerful forces in the play destroying the ability to love.

JULIET: My only love sprung from my only hate,
This first love has risen from my family's single hate,
Too early seen, unknown, and known too late,
Prematurely, I saw and didn't recognize; now recognition is too late.
Prodigious birth of love it is to me,
It is a mighty beginning of love for me
That I must love a loathed enemy.
In being compelled to love a hated foe.

THREE STEPS IN PREPARING TO PLAY ACT III, SCENE V, "THE NIGHTINGALE SCENE"

I. Romeo and Juliet speak about their histories and throughlines leading up to Act III, scene v.

II. The actors paraphrase the scene.

III. The actors break down their scene for action, subtext, and intention, as well as for sensory tasks.

Romeo

I am Romeo, the only son and heir of the Montagues. I have been brought up as an educated Renaissance gentleman. A man of honor, I am a good swordsman and I can dance. At the start of the play, I am a very enthusiastic sixteen-year-old. I am in love with Rosaline, but she has rejected me. I am pining away, hurt. Feeling pain over the rejection, I want to be alone. I hide from the daylight. My cousin, Benvolio tries to cheer me up. He discovers that Rosaline will be at a masked ball at the Capulet's. I must see her. I am a very impulsive, young Italian.

When I see Juliet, I immediately forget Rosaline. I go to her, even though I don't know who she is. We play a game, improvising a sonnet that puns on pilgrims and palms. I cleverly ask for a kiss. This girl has confidence, wit, and enjoys challenging me. She is special. She is beautiful. She is dangerous. I win a kiss. I must find out more about her. Who is she? I discover she is a Capulet. My family hates the Capulets. It is a very old and bloody feud. I have a responsibility to the honor of my family. But I cannot stop loving Juliet. I am passionately in love with her.

I go to her balcony. I am drawn to her. I overhear her confess she loves me! We speak. She makes me realize this is more than an infatuation. She makes me promise marriage. Our marriage is secretly and swiftly arranged. We wed.

Then comes the encounter between Tybalt and Mercutio. Because I am married to Juliet, I am Tybalt's cousin. But also because I love her, I try to avoid fighting. My attempt to keep peace results in a mortal blow to my best friend, Mercutio, from Tybalt. They carry Mercutio out to be examined. My love for Juliet made me betray my manly code of honor with my kinsmen. I have lost my valor.

Benvolio returns with the news of Mercutio's death. Tybalt comes back. Fury is my passion now. I kill Tybalt to revenge the sudden death of my friend.

I am ashamed for betraying Juliet. I am banished. I want to kill myself. The Friar and the Nurse persuade me to return to Juliet. We spend our wedding night together before I leave for Mantua. It is dawn. We have spent the night making love. I try gently to make Juliet understand that I must leave in order to live. I promise we will be together again soon.

Juliet

I am Juliet. I am almost fourteen years old. As far as I know, I am the only child and therefore heir of the Capulet family. I may have had brothers and sisters, but they died in infancy. I am loved by my father. I am the apple of his eye; that is, until I cross him. I have been educated, but cloistered from the world. My nurse educates me in life's ironies. I am totally dependent on her for all information. I trust her and have always loved her. In some ways she is more my mother than my mother.

I am a gracious child. I have a quick intelligence. I am very witty, but usually prefer to remain quiet. I know my duty to obey my parents. I have been taught the Montagues are my family's enemies.

My mother informs me that I am to be married to the Counte of Paris. I do not know him. When I meet him, I have no feelings either way about him.

A masked ball and banquet is given by my father. While dancing, I meet a stranger. He is exciting. We play a game which ends in a kiss. I begin to fall in love with him. He is exciting, new, challenging, interesting, bold, and dangerous. He likes me, I think. Love is a new, unexpected feeling. I am experiencing something totally new. I enjoy the challenge of creating a sonnet with him and flirting at the same time. When we kiss, I know he is the one. I need to find out who he is. I learn he is Romeo Montague. I am afraid and desperately fear life will not be worth living without him. I know it is dangerous in more ways than one to love him.

After the dance, I step out onto my balcony to dream about Romeo and ask why he is the one I must love. When he surprises me from below, I realize how much he loves me and how much I want to love him, but I know these feelings are dangerous. I know we are going too fast.

> Well do not swear, although I joy in thee:
> I have no joy of this contract tonight,
> It is too rash, too unadvis'd, too sudden,
> Too like the lightning which doth cease to be
> Ere, one can say, it lightens. Sweet good night:
> This bud of love by summer's ripening breath,
> May prove a beautious flower when next we meet:

Love and fear are communicated by images of speed and light (mostly celestial) throughout this play. But my passion for Romeo wins out over my restraint. I fully confess my love for him.

> And yet I wish but for the thing I have,
> My bounty is as boundless as the sea,
> My love as deep, the more I give to thee
> The more I have, for both are infinite:

In expressing my love for Romeo, I evoke images of nature and water. They are symbols of life. My body feels alive with all the universe. And our love is honorable, as Romeo agrees to send word tomorrow where and when we will be married. I am going to be married after all! My life is changing so rapidly.

I tell the Nurse about Romeo and send her to Romeo. Then I impatiently wait for her return. At last, she comes back and teases me about Romeo, but finally she tells me we will be wed today! Friar Lawrence marries us.

Then tragedy strikes. I learn that Romeo has killed my cousin Tybalt and that he has been banished for it. At first, I curse Romeo, but I cannot stop loving him. If Romeo is banished, I have no choice but to make death my wedding partner. The nurse tells me she knows where Romeo is hiding and she will fetch him for our wedding night. I send my ring to him, hoping he will come.

Act III, scene v, The Second Balcony Scene (Paraphrase)

JULIET: Wilt thou be gone? It is not yet near day:
You want to leave? The time is not close to dawn.
It was the nightingale, and not the lark,
I assure you the nightingale, and certainly not the lark
That pierc'st the fearfull hollow of thine ear,
Struck fright in your inner ear with its song
Nightly she sings on yond pomgranate tree,
Every night, the nightingale sits singing on that same pomegranate tree.
Believe me love, it was the nightingale.
Trust me my dearest, it was the nightingale.
ROMEO: It was the lark the herald of the morn:
Wrong, it was the morning lark's song that announced the dawn:
No nightingale: look love what envious streaks
Not the nightingale. Look, sweetheart, how jealous rays
Do lace the severing clouds in yonder east:
Adorn the separating cumulus along the horizon.
Night's candles are burnt out, and jocund day
The stars are extinguished and happy light
Stands tiptoe on the misty mountain's tops,
Stretches on its toes on the dewy mountain tops.
I must be gone and live, or stay and die.
I have to leave so I can live, because if I remain, I will be killed.
JULIET: Yond light is not daylight, I know it I:
Those distant rays are not the morning. I am sure.
It is some meteor that the sun exhales,
The light is a shooting star breathed out by the sun
To be to thee this night a torch-bearer,
To serve (in the darkness) as your personal flame carrier
And light thee on thy way to Mantua.
Guiding you on the way to Mantua.

Act III (Cont'd)

Therefore stay yet, thou need'st not be gone.
So remain longer, you do not have to leave.
ROMEO: Let me be tane, let me be put to death,
Allow me to be captured, allow them to kill me,
I am content, so thou wilt have it so.
It pleases me, if that is what you want.
I'll say yon gray is not the morning's eye,
I will say that distant haze is not the daylight's gaze,
'Tis but the pale reflex of Cynthia's brow.
But it is the weak reflection of the moon.
Nor that is not the lark whose notes do beat
Also that is not the lark's song that strikes the
The vaulty heaven so high above our heads,
Cathedral sky so distant above us.
I have more care to stay, then will to go:
I have more desire to remain, than strength to leave;
Come death and welcome, Juliet wills it so.
Approach death, and happily, my beloved wants it that way.
How is't my soul, let's talk, it is not day.
So how goes things my inner/other self? Shall wetalk?
Day has not come yet.
JULIET: It is, it is, hie hence be gone away:
Morning is here! Therefore, quickly leave—go away!
It is the lark that sings so out of tune,
It is the morning bird, who warbles very inharmoniously,
Straining harsh discords, and unpleasing sharps.
Pushing dissonant harmonies and distasteful rising halfsteps.
Some say the lark makes sweet division;
People remark how the lark sings melodious divergence,
This doth not so: for she divideth us.
This lark does not, because her song separates us.
Some say, the lark and loathed toad change eyes,
People remark the lark and the hated toad exchange sight,
O now I would they had chang'd voices too:
Ah, now I wish they had exchanged their voices also,
Since arm from arm that voice doth us affray,
Because your limb from my limb that song frightens,
Hunting thee hence, with "Hunt's up" to the day,
Chasing you from here, arousing the day,
O now be gone, more light and it light grows.
Ah, presently leave, bright and still more bright it's getting.
ROMEO: More light and light, more dark and dark our woes.
*The brighter and brighter it gets, the worse and
still worse our troubles.*

[*Enter Nurse.*]

NURSE: Madam.
    Married lady.

Act III (Cont'd)

JULIET: Nurse.
    My foster mother.
NURSE: Your lady mother is coming to your chamber,
    Your noble mother is coming to your room,
  The day is broke, be wary, look about.
    It is daylight, beware, see to yourself.
[*The Nurse exits.*]
JULIET: Then window let day in, and let life out.
    So window, allow light to enter and permit Romeo to leave.
ROMEO: Farewell, farewell, one kiss and I'll descend.
    Goodbye, goodbye, a single kiss and I will go down.
[*They kiss.*]
JULIET: Art thou gone so: Love, lord, aye husband, friend,
    Do you leave like that? My heart, master, yes mate, companion,
  I must hear from thee every day in the hour,
    I require word from you all the days there are in an hour,
  For in a minute there are many days,
    Because each minute willseem so long that it will
    contain many days,
  O by this count I shall be much in years,
    Ah in this computation I will grow very old,
  Ere I again behold my Romeo.
    Before I see my love again.
ROMEO: Farewell:
    Goodbye.
  I will omit no opportunity,
    I will seize every chance,
  That may convey my greetings love, to thee.
    To send my best wishes, Love, to you.
JULIET: O thinkest thou we shall ever meet again?
    Ah, do you imagine we will ever see each other again?
ROMEO: I doubt it not, and all these woes shall serve
    I do not question that, also this unhappiness will offer
  For sweet discourses in our time to come.
    Pleasant conversations in our future days together.
JULIET: O God! I have an ill-divining soul,
    Oh deity, I have a sick premonition,
  That thinks I see thee now, thou art so low,
    Which believes with my inner eye, you are now down under me
  As one dead in the bottom of a tomb,
    As a corpse expired and laid to be buried,

Act III (Cont'd)

Either my eye-sight fails, or thou look'st pale.
Else my vision falters or you appear ashen.

ROMEO: And trust me love, in my eye so do you:
Believe me love, to my mind you also look pale.
Dry sorrow drinks out blood.
Adieu, adieu.
Scorching unhappiness saps our life. Goodbye, goodbye.

[Exit.]

JULIET: O Fortune, Fortune, all men call thee fickle,
You, goddess of fate, every man says you change your lovers often,
If thou art fickle, what dost thou with him
Should you be easy, why would you need Romeo
That is renown'd for faith? be fickle Fortune:
Who is reputed for his devotion? Go ahead and flirt, woman,
For then I hope thou wilt not keep him long,
*For once you have him, I hope you will not possess
him for a long time,*
But send him back.
But return him to me.

Table 13.1 *ROMEO AND JULIET*, ACT III, SCENE V

	Text	Action/Subtext/Intention	Sensory Tasks
JULIET:	Wilt thou be gone? It is not yet near day: It was the nightingale, and not the lark, That pierc'st the fearfull hollow of thine ear, Nightly she sings on yond pomgranate tree, Believe me love, it was the nightingale.	*Tactic:* To keep Romeo near, must prove it is still night. To make Romeo believe he heard the nightingale	Fear of tactile separation. Seeing the tree. Looking at Romeo/touching him.
ROMEO:	It was the lark the herald of the morn: No nightingale: look love what envious streaks Do lace the severing clouds in yonder east: Night's candles are burnt out, and jocund day Stands tiptoe on the misty mountain's tops, I must be gone and live, or stay and die.	Contradicting her, to make her realize the time has come to part. I use language to make Juliet see the light of dawn,.... the stars,.... the mist. I make a decision to leave.	Seeing the light of dawn. Seeing the stars go out. Seeing the mists on the horizon. Physical separation from Juliet.
JULIET:	Yond light is not daylight, I know it I: It is some meteor that the sun exhales, To be to thee this night a torch-bearer, And light thee on thy way to Mantua. Therefore stay yet, thou need'st not be gone.	Fighting reality	Desire to keep touching Romeo.
ROMEO:	Let me be tane, let me be put to death, I am content, so thou wilt have it so. I'll say yon gray is not the morning's eye, 'Tis but the pale reflex of Cynthia's brow. Nor that is not the lark whose notes do beat The vaulty heaven so high above our heads, I have more care to stay, than will to go: Come death and welcome, Juliet wills it so.	*Tactic change:* Playing a game of imagination. Looking at the sky Sharing "I love you." Humor	Giving in to desire to touch. Denial of sensory condition. Denial of sensory condition of lark's song. Sense of death.

(continued)

Table 13.1 (Cont'd)

	Text	Action/Subtext/Intention	Sensory Tasks
	How is't my soul, let's talk, it is not day.		Looking at/desire to touch Juliet. Tactile: actual touching.
JULIET:	It is, it is, hie hence be gone away: It is the lark that sings so out of tune, Straining harsh discords, and unpleasing sharps. Some say the lark makes sweet division; This doth not so: for she divideth us.	Realizing the truth—that Romeo could die— I want him to leave	Hearing the lark like an alarm.
	Some say, the lark and loathed toad change eyes, O now I would they had chang'd voices too: Since arm from arm that voice doth us affray,	Preparing self for separation.	Tactile: touch of a toad.
	Hunting thee hence, with "Hunt's up" to the day, O now be gone, more light and light it grows.	My Romeo must leave, now!	Image of Romeo being hunted. Seeing the daylight in the sky.
ROMEO:	More light and light, more dark and dark our woes.	Recognizing the pain of the truth.	Seeing the sky—gut sensations of the truth.
[Enter Nurse.]			
NURSE:	Madam.		
JULIET:	Nurse.		
NURSE:	Your lady mother is coming to your chamber, The day is broke, be wary, look about.	To warn Romeo and Juliet.	Juliet: image of mother and discovery..
JULIET:	Then window let day in, and let life out.		
ROMEO:	Farewell, farewell, one kiss and I'll descend.	Asking for a kiss.	Need for touch/act of kissing. Aroma and taste of beloved.

JULIET: Art thou gone so: Love, lord, aye husband, friend,
I must hear from thee every day in the hour,
For in a minute there are many days,
O by this count I shall be much in years,
Ere I again behold my Romeo.

Fear of loss, realization of his leaving. Imploring Romeo.

Feeling cold. Awareness of time and loss of touch.

ROMEO: Farewell!
I will omit no opportunity,
That may convey my greetings love, to thee.

Preparing to descend. Promising.

JULIET: O thinkest thou we shall ever meet again?

Pain of separation/cold morning air.

ROMEO: I doubt it not, and all these woes shall serve
For sweet discourses in our time to come.

To reassure Juliet.

Image of old age together.

JULIET: O God! I have an ill-divining soul,
That thinks I see thee now, thou art so low,
As one dead in the bottom of a tomb,
Either my eye-sight fails, or thou look'st pale.

Seeing Romeo below balcony.

Shiver through body; cold air.

Image of Romeo dead

ROMEO: And trust me love, in my eye so do you:
Dry sorrow drinks out blood. Adieu, adieu.

Assuring her that I love her too. To say goodbye, parting.

Moving away from Juliet.

[Exit.]

JULIET: O Fortune, Fortune, all men call thee fickle,
If thou art fickle, what dost thou with him
That is renown'd for faith? be fickle Fortune:
For then I hope thou wilt not keep him long,
But send him back.

Questioning, pleading.

After last line, prepare to greet mother.

Aroma of Romeo is still present. Image of their love-making.

Act III, scene v is loaded with sensorial requirements. There are visual and aural images conjured by the lovers as they view the approaching dawn. Starlight and firelight burn and wane. The aural images of the nightingale and the morning lark are debated. There are tactile sensations as Romeo and Juliet struggle to part. Smell is an important element in this scene: Romeo and Juliet have just spent the night making love. Each has private images of the other. The intensity of their passion is expressed in the wealth of sensory images evoked by Shakespeare's language. And even as Romeo and Juliet's physical/emotional fire continues to burn, the fear of cold death haunts the scene, foreshadowing their end.

In the short analysis of two scenes from *Romeo and Juliet,* it is easy to see that some roles require more than a fertile imagination and flexible sensorial skill. Romeo and Juliet are roles of a complex psychology. The actors who undertake these roles must thoroughly familiarize themselves with their sensorial journey from the first entrance to their deaths in the tomb. That process of work has been investigated so far by our close look at the language of Palmer's Sonnet, the imagery of the Banquet Scene, and in the images invoked during the unwilling parting of the Nightingale Scene. The next step for the actors might involve the homework of experiencing the sensorial conditions or tasks in the soliloquies. For both roles, the soliloquies are loaded with sensory life which will enable the actors to understand this particular sensorial journey of unlimited passion.

Actors need to take the time to explore and experience their sensorial life. Soliloquies are the perfect opportunity for actors to do this work in private. Once actors are in the middle of the play, there is no time to wait for private responses. The sensorial throughline must be immediately accessible, and Romeo and Juliet's sensorial throughline is mammoth.

To be successful, actors must have not only a full sensorial technique, but also a great capacity for imagination. Imagination is the actor's talent. Imagination means making the *impossible possible*! The *unreal* real! Fantasy a reality! An actor's responsibility is to create a panorama of passionate, exciting, fearful, tragic, comic, and mysterious lives. To do this, an actor must use himself, but s/he does not play his/herself. Only through imagination can an actor discover his/her creative persona. Sensorial power (skill) enables the actor to dig deeply into creative sensations in order to breathe life into a character. When an actor can experience sensorially the character's vocal and physical life, his/her imagination will be ignited.

Actors who have not developed their imaginations may have a happy accident in some special role. They may know what it means to be creative. However, good actors cannot rely on accident. A skilled actor is one who has imaginative power. This is an actor who is able to perform a variety of roles.

Chapter 14

Rehearsing Multiple Sensory Demands in Williams' *A Streetcar Named Desire*

The struggle to survive is a painful process. Often, those who get in the way get trampled down. Tennessee Williams' *A Streetcar Named Desire*, set in 1947, is a play about survival in a cruel, godless, materialistic, selfish, and lustful world. The characters in *A Streetcar Named Desire* are loaded with fear, anger, hatred, and jealousy. They also have the human need for beauty, compassion, understanding, and love. Tennessee Williams' world is one of desire, joy, pain, conflict, and destruction. The key word, of course, is desire.

Following World War II, the United States celebrated the virility of winning. The returning men were cocky, assured, and confident of their ability to protect what belonged to them. The women, on the other hand, had learned to survive, often by taking on the vacant industrial jobs left open by the men who were fighting overseas. Women, therefore, were more aware of the struggle it takes to endure life's cruelties.

In preparing to work on any Tennessee Williams play, there is a lot of reading to consider. His *Memoirs,* written in the late sixties, offer some insight into this period of his life and also recall his first meetings with Brando and Kazan. This can be augmented by looking at his letters to Maria St. Just, his "Five O'Clock Angel," as well as his correspondence with Donald Windham. His short stories, particularly the collection entitled *One Arm*, often provide the earliest sketches for several of his plays. Of course, every student of the theatre should be familiar with Tennessee Williams' plays, *The Glass Menagerie, Cat on a Hot Tin Roof, Sweet Bird of Youth, The Rose Tattoo, Night of the Iguana*, and his one-acts, particularly *The Mutilated*, from the collection entitled *Dragon Country. The Mutilated* is especially interesting for the actress playing Blanche, even though it was written almost twenty years after *Streetcar*. It offers a view of Blanche's vagrant loneliness before coming to New Orleans, or possibly the life she will know years after the events of this play.

Throughout the second part of this text I have been stating that after reading as much as possible, the actors should write a biography for their character, answering the questions outlined in the Egri Three-Dimensional Chart, as well as the additional questions posed in Chapter 10. The following section contains biographies for Blanche, Stella, and Stanley, as they might be written by the actors playing these roles. They are written in the first person. I believe that this is important. Often, in rehearsal, when an actor, speaking of his/her character, says "Well, he wants to. . . ," I stop the actor and say *"Who* wants to?" When talking about a role, an actor should attempt to personalize the character by talking as if s/he is that character. It makes the emotions more directly accessible and personal.

Blanche

My name is Blanche. It comes from the French, "blanc" meaning white, which is the color of virgins. This is ironic, since my physical/psychological center is in my sex. My last name is DuBois, which means "woods." In my first meeting with Mitch, I explain the meaning of my name. "It's a French name. It means woods and Blanche means white, so the two together mean white woods. Like an orchard in spring!" My home was a great plantation, an orchard called Belle Reve. This is also ironic, since the translation of "Belle Reve" is "beautiful dream." I live in a dream.

When I arrive in the French Quarter of New Orleans, I am immaculately dressed in a white suit and a fashionable hat. I appear out of place to those who live here, and I feel out of place. I am repulsed by the vulgarity and the dirt of Elysian Fields. I was raised and educated as a lady of the Old South. In the southern tradition, sensitive, delicate women were looked after.

I want to go back to Belle Reve. I belong to that past life. I cannot admit to the decaying traditions of the South. But I have lost Belle Reve. I have buried all my relatives and servants—everyone I loved, except Stella. Their ugly deaths haunt me.

When I was younger, I married a beautiful, sensitive, poetic man—Allan Grey. He had all the refined qualities educated, polite society can offer. He was the opposite of Stanley Kowalski. During our brief marriage, I could not understand why he could not satisfy me sexually. Then I walked in on him suddenly, unexpectedly, in a room that I thought was empty. He was with an older man. I discovered Allan in a homosexual relationship. Later, I viciously attacked him with verbal abuse. It made him feel weak and vulgar. It destroyed him. He shot himself. His suicide traumatized me. Allan's death haunts me. I am responsible for his ugly death. I have several inner images that continually haunt me. I can see the moment between him and his friend, having sex. I remember the three of us, very drunk, driving out to Moon Lake Casino. I remember the look on Allan's white face when I said, "I know! I saw! You disgust me!"

Since that experience, I have been trying to run away from the past. The harder I try to escape, the more crushing my images of Allan become. I try to escape through sex. I am searching for love and kindness. I have come for help to my sister Stella here in New Orleans.

The people who live in Elysian Fields are vulgar and crude. In order to escape the muggy heat and the dirty environment, I flee into the bathroom (the only private place) to take hot baths. They calm my nerves, desires, fears, and anxieties. I have an overwhelming need to be purified, cleansed, but I also have tremendous physical yearnings and responses.

Before my arrival, I had to leave Belle Reve and my home town. I was fired from my position as a teacher by Mr. Graves, the principal. I seduced a seventeen-year-old boy. I was run out of town for this and my other "fornications."

I am homeless. I have no money. My last hope is my married sister, Stella. She is actually younger than me, although I claim to be the youngest. Stella deserted Belle Reve and me. She came to the French Quarter, met Stanley Kowalski, and married him.

In the stage directions preceding my first entrance, Tennessee Williams describes my movement as having an "uncertain manner that suggests a moth." The dictionary states that a moth is an animal "that gradually eats away, wastes, or consumes something." This suggests the appetite to devour. In relation to the various "hungers," my appetite is sexual. But there is a sense that I have come here to eat away at the marriage of Stella and Stanley. There is also the feeling that my world is being eaten away. I am losing my rational self and am increasingly forced to survive through a world of fantasy.

My rhythm/tempo suggested by this stage direction is that of a moth in "uncertain" flight.

I am super-sensitive to all sensory conditions. My tactile sense is especially overpowering. My skin tingles with each thing I see or hear. I respond kinesthetically to the feel and touch of others, whether they are touching me or not. As I work on improvising my arrival, I respond to the muggy heat, the dirt, the smell. When entering the cramped Kowalski apartment, I feel suffocated by the close quarters. I have difficulty breathing, and my ribs and chest feel tight. My hands are restless to touch, but they are also repulsed. Feelings of loneliness, anxiety, and fear come up. This is not Belle Reve. I am homeless. I have no money. My last hope is my married sister, Stella. Will I have a home here?

I need a drink. I search for liquor. I drink, clandestinely. I am preparing myself to face my sister Stella, whom I have not seen in many years.

Stella

My name is Latin for "star." I shine with life. I am pregnant. I am twenty-five and Stanley Kowalski's wife. I am a happy woman.

When I lived at Belle Reve, I was dominated by Blanche. She was the older and more beautiful one. I tried to compete with her, but lost out. I could not survive in that decaying society. I had to abandon it. I love my sister, but I had to get away.

I ran away in search of excitement, work, and a new life. I found a loving, passionate life with Stanley Kowalski in New Orleans. We met during the War, while Stanley was on leave. Our relationship is very physical and sexual. I am deeply in love with him. I also love the feeling of approaching motherhood. I am proud to be able to mother Stanley's child. It makes me feel vital.

Until Blanche arrives, I had given up any desire for my past. But Blanche succeeds in making me feel guilty about deserting Belle Reve and my family responsibilities. She stimulates anxiety and conflict over the past I had buried.

Blanche prolongs her stay. The tension between her and Stanley grows. I feel trapped, caught between them. I love them both. Each pulls on me.

In the fourth scene, Blanche tries to convince me to leave Stanley. She wants to rip me apart from him. I realize that she is afraid of being alone, but at times she is irrational. She doesn't understand me anymore. I worry that if Blanche continues to stay in the middle of my life, she will destroy my marriage. I must find a way to get rid of her. Blanche meets Mitch. They show an interest in one another. I hope that Blanche will marry Mitch. If Blanche can find love and a home, and feel protected, she will leave me alone with Stanley.

When Blanche collapses and tells me she has been raped, I must make a decision about whether to believe her or to believe that her mental state has become deluded by the rejection she suffered from Mitch. My love and passion for Stanley and especially for my child wins out. I must not believe her story. I want life to shine again. Perhaps it can through our son.

Stanley

My name "Stanley Kowalski" is Polish for "Stone Smith." According to Leonard Quirimo, in his essay "The Cards Indicate a Voyage on A Streetcar Named Desire," this name suggests the stone-age man. I am a healthy, earthy, sexual, passionate man in my early thirties. Stella is my wife. She is pregnant with my child. We make love often. I am the boss in my home.

As Tennessee Williams tells me in the description of my character preceding my first entrance Scene One, A Streetcar Named Desire by Tennessee Williams, (New Directions; 8th printing, 1980, pp. 24–25), all my relationships are physical.

> Stanley throws the screen door of the kitchen open and comes in. He is of medium height, about five feet eight or nine, and strongly, compactly built. Animal joy in his being is implicit in all his movements and attitudes. Since earliest manhood the center of his life has been pleasure with women, the giving and taking of it, not with weak indulgence, de-

pendently, but with the power and pride of a richly feathered male bird among hens. Branching out from this complete and satisfying center are all the auxiliary channels of his life, such as his heartiness with men, his appreciation of rough humor, his love of good drink and food and games, his car, his radio, everything that is his, that bears his emblem of the gaudy seed-bearer. He sizes women up at a glance, with sexual classifications, crude images flashing into his mind and determining the way he smiles at them.

My energy is very masculine and my physical/psychological center is in my pelvis, or sex. I have a "can do" attitude. I get what I want and I am eager and able to fight for it.

During the Second World War, I was a Master Sergeant in the Engineers' Corps. I was decorated for bravery. I was responsible for my outfit. I still feel in charge of my men, my friends. Mitch was under my command in the army.

I enjoy being challenged, but I hate being cheated or proven wrong. In any competition, I must be the winner, especially in my own home. When I am challenged and threatened with loss, I become dangerous. I am very vulnerable and easily hurt, but I hide my vulnerability by becoming destructive and dangerous. No one will ever hurt me and get away with it. I cannot become weak by being vulnerable.

When I realize Blanche is trying to destroy my marriage and ruin my home, and especially after she ridicules me to Stella, calling me an ape and making me feel like an animal, I know I must destroy her. I am ready to kill. I am on the prowl. I must discover "Who is this broad?"

In our first meeting, Blanche gives me the impression she is sexually available to me. I suspect she is a drinker and test this theory when I examine the whiskey bottle. In the next scene, I learn from Stella that Blanche has lost Belle Reve and possibly cheated me out of my share of the plantation. In Scene Three, Blanche's entrance disrupts my poker game. She is distracting, especially to Mitch. She flirts with him. I am jealous. Her constant flirtations and intrusions cause me to lose my temper. Stella calls me an *animal*. I am reduced to the behavior of an ape. Blanche is trying to take Stella away from me. I must get Stella back. I am fighting for my survival, my wife, my child, and my home. The war is on! I must destroy my enemy to protect my home.

ACT I, SCENE I: FIRST MEETINGS

Our first impressions of others are often the most important. On stage, actors too often give short shrift to the drama of first meetings. In Act I, scene one, Blanche and Stella see each other for the first time after many years of separation. Their greeting of one another includes recognizing each other and physically responding to the effects of time and experience on their appearances since the last time they were together at Belle Reve. These sisters have aged. Perhaps the last memory each has of the other is from the last stages of their childhood. Stella especially senses in Blanche something tragic, something that Blanche has suffered deeply.

With the first eye contact they make, Stella can already read Blanche's desperate questions. This is not the Blanche she once knew.

This scene also includes the *very* first encounter between Blanche and Stanley. This has more dramatic significance, as the entire action of the rest of the play depends on the physical relationship of these two antagonists. They are the instigators or driving forces behind the action, with Stella unfortunately caught in the middle.

In the opening scene, the challenge for the actor playing Stanley is to include through his sensory skills the physical/sexual awareness he immediately has of Blanche and to respond with the intimidating subtext (which frightens and excites Blanche) saying, "This is my territory. How long are you going to be here?" Blanche, on the other hand, has multiple sensory tasks to explore which conflict with each other. She is both excited and frightened by Stanley's presence. Her immediate sexual attraction for him is in conflict with her need for sanctuary in his home with Stella, her sister. In addition, her romantic pretenses for the idyllic life abandoned at Belle Reve are in conflict with the common environment she has lowered herself to in this poor, working class section of New Orleans.

As preparation for working on the scene, a nonverbal improvisation exploring the heat, both in the muggy temperature of a hot New Orleans evening and in the sexual energy between Blanche and Stanley, is a valuable way to work on the relationship between the two actors playing these roles. The suggestions below are another variation on the touch exercise from Chapter 5 (Experience/Exercise 12). The imagination of the actors and their knowledge of the sensory requirements for the scene might elaborate themselves into a physical score loosely following the first meeting between Blanche and Stanley.

IMPROVISATION: THE FIRST SEXUAL MEETING OF STRANGERS

Objective   To discover the sexual energy between Blanche and Stanley established in the opening scene.

Format   The actors dress in neutral apparel. The space is empty.

1. The actress playing Blanche should prepare by exploring the sensory condition of heat.
2. The actor playing Stanley should prepare by doing a short, invigorating physical workout.
3. Sweating, Stanley runs into the space.
4. Stanley and Blanche see each other.
   a. sizing each other up
   b. giving/receiving sensous signals
5. Stanley and Blanche circle each other.
   a. exploring the tactile desire to touch
   b. cat and mouse game of intimidation
6. Sensing Blanche's desire.
   a. both actors are aware of it

7. Blanche hears a cat scream.
    a. frightened, she jumps into Stanley's arms
    b. they sizzle for a few seconds
8. Stanley throws her to the ground.
    a. rejection, he leaves
9. Blanche explores inner-eye images of Allan.
    a. also explores inner-eye images of Stanley
    b. alternates between the two
10. Blanche explores the sensation of physical illness.
11. The actors dress for their first scene.

Table 14.1 is a breakdown of the first meeting between Blanche and Stanley. The pervading sensory condition of the scene is the New Orleans heat. (This is augmented by the sexual heat between Blanche and Stanley. This energy can also be stimulated by the heat/sweat-smell of Stanley's body.) This sexual/sensory condition is in conflict with Blanche's overall intention, her need to win Stanley's friendship in order to secure a home. Stanley's instincts are driven by his curiosity to know "Who is this broad?" My title for the scene is "Casing Each Other Out" or "Cat and Mouse Game."

Table 14.1 *A STREETCAR NAMED DESIRE*, ACT I, SCENE I

Text	Action/Subtext/Intention	Sensory Tasks
[*Drawing involuntarily back from his stare.*]	Stanley stares at Blanche.	
BLANCHE: You must be Stanley. I'm Blanche.	Introduces herself.	Feeling the heat.
STANLEY: Stella's sister?	Questions/recognizes.	
BLANCHE: Yes.	Blanche advances slowly.	
STANLEY: H'lo. Where's the little woman?	Greeting/questions.	Image of Stella—wife/lover.
BLANCHE: In the bathroom.	Answers.	
STANLEY: Oh. Didn't know you were coming to town.	*Subtext:* "What is she doing here?"	
BLANCHE: I—uh—	Attempting response.	Blanche aware of Stanley physically; staring at his body.
STANLEY: Where you from, Blanche?		
BLANCHE: Why, I—live in Laurel.	*Subtext:* "What does he know?"	Image of Laurel; fear of being discovered; scandal. Stanley: thirst, desire to relax. Blanche: conflicting desire for alcohol, need for control
[*He has crossed to the closet and removed the whiskey bottle.*]		
STANLEY: In Laurel, huh? Oh, yeah. Yeah, in Laurel, that's right. Not in my territory. Liquor goes fast in hot weather.	Making conversation/examining bottle.	

[He holds the bottle to the light to observe its depletion.]	Subtext: "Who's been drinking out of this bottle?"	
Have a shot?	Testing Blanche/pours a drink.	
BLANCHE: No, I—rarely touch it.	Lying; trying to convince.	Need for alcohol.
STANLEY: Some people rarely touch it, but it touches them often.	Drinking whiskey; infers with joke that Blanche is a drinker.	
BLANCHE: Ha-ha.	Blanche denies need with a laugh.	Blanche has cold hands.
STANLEY: My clothes're stickin' to me. Do you mind if I make myself comfortable?	Playing sexual game.	
[He starts to remove his shirt.]	Subtext: "She is impressed with my body."	Blanche aware of Stanley physically; has difficulty breathing; sensing smell of his sweat.
BLANCHE: Please, please do.		
STANLEY: Be comfortable is my motto.		Sees his body.
BLANCHE: It's mine, too. It's hard to stay looking fresh. I haven't washed or even powdered my face and —here you are!	Overcoming attraction; putting cologne-soaked handkerchief to face	
STANLEY: You know you can catch cold sitting around in damp things, especially when you been exercising hard like bowling is. You're a teacher, aren't you?	Sizing up her response; makes excuses for his nakedness. Changes subject.	Aware of sexual energy.

(continued)

185

Table 14.1 (Cont'd)

Text	Action/Subtext/Intention	Sensory Tasks
BLANCHE: Yes.		
STANLEY: What do you teach, Blanche?	Curious.	
BLANCHE: English.	Answers.	
STANLEY: I never was a very good English student. How long you here for, Blanche?	Dismissing/direct question.	
BLANCHE: I——don't know yet.	*Subtext:* "No place to go."	Fear, uncomfortable physically; feels the heat.
STANLEY: You going to shack up here?	*Tactic:* Checking her out.	
BLANCHE: I thought I would if it's not inconvenient for you all.		
STANLEY: Good.	Positive response. *Subtext:* "Not for long."	
BLANCHE: Traveling wears me out.	Desire to be alone.	Fatigue.
STANLEY: Well, take it easy.	Excuses himself from her.	
[A cat screeches near the window. Blanche springs up.]		Startled by cat's screech, involuntarily touches Stanley.
BLANCHE: What's that?	Recovering from touch.	
STANLEY: Cats . . . Hey, Stella!	Jokes.	Needs Stella: wife/lover.

[Faintly, from the bathroom]

STELLA: Yes, Stanley.

STANLEY: Haven't fallen in, have you?

[He grins at Blanche. She tries unsuccessfully to smile back. There is a silence.]

Crude joke to impress Blanche.

Blanche and Stanley aware of each other.

I'm afraid I'll strike you as being the unrefined type. Stella's spoke of you a good deal. You were married once, weren't you?

Image of Allan.

Challenge/apology.

Curious; wants to know about why her husband didn't stick around.

[The music of the polka rises up, faint in the distance.]

BLANCHE: Yes. When I was quite young.

Image of Allan's face at Moon Lake Casino; hears her words, "I know! I saw! You disgust me!"

STANLEY: What happened?

BLANCHE: The boy—the boy died.

[She sinks back down.]

Trying to maintain strength.

I'm afraid I'm—going to be sick!

Impulse to be sick to stomach.

[Her head falls on her arms.]

187

Multiple Sensory Conditions

By Scene Four, when the relationship between Stella and Blanche is reaching its first crisis, the sensory conditions inherent in the scene are related directly to the development of their relationship. The presence of Stanley is everywhere. His smell is in the room, in the pajamas lying "across the threshold of the bathroom", in the sheets of the bed (where the scene begins for Stella), and finally in all the reminders of the party from the evening before, especially in the stale beer and cigarette butts. Because Blanche is an alcoholic, the stale beer has a double effect on her.

However, Stanley's presence stimulates very different images and potent responses in these two women, and these individual responses are, of course, at the heart of their conflict. Their physical responses to these sensorial reminders of their needs heighten the tension and complexity of the relationship.

In this scene, Blanche is at a crucial point in her desperate journey for survival. We begin to see her irrational behavior, her compulsive need to wrench her sister away from Stanley, her inability to cope with reality, and her escape into fantasy. The actress playing Blanche is challenged to discover and communicate these needs in a manner that is logical to the character. Blanche does not consider her behavior irrational. She is simply trying to survive.

Stella recognizes shifts in Blanche's personality and behavior, and feels the threat of her sister's attempt to undermine her life with Stanley. Stella must make some pertinent decisions in this scene. Williams gives her a lot of physical activity which includes putting her house (i.e., her priorities) in order. The actress performing this housekeeping activity can establish her need for Stanley, her desire for motherhood and home, and how it is in conflict with her sister's demands. That's where the difficulty for Stella comes in, because she has definite questions and opinions about Blanche's suggestions, hints, and questionable behavior, and yet her inner voice, as she listens to this sister, whom she loves as the only family she has, tells her to behave in a subtle, careful way in dealing with her conflicts with Blanche.

At the end of the scene, Stanley secretly overhears Blanche's harangue and realizes she is trying to take Stella away by destroying his character. With a viper's instinct, Blanche has struck at Stanley's vulnerability by calling him an ape and brute. The challenge for any actor playing Stanley is to be stung by her vicious attack, but upon entering the scene, to mask its effect through gregarious behavior.

Because the relationships between Stella, Stanley, and Blanche have developed into a three-way triangle of sexual complexity, one way to prepare for Scene Four is through an improvisation which explores these physical relationships directly. The silent physical score outlined below offers a possible springboard for an improvisation exploring Blanche's need to coerce Stella away from Stanley, Stella's struggle to secure her life with Stanley, and Stanley's claim on Stella, wanting to sexually pull her out of Blanche's grasp.

Physical/Silent Improvisation: "Who Is the Winner?"

Place   An open, neutral space, with a bench or bed.

1. Stanley and Stella run to greet each other.
   a. They dance.
   b. movements suggesting physical love
   c. lying down on the bench/bed, embracing
2. Blanche enters.
   a. circles the couple
   b. wants to touch Stanley
   c. wants to drag Stella out of bed
3. Blanche retreats.
4. Stanley kisses Stella, gets up, and leaves.
5. Stella lies comfortably on bench.
   a. recalls sensuous tactile images
6. Blanche re-enters.
   a. embraces Stella
   b. continues to cling to Stella
7. Stella gets out of bed.
8. Blanche follows Stella.
   a. The tug of war starts as Blanche tries to coerce/drag Stella out of her space.
9. Stanley re-enters.
   a. He watches.
10. Stella runs into Stanley's arms.
11. Blanche pulling on Stella
12. Stella pushes Blanche.
   a. Rejection
13. Stanley lifts Stella and carries her to the bed.
   a. Blanche watches Stanley and Stella.

What's Before?

Another area of preparation necessary to working successfully on Scene Four is to investigate the sensorial echoes of the evening before. Rehearsing the entire play will give some of this to the actors, but especially in the case of Tennessee Williams as playwright, images from a previous scene often exert a strong affect on the following sensory life of the characters and should be actively nurtured to feed the emotional life which follows.

At the end of Scene Three, after Stella returns to Stanley in the night, Blanche "slips fearfully down the steps" and "stops before the dark entrance of her sister's flat." The acting version and the published version differ slightly in their specific directions here, but both ascribe a reaction to Blanche and my interpretation of what she sees/hears through that door is Stanley and Stella having intercourse. When Blanche enters in Scene Four and sits on the bed with Stella, she carries those sight and sound images with her.

Some questions the actress playing Blanche should therefore consider are:

1. Does Blanche want to go to bed with Stanley?
2. Is Blanche aware that she is jealous of Stella?
3. Either consciously or subconsciously (that is through her behavior), does Blanche admit these feelings?

My feeling is that Blanche realizes her emotional needs, but she has difficulty coping with them. She pushes them away, to focus her energy on her main intention—to persuade Stella to leave Stanley. Inside, with each sensorial distraction, she keeps saying "I must wrench my sister away from Stanley, from this apartment. We both must escape."

As with Scene One, Table 14.2 is a breakdown of Scene Four, listing the "Action Subtext Intention" and "Sensory Tasks" suggested by the script and the conditions of the scene. The breakdown is an outline of the rehearsal objectives. Once the scene has been rehearsed, the actors do not have time to be aware of their homework, that is, actors should not be conscious of choices or conditions, their sensory responses arise involuntarily as a result of the rehearsal process. When actors are in the performance of a scene, they must concentrate on hearing/seeing each other. Everything else is a plus.

Table 14.2   *A STREETCAR NAMED DESIRE*, ACT I, SCENE IV

Text	Action/Subtext/Intention	Sensory Tasks
It is early the following morning. There is a confusion of street cries like a choral chant.		Early morning in New Orleans. The temperature is warm (it gets warmer throughout the scene).
Stella is lying down in the bedroom. Her face is serene in the early morning sunlight. One hand rests on her belly, rounding slightly with new maternity. From the other dangles a book of colored comics. Her eyes and lips have that almost narcotized tranquility that is in the faces of Eastern idols.	Stroking baby.	Smell of Stanley in bed. Inner-eye images of him at peace with motherhood and being loved.
The table is sloppy with remains of breakfast and the debris of the preceding night, and Stanley's gaudy pyjamas lie across the threshold of the bathroom. The outside door is slightly ajar on a sky of summer brilliance.		
Blanche appears at this door. She has spent a sleepless night and her appearance entirely contrasts with Stella's. She presses her knuckles nervously to her lips as she looks through the door, before entering.	Blanche invades Stella's space.	Blanche's psychological center is in her sex. Cold hands.
BLANCHE: Stella?	Checking: "Is Stanley home?"	
STELLA: *[stirring lazily]* Hmmmh?		

(continued)

191

Table 14.2 (Cont'd)

Text	Action/Subtext/Intention	Sensory Tasks
[*Blanche utters a moaning cry and runs into the bedroom, throwing herself down beside Stella in a rush of hysterical tenderness.*]		
BLANCHE: Baby, my baby sister!	To be a loving sister. To protect/console Stella.	Touching Stella.
STELLA: [*drawing away from her*] Blanche, what is the matter with you?	Rejecting Blanche's touch. Cannot understand her behavior	
[*Blanche straightens up slowly and stands beside the bed looking down at her sister with knuckles pressed to her lips.*]	To overcome her anxiousness.	Blanche has image of Stanley —what she saw/heard last night at poker game; cold hands.
BLANCHE: He's left?		
STELLA: Stan? Yes.		
BLANCHE: Will he be back?	*Subtext:* "Will it be safe?"	Tactile: body needs to know.
STELLA: He's gone to get the car greased. Why?	Explains.	
BLANCHE: Why! I've been half-crazy, Stella! When I found out you'd been insane enough to come back in here	Beginning attack on Stella.	Chill; hands cold. Image of night before— their love-making.
after what happened—I started to rush in after you!		
STELLA: I'm glad you didn't.		Stella has image of Stanley making love with her.
BLANCHE: What were you thinking of?	Accusation.	

[Stella makes an indefinite gesture.]	Stella doesn't want to explain.
Answer me! What? What?	Older sister attitude, demanding.
STELLA: Please, Blanche! Sit down and stop yelling.	Trying to calm Blanche. / Blanche's voice irritating to Stella.
BLANCHE: All right, Stella. I will repeat the question quietly now. How could you come back in this place last night? Why, you must have slept with him!	To control emotions. / Slower tempo. Accusation/outrage. / Image of sex.
[Stella gets up in a calm and leisurely way.]	To get away from Blanche; calm rejection.
STELLA: Blanche, I'd forgotten how excitable you are. You're making much too much fuss about this.	Image of Blanche as a girl.
BLANCHE: Am I?	Trying to control self.
STELLA: Yes, you are, Blanche. I know how it must have seemed to you and I'm awful sorry it had to happen, but it wasn't anything as serious as you seem to take it. In the first place, when men are drinking and playing poker anything can happen. It's always a powder-keg. He didn't know what he was doing.... He was as good as a lamb when I came back and he's really very, very ashamed of himself.	To calm Blanche. Trying to be rational with an irrational person. / Blanche has cold hands. Stella has image of tender Stanley.
BLANCHE: And that—that makes it all right?	Defending her lover. Rejecting.

(continued)

193

Table 14.2 (Cont'd)

Text	Action/Subtext/Intention	Sensory Tasks
STELLA: No, it isn't all right for anybody to make such a terrible row, but—people do sometimes. Stanley's always smashed things. Why, on our wedding night—soon as we came in here—he snatched off one of my slippers and rushed about the place smashing the light-bulbs with it.		Memory of wedding night and first sense of own sensuality.
BLANCHE: He did—*what?*	Disbelief; outrage.	
STELLA: He smashed all the light-bulbs with the heel of my slipper!		Sound of light bulbs smashing.
[*She laughs.*]		
BLANCHE: And you—you *let* him? Didn't *run*, didn't *scream?*	Covering feelings with anger.	
STELLA: I was—sort of thrilled by it.		Remembering first orgasm.
[*She waits for a moment.*]	Realizing Blanche doesn't understand.	Psychological distance grows between them
Eunice and you had breakfast?	Tactic: changing subject.	
BLANCHE: Do you suppose I wanted any breakfast?	Continuing to reproach.	
STELLA: There's some coffee left on the stove.		
BLANCHE: You're so—matter of fact about it, Stella.	Can't understand/won't understand. Has never felt the way Stella feels.	

(continued)

STELLA: What other can I be? He's taken the radio to get it fixed. It didn't land on the pavement so only one tube was smashed.	Amused love for Stanley.
BLANCHE: And you are standing there smiling!	Seeing her love for Stanley.
STELLA: What do you want me to do?	Making a joke. Amused by it all,
BLANCHE: Pull yourself together and face the facts.	Condemning.
STELLA: What are they in your opinion?	Direct question.
BLANCHE: In my opinion? You're married to a madman!	Gently must discover what Blanche thinks/feels.
STELLA: No!	Direct approach, to debase Stanley.
BLANCHE: Yes, you are, your fix is worse than mine is! Only you're not being sensible about it. I'm going to *do* something. Get hold of myself and make myself a new life!	Rejects Blanche's opinion.
STELLA: Yes?	Attempting to be rational, to calm her sensations; beginning plan of escape.
BLANCHE: But you've given in. And that isn't right, you're not old! You can get out.	*Subtext: "How?"*
STELLA: [*slowly and emphatically*] I'm not in anything I want to get out of.	Direct approach to scene's main objective.
	Making Blanche understand "This is my space. I am Stanley's wife; he is my husband."

195

Table 14.2 (Cont'd)

Text	Action/Subtext/Intention	Sensory Tasks
BLANCHE: [*incredulously*] What—Stella?		Hearing rejection with inner ear.
STELLA: I said I am not in anything that I have a desire to get out of. Look at the mess in this room! And those empty bottles! They went through two cases last night. He promised this morning that he was going to quit having these poker parties, but you know how long such a promise is going to keep. Oh, well, it's his pleasure, like mine is movies and bridge. People have got to tolerate each other's habits, I guess.	Putting my house in order. *Action:* housecleaning. *Subtext:* "This is my home." Defending the contract of their relationship/marriage	Inner-eye image of Stanley.
BLANCHE: I don't understand you.	Trying to understand.	
[*Stella turns toward her.*]	Stella gives attention directly to Blanche; leaves off housework, momentarily.	
I don't understand your indifference. Is this a Chinese philosophy you've—cultivated?	Ridicule.	
STELLA: Is what—what?		
BLANCHE: This—shuffling about and mumbling—'One tube smashed—beer-bottles—mess in the kitchen!'—as if nothing out of the ordinary has happened!		Blanche has difficulty breathing.
[*Stella laughs uncertainly and picking up the broom, twirls it in her hands.*]	Returns to housework.	Stella's tool of protection.

Dialogue	Beat	Subtext
Are you deliberately shaking that thing in my face?	Challenging.	Feeling threatened.
STELLA: No.	Denial.	
BLANCHE: Stop it. Let go of that broom. I won't have you cleaning up for him!	Rejecting Stella's home object.	Image of Stanley.
STELLA: Then who's going to do it? Are you?	Challenging: "You want to take over?"	
BLANCHE: I? I!	Hysterical questions; senses she has lost.	Cold hands.
STELLA: No, I didn't think so.	Stella returns to housecleaning.	
BLANCHE: Oh, let me think, if only my mind would function! We've got to get hold of some money, that's the way out!	Mind confused by battle, need for new tactic: return to throughline; to get Stella to leave Stanley.	Head throbbing.
STELLA: I guess that money is always nice to get hold of.	Noncommittal agreement.	
BLANCHE: Listen to me. I have an idea of some kind.	Transition: new intention in plan to escape;separating Stella from Stanley.	
[Shakily she twists a cigarette into her holder.]		Need for nicotine; to calm self.
Do you remember Shep Huntleigh?	Question.	
[Stella shakes her head.]		Inner-eye image of Shep.

(continued)

197

Table 14.2 (Cont'd)

Text	Action/Subtext/Intention	Sensory Tasks
BLANCHE: Of course you remember Shep Huntleigh. I went out with him at college and wore his pin for a while. Well—	Tactic: trying to make Stella remember; to participate with her in the plan.	
STELLA: Well?	Mildly interested; continues cleaning her home.	Smell of home/Stanley.
BLANCHE: I ran into him last winter. You know I went to Miami during the Christmas holidays?		
STELLA: No.		
BLANCHE: Well, I did. I took the trip as an investment, thinking I'd meet someone with a million dollars.	Tempo changing, becoming faster.	Feeling warm.
STELLA: Did you?	Interested, urging Blanche on; hoping it is true. Inner monologue: "Perhaps this is a way to get rid of Blanche."	
BLANCHE: Yes. I ran into Shep Huntleigh—I ran into him on Biscayne Boulevard, on Christmas Eve, about dusk . . . getting into his car—Cadillac convertible; must have been a block long!	Faster tempo.	Blanche has clear image of Shep and the meeting; excited by the possibility of money.
STELLA: I should think it would have been—inconvenient in traffic!	Making a joke.	
BLANCHE: You've heard of oil-wells?		

STELLA: Yes—remotely.

Stella not sure she believes Blanche, but wants to.

BLANCHE: He has them, all over Texas. Texas is literally spouting gold in his pockets.

Blanche informing Stella of opportunity, trying to entice her.

STELLA: My, my.

BLANCHE: Y'know how indifferent I am to money. I think of money in terms of what it does for you. But he could do it, he could certainly do it!

Image of Shep giving them money = dream of security.

STELLA: Do what, Blanche?

Trying to understand Blanche; realizing she lives in fantasy.

BLANCHE: Why—set us up in a—shop!

Reveals dream.

STELLA: What kind of a shop?

Probing to understand Blanche.

BLANCHE: Oh, a—shop of some kind! He could do it with half what his wife throws away at the races.

Image of Shep's wife throwing away money.

Realizing Blanche is on a fantasy.

STELLA: He's married?

Making a joke.

BLANCHE: Honey, would I be here if the man weren't married?

New tactic: action of pursuing dream

[*Stella laughs a little. Blanche suddenly springs up and crosses to phone. She speaks shrilly.*]

Hearing Stella's laugh. Physical transition; hysterical.

How do I get Western Union?—Operator! Western Union!

(continued)

199

Table 14.2 (Cont'd)

Text	Action/Subtext/Intention	Sensory Tasks
STELLA: That's a dial phone, honey.	Sensing Blanche's panic.	
BLANCHE: I can't dial, I'm too—	Feeling she is losing.	Blanche has ice-cold hands.
STELLA: Just dial O.	Attempting to calm Blanche.	
BLANCHE: O?		
STELLA: Yes, "O" for Operator!	Explaining.	
[Blanche considers a moment; then she puts the phone down.]		
BLANCHE: Give me a pencil. Where is a slip of paper? I've got to write it down first—the message, I mean . . .	Overcoming panic; new tactic.	
	Trying to control hysteria.	
[She goes to the dressing table, and grabs up a sheet of Kleenex and an eyebrow pencil for writing equipment.]	To present a controlled front.	
Let me see now . . .		
[She bites the pencil.]		
BLANCHE: "Darling Shep. Sister and I in desperate situation."	To include Stella in plan.	Image of Stanley.
STELLA: I beg your pardon!	Subtext: "What the hell are you talking about?"	

BLANCHE: "Sister and I in desperate situation. Will explain details later. Would you be interested in—?"	Insisting on including Stella. Hoping for Stella's help in writing note.
[*She smashes the pencil on the table and springs up.*]	Fingers not working. Hands cold.
You never get anywhere with direct appeals!	Realizes rejection.
STELLA: [*with a laugh*] Don't be so ridiculous, darling!	Need for new tactic. Getting hot.
BLANCHE: But I'll think of something, I've got to think of—*something!* Don't don't laugh at me, Stella! Please, please don't—I—I want you to look at the contents of my purse! Here's what's in it!	Trying to find a way to escape. Reveals vulnerability, need for money. Body hears Stella's laughter. Head throbbing.
[*She snatches her purse open.*]	
Sixty-five measly cents in coin of the realm!	
STELLA: [*crossing to bureau*] Stanley doesn't give me a regular allowance, he likes to pay bills himself, but—this morning he gave me ten dollars to smooth things over. You take five of it, Blanche, and I'll keep the rest.	Sharing what Stanley gives her. Offering to help.
BLANCHE: Oh, no. No, Stella.	Cannot depend on Stanley. Image of Stanley.
STELLA: [*insisting*] I know how it helps your morale just having a little pocket-money on you.	Trying to understand.
BLANCHE: No, thank you—I'll take to the streets!	Feeling dirty/soiled.

(continued)

Table 14.2 (Cont'd)

	Text	Action/Subtext/Intention	Sensory Tasks
STELLA:	Talk sense! How did you happen to get so low on funds?	Stella: new tactic, questions Blanche to uncover reality.	Image of Belle Reve.
BLANCHE:	Money just goes—it goes places.		
	[She rubs her forehead.]		Throbbing headache; needs alcohol, losing control.
BLANCHE:	Sometime today I've got to get hold of a bromo!	Avoids explanation.	
STELLA:	I'll fix you one now.	Trying to help Blanche.	
BLANCHE:	Not yet—I've got to keep thinking!	Rejection of help.	
STELLA:	I wish you'd just let things go, at least for a—while . . .	Trying to comfort Blanche.	Desire to hold Blanche, hug her.
BLANCHE:	Stella, I can't live with him! You can, he's your husband. But how could I stay here with him, after last night, with just those curtains between us?	*Subtext:* strong feelings for Stanley, trying to overcome them.	Hearing/seeing their love-making. Blanche's tactile need.
STELLA:	Blanche, you saw him at his worst last night.	Not understanding Blanche's fear.	
BLANCHE:	On the contrary, I saw him at his best! What such a man has to offer is animal force and he gave a wonderful exhibition of that! But the only way to live with such a man is to—go to bed with him! And that's your job—not mine!	Vehemently rejects	Repulsed; sick to stomach.
		Angry/jealous; the truth slips out.	
STELLA:	After you've rested a little, you'll see it's going to work out. You don't have to worry about anything while you're here. I mean—expenses . . .	Stella in conflict, trying to hang on to priorities, trying to reassure Blanche.	Lower region very energized.

202

BLANCHE: I have to plan for us both, to get us both—out!	Return to throughline: needs Stella to join with her.	
STELLA: You take it for granted that I am in something that I want to get out of.	Rejection of Blanche.	
BLANCHE: I take it for granted that you still have sufficient memory of Belle Reve to find this place and these poker players impossible to live with.	Reminds Stella of Belle Reve to make her feel guilty.	
STELLA: Well, you're taking entirely too much for granted.		Images of Belle Reve and relatives she rejected.
BLANCHE: I can't believe you're in earnest.	Frozen to spot.	
STELLA: No?	Direct.	
BLANCHE: I understand how it happened—a little. You saw him in uniform, an officer, not here but—	Tactic: trying a rational approach.	
STELLA: I'm not sure it would have made any difference where I saw him.	Trying to make Blanche understand about love.	Image of Stanley.
BLANCHE: Now don't say it was one of those mysterious electric things between people! If you do I'll laugh in your face.	Vicious attack.	Image of Stanley.
STELLA: I am not going to say anything more at all about it!	Rejecting Blanche.	Sense of heat, from the work.

(continued)

203

Table 14.2 (Cont'd)

Text	Action/Subtext/Intention	Sensory Tasks
BLANCHE: All right, then don't!	Rejection.	
STELLA: But there are things that happen between a man and a woman in the dark—that sort of make everything else seem—unimportant.	Tactic: to teach Blanche about intimate sexual love—it is beautiful, not dirty.	Tactile sense of sex with Stanley. Lower region energized with images of Stanley and the unborn baby.
[*Pause*].		Uncomfortable silence between them.
BLANCHE: What you are talking about is brutal desire—just Desire!—the name of that rattle-trap street-car that bangs through the Quarter, up one old narrow street and down another . . .	Fighting own desires. Tactic: verbal slamming = quick tempo.	Body energized with images of sex. Sense of being out of control. Sense of being dirty.
STELLA: Haven't you ever ridden on that street-car?	Question which gently suggests Blanche can't understand because she doesn't know what real love is.	
BLANCHE: It brought me here.—Where I'm not wanted and where I'm ashamed to be . . .	Attacks Stella while playing the martyr. Tactic: to make Stella feel sorry for me.	Feels dirty.
STELLA: Then don't you think your superior attitude is a bit out of place?	Challenging.	

BLANCHE: I am not being or feeling at all superior, Stella. Believe me I'm not! It's just this. This is how I look at it. A man like that is someone to go out with—once—twice—three times when the devil is in you. But live with? Have a child by?

Images of her life of sexual activity.

STELLA: I have told you I love him.

Entire body energized with love.

Subtext: jealous of Stella.

BLANCHE: Then I *tremble* for you! I just—*tremble* for you . . .

Beginning of peak of crisis = desperately trying to make Blanche understand.

Subtext: "I am losing the battle."

STELLA: I can't help your trembling if you insist on trembling!

Fear of the unknown; hands cold.

Heat of the fight.

[*There is a pause.*]

Rejection.

Spine, groin, and total body energized.

BLANCHE: May I—speak—plainly?

Blanche preparing to play final trump card against Stanley/Stella finishes housecleaning; asks permission.

STELLA: Yes, do. Go ahead. As plainly as you want to.

Stella confronting Blanche.

[*Outside, a train approaches. They are silent till the noise subsides. They are both in the bedroom.*]

Body energized by the rhythm of the train and whistle/can't bear the sound.
Bed = Stanley, his smell, his sexuality.

(continued)

Table 14.2 (Cont'd)

Text	Action/Subtext/Intention	Sensory Tasks
[*Under cover of the train's noise Stanley enters from outside. He stands unseen by the women, holding some packages in his arms, and overhears their following conversation. He wears an undershirt and grease-stained seersucker pants.*]		Stanley recognizes Blanche's voice, realizes the conversation is about himself.
BLANCHE: Well—if you'll forgive me—he's *common!*	Playing her trump card.	
STELLA: Why, yes, I suppose he is.	Endorses Stanley.	Body instinctively responds; likes him that way.
BLANCHE: Suppose! You can't have forgotten that much of our bringing up, Stella, that you just *suppose* that any part of a gentleman's in his nature! *Not one particle, no!* Oh, if he was just—*ordinary!* Just *plain*—but good and wholesome, but—*no.* There's something downright—*bestial*—about him! You're hating me saying this, aren't you?	To make Stella feel guilty.

Blanche needs to prove Stanley is not good enough for her little sister. | Stanley hears himself degraded into a beast.
Blanche senses Stella's physical response. |
| **STELLA:** [*coldly*] Go on and say it all, Blanche. | | |
| **BLANCHE:** He acts like an animal, has an animal's habits! Eats like one, moves like one, talks like one! There's even something—subhuman—something not quite to the stage of humanity yet! Yes, something—apelike about him, like one of those pictures I've seen in—anthropological studies! Thousands and thousands of | Tempo quickening | Blanche overpowered by images of Stanley and animal feelings.

Images of dark bestial power. |

years have passed him right by, and there he is—Stanley Kowalski—survivor of the stone age! Bearing the raw meat home from the kill in the jungle! and you—*you here*—*waiting* for him! Maybe he'll strike you or maybe grunt and kiss you! That is, if kisses have been discovered yet! Night falls and the other apes gather! There in front of the cave, all grunting like him, and swilling and gnawing and hulking! His poker night!—you call it—this party of apes! Somebody growls—some creature snatches at something—the fight is on! *God!* Maybe we are a long way from being made in God's image, but Stella—my sister—there has been *some* progress since then! Such things as art—as poetry and music—such kinds of new light have come into the world since then! In some kinds of people some tenderer feelings have had some little beginning! That we have got to make *grow!* And *cling* to, and hold as our flag! In this dark march toward whatever it is we're approaching. . . . *Don't—don't hang back with the brutes!*

[*Another train passes outside. Stanley hesitates, licking his lips. Then suddenly he turns stealthily about and withdraws through front door. The women are still unaware of his presence. When the train has passed he calls through the closed front door.*]

STANLEY: Hey! Hey, Stella!

Stanley is dangerous; fear of the unknown.

Stella has images of Stanley's violent streak. Blanche arouses self; dirty images. Visual and aural images of the poker night. Inner-eye images of fight.

Must make Stella see the images; make her feel dirty/common as well.

Blanche gets physically close with Stella.

Transition: gentler.

Blanche's truth = her battle cry.

Stanley has heard enough = feels bestial, must not be discovered. Climax of scene = train whistle = call for action which increases Blanche's sensations.

Stanley's tactic: to act innocent.

Stanley: inner rage. Blanche alerted to Stanley's presence (intake of breath).

(*continued*)

Table 14.2 (Cont'd)

Text	Action/Subtext/Intention	Sensory Tasks
STELLA: [who has listened gravely to Blanche] Stanley!	Answering Stanley's call, Stella leaves Blanche.	
BLANCHE: Stell, I—	Blanche needs a response from Stella.	
[But Stella has gone to the front door. Stanley enters casually with his packages.]		Stella between Stanley and Blanche.
STANLEY: Hiyuh, Stella. Blanche back?		
STELLA: Yes, she's back.		
STANLEY: Hiyuh, Blanche.	Subtext: playing a game.	
[He grins at her.]	Subtext: "I know what you are. You are the enemy."	Blanche has cold hands.
STELLA: You must've got under the car.	Blanche asks herself "What will Stella do? Did I win?"	Stella sees what she likes = Stanley.
STANLEY: Them darn mechanics at Fritz's don't know their ass fr'm—Hey!		

	Blanche sees love between Stella and Stanley; feel ng sick, Blanche is lost, rejectec, and alone.
[Stella has embraced him with both arms, fiercely, and full in the view of Blanche. He laughs and clasps her head to him. Over her head he grins through the curtains at Blanche.]	Stella rejects Blanche, embraces Stanley. *Subtext: "I've won."*
[As the lights fade away, wfith a lingering brightness on their embrace, the music of the "blue piano" and trumpet and drums is heard.]	

Discovering the Overall Sensory Condition

Sometimes an actor can be engulfed by a role such as Blanche where there are multiple conflicting sensory needs of overwhelming intensity. When there is such a wealth of sensory work, personalizing all the behavioral factors can be difficult. An actor becomes lost in the many physical and psychological demands of the role. When this happens and an actor is unable to sufficiently develop a sensorial kinesthetic throughline, either in a scene or in his/her journey through the entire play, I recommend an approach I call the *overall sensory condition* (or the "OSC").

Developing an OSC involves discovering a sensory condition lodged in the actors' Pandora's Box which is somehow appropriate to the psychological center of the role and can serve as a link between all the demands of the role. The choice is not made at random. The actor must have invested time in researching the text, the subtext, the many and various sensorial demands suggested by the playwright, and the actor must have been allowed to explore all the sensorial life and relationships in rehearsal. These are prerequisite to choosing an OSC. In other words, the actor must have a thorough and intimate connection with the role he/she is playing.

Having looked with some detail at the requirements for playing Blanche in two scenes from *Streetcar,* we have a good opportunity to explore how an OSC is chosen and used.

Blanche is a complicated role, psychologically. She is an alcoholic and a nymphomaniac. Continually on edge, fighting all her ghosts, Blanche is in trouble. She is hot. She feels dirty. She needs sex. She needs a drink. She needs a hot bath to calm her. She is never totally calm. The actor creating this role discovers all these challenges in the text, the subtext, and the given sensorial conditions of the play.

Because Tennessee Williams gives the actor so much to work with, after exploring each separate condition or need in rehearsal, the actor creating Blanche will benefit from using one overall sensory condition to focus her energy. In the case of Blanche, the sensory condition I recommend is an itch, an itch in the lower regions of the body, an itch that cannot be scratched. An itch is an irritating sensation. Imagining and believing in an itch will heighten the physical and emotional conditions in each moment. Blanche would not allow herself to scratch in public, therefore all her frustrations and needs will become more intense, that is, more neurotic.

Using the overall sensory condition is a process that is explored in rehearsal and not in performance. Directors should note that the actor must be allowed to explore this sensory condition to its fullest extreme. At first, it might seem that the itch will become the role, but the actor must be allowed to explore its ability to stimulate her behavior fully. Eventually, the itch will internalize itself and the actor will have discovered a physical behavior that automatically stimulates need. The overt sensation of the itch will disappear, even while its stimulation of a behavior remains.

As always, the actor must continue to ask those basic questions of character and motivation which address the requirements of the script and of the particular director's vision. It is important to remember that the performance is not about the sensory condition, but about Blanche's life, that is, her needs. The overall sensory condition must not take over the role, but enhance it, heightening the ability to see, hear, and respond in the moment.

In the case of Blanche, when the itch is used as the overall sensory condition, it modulates all the other sensory conditions of the scene. Physical/psychological transitions occur when the energy center moves out of Blanche's groin into the other parts of her body, as in her need for a Bromo (her throbbing headache), her need for alcohol, her cold hands, the New Orleans heat, the smell of Stanley, the screech of a cat, the loud whistle of a train, the haunting polka of the Moon Lake Casino, the images of Allan, her need for nicotine (cigarettes), her difficulty breathing, her continual hot baths, and finally her sullied response to the French Quarter of New Orleans, as well as the remembrance of her sexual experiences in the Flamingo Hotel. Transitions from the itch to each of these conditions as they come up in the scene, and then back to the itch of her sexuality, give Blanche her particular rhythm, as well as focus the throughline of her kinesthetic sensory life.

Again, it is important to note that an actor does not begin his/her investigation of the role by choosing an overall sensory condition. The OSC will arise sometimes as a natural consequence, sometimes through the need to focus the psychological life of a role, but only after extensive rehearsal and exploration. Other examples of OSCs might be: extreme hunger, a nauseating smell, itchy feet, toes, and fingers, a very bad sunburn, or any condition that stimulates physical discomfort. For the experienced actor in the long run of a successful play, I sometimes recommend incorporating an OSC to keep the role fresh and interesting for the performer. But as I stated earlier, the condition should be explored first in a rehearsal situation, and then incorporated at the actor's discretion into the performance.

The ability to use an OSC is a complicated process and the test of an actor who has fully developed his/her sensory abilities.

Epilogue

When I sat down to write this book, I think I envisioned something different in form and content than what was finally arrived at. The act of writing demands a kind of explicit definition which can negate the true process of sensorial acting. Several times, in re-reading the text, I found myself uncomfortable with the "analysis" of the process. A clinical approach to solving the acting issues of beats, intentions, subtext, and sensory life paralyzes the instinctive actor. I don't want to deny the value or importance of this type of work—it has been my life's study—but it is important to remember that actors cannot do their homework on stage. It is the premise of this book that the actor must ask about and explore beat intentions, sensory conditions, and the throughline of a role before walking into a scene. This is the only way to successfully allow kinesthetic responses to take over when exploring in rehearsal. In training, an actor must learn to trust his/her kinesthetic, sensorial responses. This opens up the technique, incorporates good vocal and physical work into the process as well, and allows the actor to come on stage and simply "be" the role. A sensorial actor's *behavior* will subscribe naturally to telling the story of the play.

The process is to prepare. The performance is just do it.

In real life, we often don't know why we react in the way we do. We just react. Characters, too, often don't know why they respond physically/emotionally in a scene, even if the actor playing that role does. But the process of organic responses frees an actor to be in-the-moment, rather than in the head or anticipating the whys and wherefores of any motivation. The body's kinesthetic responses stimulate the imagination to a much more effective result than vice versa.

If an actor anticipates "choices," "beats," "intentions"—all those catch phrases of trained actors—then we see an actor playing "choices" rather than inhabiting a believable, instinctive, creative life. Choices are destructive, if that's what we see. And for an actor, they can too easily become set in concrete; they can too easily become safe. They evade the dangerous mystery of unanticipated, unexpected, instinctive responses.

Knowing your intentions is good, but you cannot overtly play an intention. How interesting can that get? Ask yourself about seeing, and hearing, and touching, and wanting to touch. These actions will inform you about the character's needs and desires, as well as focus your technique as an actor.

What I am ultimately advocating after all the analysis, after all of the sensory homework, after all the rehearsing, is a style of acting (of behavior), that is exciting because it is natural. It is natural because it is instinctive. It is instinctive because it is kinesthetic, sensorially. And it is confident, because the actor is able to relax his/her instrument through a process of trusting the moment. This will lead to a life energized with the electricity of spontaneous responses.

Glossary

actions   Physical, sensorial, and verbal doing.

ambivalent response   (a) Conflict emotions; (b) Feeling more than one emotion at a time.

as if   "Ask yourself: What would I do if the same thing should happen to me as it does to the character I am playing?" (From *Stanislavski's Legacy: Constantin Stanislavski*, edited and translated by Elizabeth Reynolds Hapgood. Published by Theatre Art Books, 1956, page 12.)

auditory image   (a) Hearing a sound in your imagination; (b) a sound sensation that merges with or stimulates inner images from any of the other senses.

beat intention   A need, desire, or purpose which motivates the behavior of a character; as beats meet with conflict or are accomplished, they will immediately segue into a new intention, thereby beginning a new beat.

behavior   What a person physically does or says.

body language   (a) The physical characteristics of a person. and how those characteristics communicate an emotional life; (b) any part of the body that signals a need or desire; (c) a complete sensorial life.

character's journey   The sequence of behavior (including discoveries, changes in motivation, and throughline) from the first entrance of the character, to his/her final moment in the play.

clean slate   Wiping away all past influences. (*See* prejudicial response, and subjective response.)

conflict   Physical/mental/emotional turmoil brought in by two or more opposing responses or needs.

conflict of emotional relationship   Physical/mental/emotional turmoil stimulated in relationships with others; the obstacle is in the relationship.

diaphragm   (a) The partition of muscles and tendons between the chest cavity and the abdominal cavity; (b) the midriff or gut.

discover/uncover   (a) To allow the experience/sensation to stimulate action or emotion; (b) to discover a sensation in response to a condition and then allow that discovery to be uncovered or revealed through physical behavior.

echo of sensation   (a) The sensorial/emotional stimulation that continues in the silence following a response to a particular sound; (b) the sensorial/emotional stimulation that continues to influence behavior.

emotional thermometer   Figuratively speaking, the emotional temperature (sensations.)

energy center(s)   (a) Physical location of a response to some sensory stimulation; (b) the physical area of the body that is energized to create a sensory life.

event   An occurrence or happening.

experience/exercise   Living through an experience in order to stimulate and exercise sensory responses.

experience-through   (a) The actor senses/feels the play from beginning to end; (b) allowing the play to be experienced at its own pace in rehearsal, rather than repeated by rote. (*See* runthrough.)

floater   The unexpected additional person who enters an experience/exercise.

given sensory condition   Sensory conditions stipulated by the script. (*See* sensory task.)

gustatory image   (a) Tasting with your imagination; (b) a taste sensation that merges with or stimulates inner images from any of the other senses.

history   The background of the character or plot; what's before?

impromptu   Responding to the unexpected.

improvisation   (a) Impromptu action in a scenario; (b) a single performance of an experience/exercise that has not been rehearsed.

inner ear   (a) The psychological/creative ear; (b) the inner ear responds creatively/psychologically to all sound, often with a particular behavior; (c) the inner ear responds to the unspoken meaning or the subtext in another's voice.

inner eye   (a) the psychological/creative process of seeing; (b) the inner eye responds creatively/psychologically to all sights, often with a particular behavior.

inner monologue   (a) Stream-of-consciousness in a scene; it is a silent soliloquy that has been rehearsed; (b) the flow of one's thoughts, feelings, and images stimulated in a scenario or in a role.(*See* stream-of-consciousness.)

inner technique   Communicating sensorial, psychological, and emotional sensations on cue, usually through behavior.

intention   A need or desire communicated through physical and verbal action: each intention can have several tactics by which it is accomplished.

in-the-moment   (a) Being in the now or present; (b) a sequence of doing it now.

intuition   instinct.

involuntary   (a) A spontaneous response, often from a physical impulse; (b) a fresh response.

journal   The actor's private diary.

kinesthetic memory   (a) The involuntary remembering of an event; (b) the physical location of sensation when remembering an event.

kinesthetic response   A spontaneous physical response to a sensorial/psychological condition.

kinesthetic throughline   The involuntary flow of sensorial behavior from moment to moment in a character's life.

language experience viscerally   (a) Speaking from the gut; (b) organic sensations associated with words.

legato   Smooth, connected movement or speech.

"The Magic If "   "It helps an actor get into action." (From *Stanislavski's Legacy: Constantin Stanislavski*, edited and translated by Elizabeth Reynolds Hapgood. Published by Theatre Arts Books, 1956, page 12.) (*See* as if.)

motivation   (a) Possessed by a need/desire, a character is impelled into action; (b) inner drive that causes the character to want and/or do something.

need   Want, desire, purpose.

objectivity   A viewpoint that operates without preconceived thoughts or feelings.

obstacle   Whatever gets in the way of a character's desire/intention.

olfactory image   (a) Smelling an odor in your imagination; (b) a smell sensation that merges with, or stimulates, inner images from any of the other senses.

organic behavior   The combination of physical, sensorial, emotional, mental, and verbal impulses.

outer eye   (a) Peripheral or external vision; (b) observing strictly for information.

outer technique   (a) Overt physical or verbal communication; (b) using mental, verbal and/or physical information in order to stimulate an inner life.

overall intention   A need that occurs throughout an entire scene, act or play.

overall sensory condition/O.S.C.   A chosen, secret sensory condition that serves as a touchstone for an actor in a scene that contains multiple sensory conditions. (*See* sensory task.)

Pandora's Box   The actor's storehouse of experience.

paraphrase   (a) Translating scripted words or text into contemporary speech or dialogue personal to the actor; (b) especially in Shakespeare, discovering possible archiac meanings to the language and updating them to contemporary understanding.

physical score   A rehearsed or planned sequence of physical actions.

physical transition   (a) A change in the physical/sensorial life; (b) frequently a change in energy or psychological centers.

physiology   The physical makeup or attributes of a person.

prejudicial response   A response shaped by the past.

psyche   (a) The mind as it stimulates organic sensations; (b) the culmination of all physical, sensorial, and emotional experience.

psychological   Having to do with the emotions. When applied to the acting process, it refers to how the character reveals him/herself through behavior.

psychological patterns   A recurring rhythm in the emotional life of a character.

psychological centers   (a) The head (brain)—the gift of thought, intellect; (b) the heart—the gift of feeling, emotion; (c) the sex—the gift of life, physical desire.

psychological image   (a) Any inner eye, inner ear, smell, taste or tactile image associated with an emotion; (b) a feeling located in a particular part of the body.

psychology   (a) A person's emotional life or response to life; (b) mental/emotional behavior (habitual behavior.)

rhythm   (a) A characteristic and recurring pattern; (b) a repeated behavior, either physical or psychological, which defines the character.

runthrough   A rehearsal of the play from beginning to end without stopping. (*See* experience-through.)

scenario   A rehearsed outline of action.

sense memory   Any kinesthetic response of the five senses.

sensorial shutdown   (a) A deadening of the senses; (b) a censoring of response or awareness because of sensory overload.

sensorial throughline   (a) The unbroken connection of sensorial responses in the life of a character; (b) experiencing the flow if the entire sensory life during a character's journey in a play.

sensory condition   Any physical condition that stimulates one or more of the five senses.

sensory life   Experiencing through the senses.

sensory task   An imaginary sensory condition chosen by the actor or implied in the script. (*See* given sensory condition.)

sociology   (a) A person's cultural environment; (b) the ethnic heritage, culture, education, language, dialect, class, profession, etc., of an individual.

staccato   Rhythm made up of abrupt physical movement and/or speech.

stream-of-consciousness   (a) The flow of one's thoughts, feelings, and images in everyday life; (b) the spontaneous flow of one's thoughts, feeling, and images in an impromptu experience, exercise, or improvisation.

subjective response   Personal, preconceived thoughts or feelings which affect a response. (*See* prejudicial response.)

subtext   (a) The unspoken meaning of the words in scripted material; what is not said, but meant; (b) hearing/sensing and responding to the unspoken meaning or behavior of another; (c) the behavior that results from having a secret or from exposure to some sensory stimulation. (*See* given sensory condition, sensory task, and overall sensory condition.)

tactic   The particular moment-to-moment action of how a character attempts to achieve his/her intention.

tactile image   (a) Touching with your imagination; (b) a touch sensation that merges with or stimulates inner images form any of the other senses.

technique   (a) A way of working, the process; (b) a specific procedure that allows for responses to be spontaneously stimulated on cue.

tempo   The speed at which rhythm is played.

transformation   (a) The process of emerging into a new reality; (b) for the actor, creating a new self in the character; (c) a significant shift in physical/psychological center.(*See* character transformation.)

visual image   (a) A mental picture; seeing with your imagination; (b) a mental picture that stimulates responses or merges with inner images from any of the other senses.

vivid visual image   A vision that is full of life, stimulating strong sensations.

vulnerability   Being open to sensation.

"Who am I?"   Personally identifying with a role by talking about it in the first person.

"W" questions   Where (place) does the action take place? What does the character want? Why does the character want what they want? Who does the character want it from? What is the obstacle? Who or what is in the way? What is the season (temperature)? (What are the sensory conditions of the scene?) Why now? (Why is it important to get what you want now?) When ? (What time does the event take place?)

Credits

A Streetcar Named Desire by Tennessee Williams. Copyright 1947 by Tennessee Williams. Reprinted by permission of New Directions Publishing Corporation, 8th printing, 1980.

The Art of Dramatic Writing by Lajos Egri. A Touchstone book published by and reprinted by permission of Simon & Schuster, Inc. Copyright renewed 1988 by Charles Egri and Ruth Egri Holden.

Miss Evers' Boys by David Feldshuh. Copyright 1989. Reprinted by permission by Helen Merrill, Ltd., New York, NY. Caution: No amateur or professional performance or reading of Miss Evers' Boys may be given without obtaining in advance the written permission of Helen Merrill, Ltd., 435 West 23rd Street, #1A, New York, NY 10011.

The Elephant Man by Bernard Pomerance. Copyright 1979. Reprinted by permission of Michael Imison Playwrights, Ltd.

The Elephant Man: A Study in Human Dignity by Ashley Montagu. Published by Outerbridge and Dienstfrey, New York, and distributed by E.P. Dutton and Company.